GEOGRAPHY *of* MADHYA PRADESH

Soyhunlo Sebu

Pharos Books

ISBN: 978-93-59835-32-7
eISBN: 978-93-59831-19-0

©Publisher

Publisher: Pharos Books (P) Ltd.
Plot No.-63, Main Mother Dairy Road
Pandav Nagar, East Delhi-110092
Phone: 011-40395855, +4049916623
WhatsApp: +91 9319228272
E-mail: sales@pharosbooks.in
Website: www.pharosbooks.in
First Edition: 2024

GEOGRAPHY OF MADHYA PRADESH
By Soyhunlo Sebu

CONTENTS

To My Students

PREFACE

Geography is the study of places and the relationships between human and their environment. It seeks to understand where things are found, why they are there, and how they develop and change over time. Given its significance, it is been studied in Universities, colleges, and schools as while as an important paper for UPSC, SPSC, and other competitive examinations.

Madhya Pradesh is geographically located in the center of India and is also known as the "Hearth of India". The State is one of the largest in turns of the area and population interwind with diverse traditional culture, history, and natural resources.

This book "Geography of Madhya Pradesh" endeavors to provide a comprehensive understanding of various facets of the State's geography, encompassing both its physical and human dimensions. Divided into eight chapters, each section delves into specific themes integral to grasping the essence of Madhya Pradesh's geography.

Chapter 1 provides an overview of Madhya Pradesh's past and present, tracing its evolution from antiquity to contemporary times, including the administrative boundary reform witnessed up to 2024.

Chapter 2 explores the physiography, geology, and soil composition of the region, shedding light on the underlying geological processes shaping its terrain.

Chapter 3 delves into the intricate network of drainage systems and the climatic patternsdefining the State's environmental dynamics.

Chapter 4 focuses on natural vegetation, protected areas, and wetlands, highlighting the biodiversity hotspots and conservation efforts within the state.

Chapter5 delves into the realm of resources, discussing the mineral wealth and energy resources pivotal to Madhya Pradesh's economic landscape.

Chapter 6 examines the industrial sectors, tourism, and transportation infrastructure, elucidating their roles in shaping the state's socioeconomicfabric.

Chapter 7 delves into the agricultural practices prevalent in Madhya Pradesh, exploring the agricultural landscape and its productions.

Chapter 8 offers insights into the diverse populace and vibrant culture that characterize Madhya Pradesh, showcasing its culturalheritage and societal tapestry.

Each chapter is complemented by maps and tables to enhance comprehension and facilitate learning.

It is my sincere hope that this book proves invaluable to students, teachers, scholars, and civil service aspirants alike. Recognizing that no work is without its limitations, I welcome suggestions and feedback for further improvement.

I extend my heartfelt gratitude to the authors, government publications, and reports whose works I have referred to enriched this book. Special thanks are due to my former colleagues, Dr. Milind Baudh and Mr. Deepansh, for their unwavering support and assistance. I am deeply grateful to my family, especially my wife and two sons who provided a conducive environment for the completion of this book.

List of Figures

CHAPTER 1

MADHYA PRADESH: PAST AND PRESENT

Geographically located in the center of India, Madhya Pradesh has a rich and diverse history, with evidence of human habitation dating back to prehistoric times. The discovery of paleolithic tools in the Sagar district by W.L. Wilson in 1866 unearthed a multitude of Stone Age history, shedding substantial light on this early period. The Neolithicage imprint on the State's prehistoric landscape was accentuated by A.C. Carlyle's finding of numerous pigmy flints in Rewa during 1867-68. Dr. Vishnu Shribhar Wakankar's exploration in 1957-58 further enriched Madhya Pradesh's ancient history with the discovery of rock shelters and paintings at Bhimbetka. Among the 750 rock shelters, 500 boast intricate paintings, with cup marks on the rock surface dating back to 100,000 B.P. The Bhimbetka Rock Shelter is one of the world's largest prehistoric complexes and features India's oldest known example of rock art. These discoveries contribute significantly to our understanding of Madhya Pradesh's prehistoric past. Transitioning to the protohistoric period, the Chalcolithic culture (Copper age) observed in the locations like Besnagar, Mandsaur, Kayatha, Maheshwara-Navadotali, Modi, Awara, Eran, Nagda, Pipalyalorka, Azadnagar, and Dangvada marking a crucial phase in the region's history.

In ancient times, the region where the present Madhya Pradesh lies was ruled by various empires including the Nanda Empire, the Maurya Empire, and the Gupta Empire.

The Nanda dynasty was the first non-Kshatriya dynasty and the fifth ruling dynasty of Magadha, governed the region from 345 BCE to 321 BCE. Mahapadma was the first ruler of the Nanda dynasty, and during this period,the Avanti region was part of the Magadha empire.The culmination of the Nanda rule saw Chandragupta Maurya rise to power, aided by the strategic prowess of Chanakya. Together, they orchestrated the overthrow of the last Nanda king, Dhana Nanda. Chanakya played a crucial role in establishing the Maurya Empire, setting his historical significance in the region's political evolution.

Chandragupta Maurya unified northern India to establish the Maurya Empire (circa 1500 to 185 BCE), which encompassed present-day Madhya Pradesh. In the days of Emperor Ashoka, there were at least five provinces under the Mauryas, of which four provinces namely, Avantirattha/Avantirastra, Daksinapatha, Uttarapatha, and Pracya were integral parts of Chandragupta's empire.Ujjayini served as the capital of Avantirastraduring that period. Around 250 B.C.,Emperor Ashoka built stupas and railings at Sanchi, situated in today's Raisen district. Emperor Ashoka's reign marked a pivotal moment as he embraced Buddhism after the Kalinga War, advocating for non-violence and promoting the spread of Buddhism throughout the Indian subcontinent. Emperor Ashoka's inscriptions and edicts, such as those of Sanchi and Sarnath, are evidence of his influence in the region. Following Emperor Ashoka's demise, the Maurya Empire experienced a gradual decline, and central India emerged as a contested region among the Sakas, Sungas, Kushanas, Satavahanas, and local dynasties between the 3rd to 1st centuries BCE.

The Shunga/Sungas dynasty, founded by Pushyamitra Shunga, emerged around 185 BCE and took control, marking the end of the Maurya rule. Following the Shunga dynasty, various regional powers rose to prominence in different parts of India. In the Central region, the Satavahana dynasty rose to prominence, exerting control over a portion of what is now Madhya Pradesh. They played a crucial role in facilitating trade and ensuring stability in the Deccan.

Later on, the Gupta dynasty founded by King Sri Gupta (4th century CE to the late 6th century CE) rose to power and played a crucial role in shaping the history of ancient India. Regarded as the Golden Age of India, the Gupta period made substantial contributions to science, literature, architecture, painting, art, and philosophy. Rulers such as Chandragupta II and Samudragupta supported scholars and artists, fostering advancements in astronomy, mathematics, and classical Sanskrit literature. Great ancient Indian scholars such as Kalidasa, Aryabhata, Varahamihira, and Vatsyayana made great contributions. The Parivrajaka dynasty and the Uchchhakalpa dynasty in Madhya Pradesh ruled as feudatories of the Gupta dynasty. Following the decline of the Gupta dynasty, the Malwa region fell into the hands of Paramras under King Bhoja II. From the early 9th century till the mid-13th centuryA.D., the Malwa region, including the area that constitutesthe Sehore district, was governed by the Paramaras dynasty. Their original capital was at Ujjain subsequently shifted to Dhar during the reign of Vairisimha II. Under the rule of Munja's nephew, Bhoja, the Paramara dynasty experienced its zenith. Bhoja's realm extended from the northern city of Chittor to the southern region of Konkan, and from the western banks of the Sabarmati River to the eastern city of Vidisha. The prevailing belief suggests that the name Bhopal City originated from the renowned ruler of the Paramara dynasty, Bhoja. However, another narration is that, the name Bhopal derived from "Bhojpal", meaning Bhoja's dam, implying the great dam on the upper lake, which is said to have been built by the king's minister. The last Paramara ruler was defeated by the forces of Alauddin Khalji in the year 1305 CE. Between the 9th and 13th centuries CE, the Chandela dynasty ruled over the region.Between approximately 950 and 1050 CE, the Chandela rulers undertook the construction of the renowned temple city of Khajuraho. However, their authority dwindled in the early 13th century due to invasions by the Chahamanas and Ghurids. By the 13th century, Northern Madhya Pradesh came under the control of the Turkic Delhi Sultanate. After the dissolution of the Delhi Sultanate in the late 14th century, autonomous regionalkingdoms emerged, including the Tomara kingdom in Gwalior and the sultanate of Malwa, centered in Mandu. During the sixth year of Akbar's rule, he sent an army to the Malwa region, but it suffered defeat by Bayazid (Baz Bahadur). Consequently, Akbar dispatched Abdullah Khan Uzbeg with a formidable force to conquer Malwa, prompting Baz Bahadur to abandon the region. Emperor Akbar's reign (1556-1605) witnessed the Mughal rule extending over most of Madhya Pradesh. Nevertheless, Gondwana and Mahakoshal remained under the governance of Gond kings, recognizing Mughal authority while maintaining a certain degree of autonomy. Gwalior flourished as a hub of music and became the home of the famous Gwalior Gharana.

After the death of Aurangzeb, the Marathas made a bid for the conquest of northern India. The Marathas defeated the Mughals and the Nawab of Bhopal in the Battle of Bhopal in 1737 and started collecting tribute from the State. In the 18th century, Malwa underwent division between the Maratha rulers of Gwalior and Indore, associated with the Scindia and Holkar families, respectively. Under Sir John Malcolm's settlement, the Malwa map was redrawn. The boundaries of the two Maratha States viz., Indore and Gwalior were demarcated. Under the suzerainty of Indore and Gwalior, fifteen Rajput and a few Muhammadan States were freed from their rule and placed under British protection.

The Marathas defeated the Mughals and the Nawab of Bhopal in the Battle of Bhopal in 1737 and started collecting tribute from the State. In 1818 following the Maratha's defeat in the Third Anglo-Marath War, Bhopal becamea princely State. The conclusive events of the 1817-18 conflict marked the ultimate decline of Maratha power. The Maratha rule over Malwa had fostered a cultural revival in the region, contributing to the emergence of modern Ujjain. Twenty years before the establishment of British rule, Narmada Valley experienced conflict between the rulers of Bhopal and the Maratha generals. 1805 after the Scindiaforce seized Hoshangabad and briefly held sway over part of the district, the region was further plagued by the Pindhari pestilence, causing widespread disorder for several

    GEOGRAPHY OF MADHYA PRADESH

years. In the second Anglo-Maratha war (1803), Raghoji II (Bhonsle dynasty) sided with the Peshwa against the British but defected. After Raghoji II died in 1816, his son Parsaji was ousted and assassinated by Mudhoji II, also known as Appa Sahib. In the same year, Mudhoji II entered into a treaty with the British. Despite in treaty, Mudhoji II sided with the Peshwa in the Third Anglo-Maratha War in 1817, opposing the British. This intense conflict marked a crucial juncture as it set the stage for the decline of the Bhonsles and facilitated British controlover Nagpur city. After a brief reinstatement to the throne, Mudhoji II was disposedand the British installed Ragholi III (Ragholi II's grandson) on the throne. Throughout Ragholi III'srule, which lasted until 1840, the region was under British administrated. In 1853, with Ragholi III passing away without an heir, the State was annexed by the British following the Doctrine of Lapse. The Nagpur provinces became part of the Central Provinces and Berar which was administered by a Commissioner under the British central government from 1853 to 1861. British designated Nagpur as the capital of the Central provinces, later incorporating Berar in 1903.

The Central Provinces and Berar and the Central India Agency

Before independence, the present State of Madhya Pradesh was geographically under two distinct regions: the Central Provinces and Berar and the Central India Agency.

The Central Provinces was a British India Province. It comprises regions of the modern-day States of Madhya Pradesh, Chhattisgarh, and Maharashtra that were acquired by the British through conquest from the Mughals and Marathas in central India. Nagpur functioned as the primary winter capital of the province, while Pachmarhi served as the regular summer retreat. In 1817, a treaty of dependence was signed between the British government of India and the Nawab of Bhopal. Bhopal remained an ally of the British Government throughout their rule in India. By 1818, the British administration was established in the Saugor (Sagar) and Nerbudda (Narmada) territories. In 1861 Saugor (present Sagar) and Narmada territories were united and the administrative unit of the Central Provinces was established. Sambalpur, which had come under the possession of the British earlier in 1849 was incorporated in the province in 1862. In 1864 the Nimar district in the Narmada – Tapti valley also came under their jurisdiction.

The provincewas divided into four politically distinct divisions comprising eighteen Central Provinces British districts, the four districts of Berar, and fifteen Feudatory States. For administrative purposes, the British districts were divided into four divisions in the census reports of 1891 and 1901. However, in 1903, the addition of six districts of Berar, which the Commissioner of Berar had controlled under the Resident of Hyderabad, became anotheradministrative division under the jurisdiction of the local administration at Nagpur, increasing the number of British districts to twenty-four. In1853, the Nizam of Hyderabad leased Berar, or the Hyderabad Assigned Districts to the British Government and it was administered by the Resident at Hyderabad until1903. Subsequently, the lease terms were revised, and on 1stOctober 1903, the territory was integrated into the Central Provinces under the governance of the Chief Commissioner of the Central Provinces and Berar.

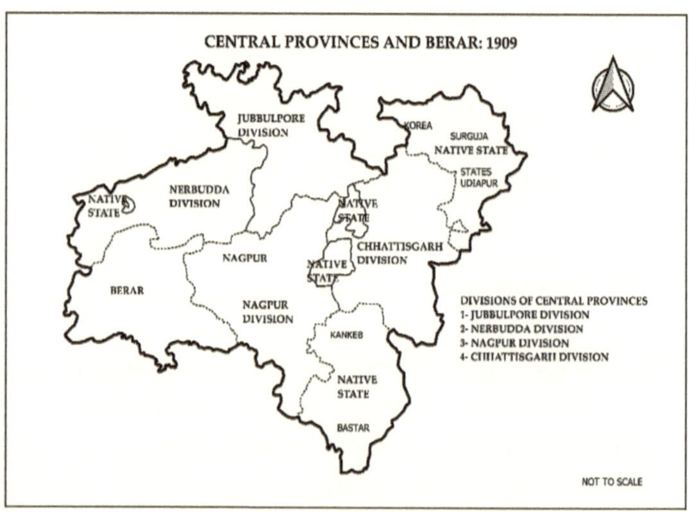

Figure 1: Central Provinces and Berar

            GEOGRAPHY OF MADHYA PRADESH

By the end of 1931, the Nerbudda (Narmada)division was abolished and the districts of Demoh, Naringpur, and Seoni were amalgamated with Saugor (Sagar), Hoshangabad, and Chhindwara. The decade (1931-41) experienced certain changes in the province. On October 24th, 1936, the Central Provinces transformed into 'Central Provinces and Berar' following g the formation of the Legislative Assembly, marking the full integration of Berar. However, Nizam retained nominal sovereignty over the Berar division. The Betul district was created in the Nagpur division.

During the decade, the feudatory State experienced a decrease in its overall territory as Surguja, Jashpur, Korea, Udaipur, and Changbhakar were transferred to the province of Bihar which became a separate Province on 1st April 1936. However, the States once again merged with Central Provinces and Berar before the first post-independence census of 1951. Extensive territorial changes took place from 1941 to 1951 with the integration of the Chhattisgarh and Bhopal Agency States after the independence when Sardar Patel called for the unification of the princely States across the country.

The Central Provinces and Berar underwent a significant administrative reorganization with the enactment of the Central Provinces and Berar Commissioners Act, 1948, which came into force on the 1st of November 1948. This legislation led to the abolition of the four commissioners Divisions. Subsequently, the province was renamed Madhya Pradesh with Nagpur as its capital. The new State comprised twenty-two districts and its administration came under the control of the State Government.

Central India Agency

In 1854, the Bundelkhand and Baghelkhand regions were incorporated into to the Malwa Agency, resulting in the establishment of the Central India Agency. The different territories that composed the Agency were at first under the charge of separate political officers, but the Residents at Indore and Gwalior directly dealt with the Government of India, while Bundelkhand and

Baghelkhand were independent charges. After 1854 these different charges were combined under the Central Control of an Agent to the Governor General of India. R. Hamilton was appointed the first Agent with his headquarters at Indore.

The Central India Agency was located between 21°52' and 26°52' north latitude and 74°0' and 83°0' east Longitude. Before the excision of the Gwalior State, the Central India Agency was bounded on the north and northeast by the Chambal River which served as a natural boundary from the United Provinces and the Rajputana Agency. On the east and along its southern boundary lay the Central Provinces, beyond the Vindhya and Satpura ranges. The southwestern boundary was delineated by the Khandesh, Rewa-Kantha, and Panch-Mahal districts of the Bombay Presidency, while its western confines were enclosed by the various States of Rajputana.

Since 1911, the political landscape of the Central India Agency has undergone significant modification with the excision of the Gwalior State, which originally formed one-third of its area. This excision was made in aligned with a policy aiming to establish closer ties between important States the Government of India, acknowledgingthe right of this great State to rank with others of the first importance and of the pre-eminent services rendered by its ruler to the Government of India.

The Central India Agency is not an administrative area, the actual units of administration being the States and Estates which number about sixty-one (twenty-eight salute States and the remaining are non-salute States), and the Pargana of Manpur. While the actual administrative units were the States and Estates in the Central India Agency, its political control remained with the Government of India working through its political offices. The political charges which were formed before 1891, have been described in the 1891 census reports as 'artificial and unstable', for these were 'merely convenient groupings of States' to exert control by the political officers. The instability of the political charges that occurred since 1891 has been plotted in Table 1.

                              GEOGRAPHY OF MADHYA PRADESH

Table1: Changes in the Political landscape since 1891

1891	1901	1911	1921	1931
(i)Gwalior Agency	(i)Gwalior Agency	(i) Gwalior Agency	(i)Indore Agency	(i)Indore Agency
(ii) Indore Agency	(ii) Indore Agency	(ii) Indore Agency	(ii) Bhopal Agency	(ii)Bhopal Agency
(iii)Bhopal Agency	(iii)Bhopal Agency	(iii) Bhopal Agency	(iii) Malwa Agency	(iii)Malwa Agency and Southern Central India States Agency
(iv)Western Malwa Agency	(vi)Western Malwa Agency	(iv) Malwa Agency	(iv) Southern Central India States Agency	(iv)Bundelkh and Agency
(v)Bhopawar Agency	(v)Bhopawar Agency	(v) Bhopawar Agency	(v) Bundelkhand Agency	(v)Baghelkhan Agency
(vi)Guna Agency	(vi)Guna Agency	(vi) Bundelkhand Agency	(vi)Baghelkh an Agency	
(vii) Bundelkhand Agency	(vii) Bundelkhand Agency	(vii)Baghelkhan Agency		
(viii) Baghelkhan Agency	(viii) Baghelkhan Agency			

Source: Census of India, 1931, Central India Agency

The political landscape change continued. In 1931, the Bundelkhand and Baghelkhand Agencies (all States except Rewa) were amalgamated into one charge, and certain States from the Malwa Agency were transferred to the Bhopal Agency. Ultimately, the system of treating the political charges as units was abandoned, and States with a population of 16,000 and above were shown as independent units. The small units with a population below 16,000 were placed as a group in the political charge to which they belonged. The Khaniadhana State though administratively outside the territorial limits of the Central India Agency was included in Central India for Census purposes.

These administrative divisions were a legacy from the first quarter of the nineteenth century and it continued for more than a decade from 1931. Thus, Central India was divided into many princely States each under a hereditary ruler and self-sufficient within itself. Gwalior, Indore, and a few other States had resources to support the administration. Another country was divided among several small States by the political officers of the British.

Following independence, a comprehensive reorganization was implemented in April 1948, leading to the abolition of all States and holdings. In its wake, three new States emerged:

Madhya Bharat, Bhopal State, and Vindhya Pradesh. Each of these entities attained the status of a State under the newly adopted constitution of India.

Madhya Bharat

On May 28th, 1948, Madhya Bharat, also known as Malwa Union, wasestablished, attaining the status of a Part 'B' State as per the constitution of India. The State lies between 20°40' and 26° 40' N Latitude and 74 °10' and 78° 40' E Longitude. The geographical area of the State was 46,478 sq. miles. It encompassed sixteen districts namely, Bhind, Gird, Morena, Shivpuri Goona, Bhilsa, Rajgarh, Shajapur, Ujjain, Indore, Dewas, Mandsaur, Ratlam, Dhar, Jhabua, and Nimar. The northern and northwest boundaries of the

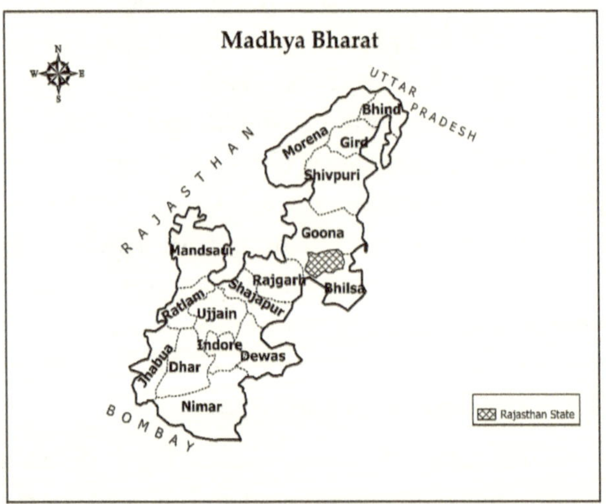

Figure 2: Map of Madhya Bharat

State were demarcated by the Chambal River on the north and northwest which separated it from Uttar Pradesh (former United

Provinces) and Rajasthan (former Rajputana Agency) States. The Vindhya Pradesh, Uttar Pradesh, Bhopal, and Madhya Pradesh lie in the eastern and southeastern of the State. On the southwestern lies the Khandesh, Rewa-Kantha, and Panch-Mahal districts of the Bombay State. The administration of the State was placed in the hands of the Rajpramukh and a Cabinet of Ministers.

Bhopal State

The Bhopal State was constituted in June 1949. The State comprises the territory of the former Bhopal state and with the political status of a Part 'C' State under the constitution of India. The Bhopal State was divided into two districts viz., Raisen and Sehore. The geographical area of the State was 6,875 sq. miles and lay between 22 °32' and 24°4' N Latitude and 76 °28' and 78° 52' E Longitude. The State was bounded by Bhilsa and Rajgarh districts of Madhya Bharat, the Ton district of Rajasthan, and the Sagar district of Madhya Pradesh on the north, on the south by the Dewas district of

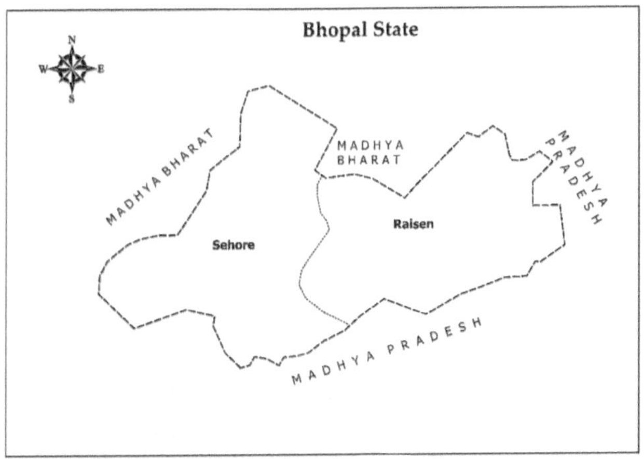

Figure 3: Map of Bhopal State

Madhya Bharat and by the Narmada River separating it from the Hoshangabad district of Madhya Pradesh. On the east by the Sagar district of Madhya Pradesh and on the west by the Rajgarh, Shajapur, and Dewas districts of Madhya Bharat.

Vindhya Pradesh: Vindhya Pradesh state was formed in 1948 by the union of thirty- fourStates of the

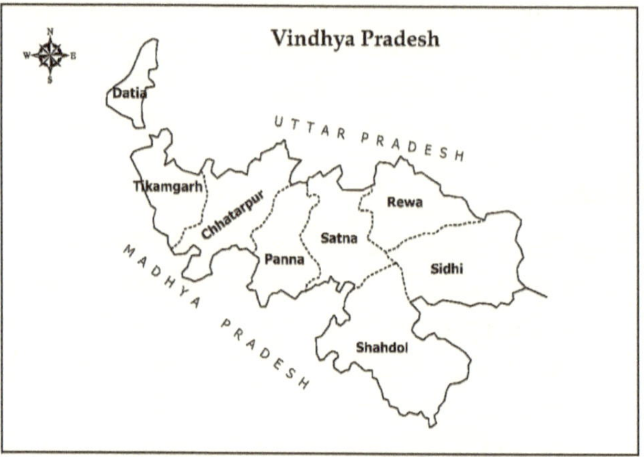

Figure 4: Map of Vindhya Pradesh

Bundelkhand Political Agency, Baghelkhan Political Agency of Central India, and the State of the Gwalior Residency, i.e., Khanniadhana.

The State was accorded the status of a Part B State in the First Schedule of the Constitution.

Nevertheless, due to its economic and political underdevelopment, the State was later transformed into a centrally administered unit, i.e., a Part 'C' State. The State is situated between 78° and 83° east longitude and 22° and 26° north latitude.

The State was bounded on the north by the Jhansi, Hamirpur, Banda, Allahabad, and Mirzapur districts of Uttar Pradesh and Surguja and Bilaspur districts of Madhya Pradesh. In the south, it is bounded by Bilaspur, Jubbulpore, and Saugor districts of Madhya Pradesh, on the west it is bounded by the Jhansi district of Uttar Pradesh and Madhya Bharat State. Vindhya Pradesh was constituted into eight districts namely Datia, Tikamgarh, Chhatarpur, Panna, Satna, Rewa, Sidhi, and Shahdol in 1951.

     GEOGRAPHY OF MADHYA PRADESH

Table 2: Princely States that joins to formed Vidhya Pradesh

Sl. No	State (Princely)	Area in sq. miles	Name of the political agency to which the state belonged in 1941
1.	Orchha	1999	Bundelkhand Political Agency
2.	Panna	2580	Bundelkhand Political Agency
3.	Chhatarpur	1170	Bundelkhand Political Agency
4.	Datia	846	Bundelkhand Political Agency
5.	Charchari	785	Bundelkhand Political Agency
6.	Bijawar	980	Bundelkhand Political Agency
7.	Ajaigarh	788	Bundelkhand Political Agency
8.	Samthar	189	Bundelkhand Political Agency
9.	Baoni	122	Bundelkhand Political Agency
10.	Alipura	73	Bundelkhand Political Agency
11.	Banka-Pahari	5	Bundelkhand Political Agency
12.	Beri	32	Bundelkhand Political Agency
13.	Bihat	16	Bundelkhand Political Agency
14.	Bijna	7	Bundelkhand Political Agency
15.	Dhurwai	12	Bundelkhand Political Agency
16.	Garrauli	39	Bundelkhand Political Agency
17.	Gaurihar	72	Bundelkhand Political Agency
18.	Jigni	22	Bundelkhand Political Agency
19.	Lugasi	45	Bundelkhand Political Agency
20.	Naigwan Rewai	12	Bundelkhand Political Agency
21.	Sarila	35	Bundelkhand Political Agency
22.	Tori-Fatehpur	27	Bundelkhand Political Agency
23.	Rewa	12830	Baghelkhand Political Agency
24.	Kothi	166	Baghelkhand Political Agency
25.	Nagod	532	Baghelkhand Political Agency
26.	Sohawal	251	Baghelkhand Political Agency
27.	Jaso	72	Baghelkhand Political Agency
28.	Maihar	412	Baghelkhand Political Agency
29.	Barondha	228	Baghelkhand Political Agency

30.	Bhaisundha	32	Baghelkhand Political Agency
31.	Kamta Rajaula	13	Baghelkhand Political Agency
32.	Pahra	27	Baghelkhand Political Agency
33.	Paldev	52	Baghelkhand Political Agency
34.	Taraon	26	Baghelkhand Political Agency
35.	Khanniadhana	101	Gwalior Residency

Source: Census of India, 1951

Madhya Pradesh: Madhya Pradesh was divided into eight districts namely., Sagar, Jabalpur, Hoshangabad, Nimar, Mandla, Betul, Chhindwara and Balaghat.

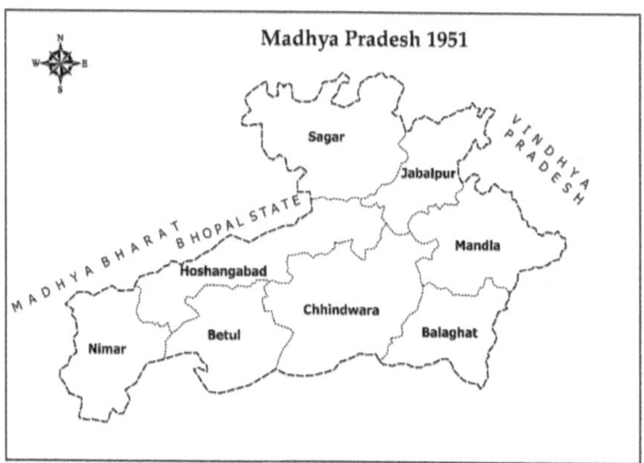

Figure 5: Map of Madhya Pradesh 1951

Reorganization of State:1956

The State of Madhya Pradesh was reconstituted in 1956 under the provision of the States Reorganization Act, 1956, broadly on a linguistic basis and the Seventh Constitutional Amendment Act, 1956, the Bhopal State, the Vindhya Pradesh, Madhya Bharat (except the Sunel enclave of the Mandsaur district), and the Sironj sub- division of the Kotah district of Rajasthan were merged in Madhya Pradesh (fourteen districts of the residuary Madhya Pradesh) to form the State of Madhya Pradesh on 1st November 1956. Bhopal became the capital of the new State. In 1956 three districts were created viz., Damoh from Sagar on 1st October 1956,

                    GEOGRAPHY OF MADHYA PRADESH

Seoni from Chhindwara on 1st November 1956 and Narsimhapur from Honshangabad on 1stNovember 1956, and a small enclave of Rajasthan merged in Vidisha district.

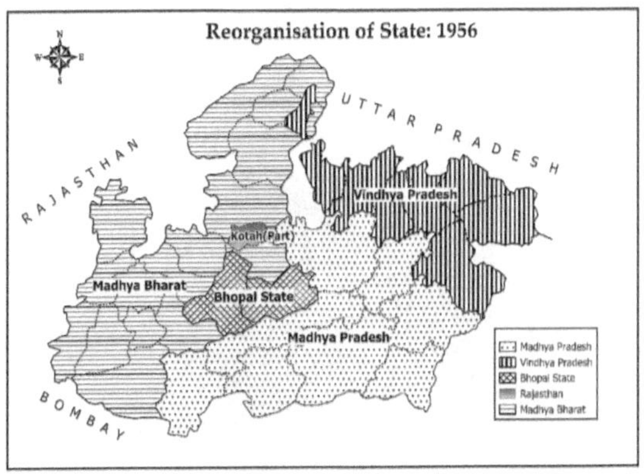

Figure 6: Map of M.P – Reorganization of State: 1956

As per the Census of India, 1961, the State was divided into 43 districts viz., Bastar, Surguja, Raipur, Bilaspur, Durg, Shahdol, West Nimar, Mandla, Raigarh, Chhindwara, Morena, Guna, East Nimar, Sidhi, Shivpuri, Mandsaur, Sagar, Jabalpur, Betul, Hoshangabad, Sheore, Balagaht, Chhatarpur, Seoni, Raisen, Dhar, Vidisha, Damoh, Satna, Panna, Dewas, Jhabua, Rewa, Shajapur, Rajgarh, Ujjain, Gwalior, Narshimhapur, Tikamgarh, Ratlam, Bhind, Indore and Datia. Bastar was

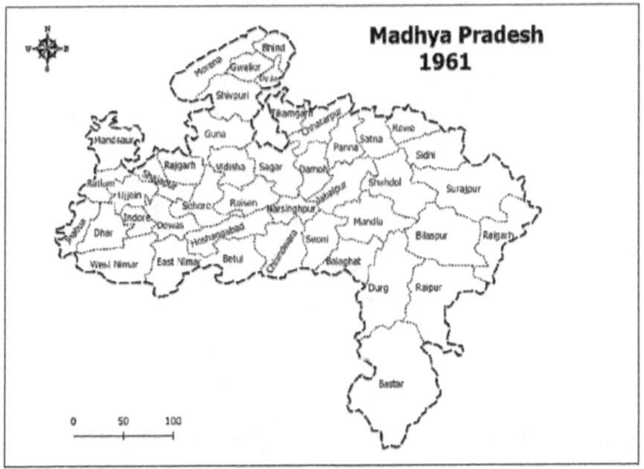

Figure 7: Map of Madhya Pradesh 1961

the largest district with a geographical area of 15,124 sq. miles and Datia district with a geographical area of 782 sq. miles was the smallest district in the State. From 1961 to 1971,no jurisdictional change has occurred in the State's territory.

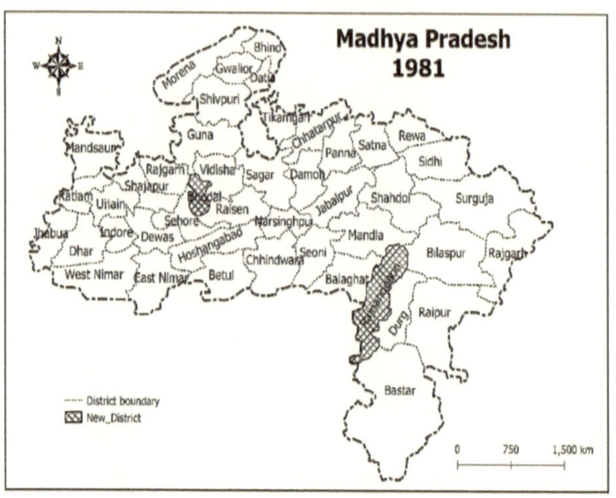

Figure 8: Map of Madhya Pradesh 1981

Significant internal boundary re-demarcation occurred between 1971 to 1981resulting in the division of the State into nine distinctdivisions namely Chambal, Gwalior,Sagar, Rewa, Ujjain, Indore, Bhopal, Hoshangabad, and Jabalpur.

On 13th September 1972, the Bhopal district was created, consisting of Bhopal (Huzur) and Berasia tehsil from the erstwhile Sehore district, and in 1973, Rajnandgaon was curved out from Durg district. In 1998, 16 (sixteen) districts namely., Neemuch (02/07/1998), Barwani (25th May 1998), Khargone (24th May 1998),Sheopur (1998), Harda (02/07/1998), Katni (1998), Umaria (02/07/1998), Dindori (1998), Koria (01/01/1998), Surguja (01/01/1998), Jashpur (01/01/1998), Korba(01/01/1998), Janjgir-Champa(01/01/1998), Mahasamund (01/01/1998), Kawardha (06/07/1998) and Surajpur (01/01/1998) were created and the number of districts increased to 61 (Sixty one).

Madhya Pradesh Reorganization Act 2000

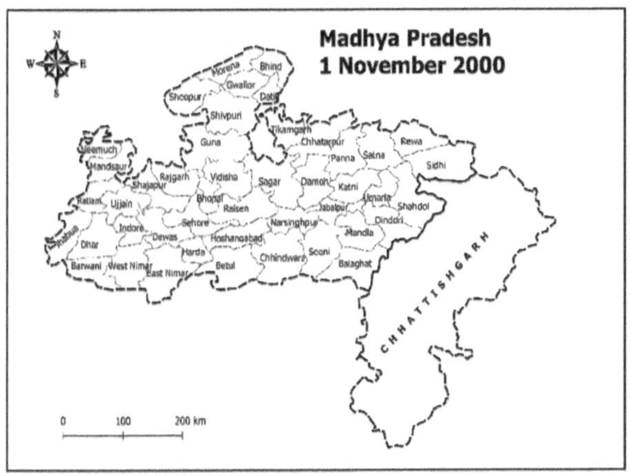

Figure 9: Map of Madhya Pradesh on 1 November 2000

Under the Madhya Pradesh Reorganization Act 2000, Chhattisgarh was curved out as a separate State from Madhya Pradesh, officially coming into existence on November 1, 2000. With the formation of Chhattisgarh State, Madhya Pradesh was left with forty-five districts and nine divisions as shown in the table.

Table 3: Madhya Pradesh- Division and Districts

Sl.No	Division	Districts
1	Chambal	1. Sheopur, 2. Morena, 3. Bhind
2	Gwalior	4. Gwalior, 5. Datia, 6. Shivpuri, 7. Guna
3	Sagar	8. Tikamgarh, 9. Chhatarpur, 910 Panna, 11. Sagar, 12. Damoh
4	Rewa	13. Satna, 14. Rewa, 15. Umaria, 16. Shahdol, 17. Sidhi
5	Ujjain	18. Neemuch, 19. Mandsaur, 20. Ratlam, 21. Ujjain, 22. Shajapur, 23. Dewas

6	Indore	24. Jhabua, 25. Dhar, 26. Indore, 27. Khargone (West Nimar), 28. Barwani(West Nimar), 29. East Nimar
7	Bhopal	30. Rajgarh, 31. Vidisha, 32. Bhopal, 33. Sehore, 34. Raisen, 35. Betul
8	Hoshangabad	36. Harda, 37. Hoshangabad
9	Jabalpur	38. Katni, 39. Jabalpur, 40. Narsimhapur, 41. Dindori, 42. Mandla, 43. Chhindwara, 44. Seoni, 45. Balaghat

Source: Part II. Administrative Division Census 1951-2001

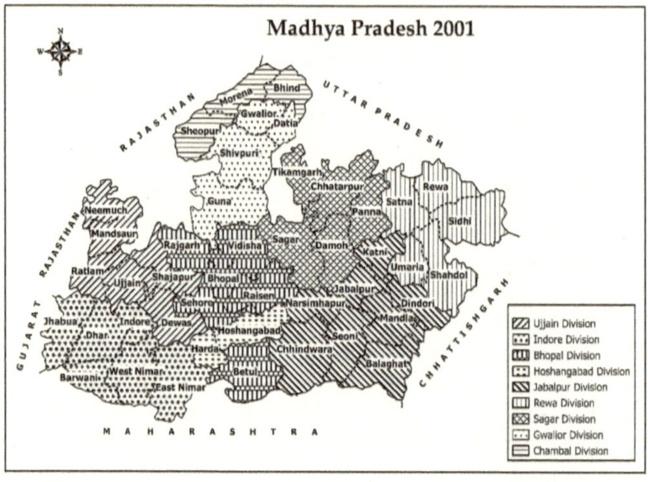

Figure 10: Madhya Pradesh 2001

On 15th August 2003, the East Nimar district underwent division, resulting in the formation of two districts namely., Khandwa and Burhanpur. Additionally, on the same date, Anuppur and Ashoknagar districts were established. Subsequently, Singrauli district was inaugurated on 24th May 2008, followed by the creation of Alirajpur district on 17th May 2008. Furthermore,the Agar-Malwa district was established on 16th August 2013 and the Niwari district was created on 1stOctober 2018.

   GEOGRAPHY OF MADHYA PRADESH

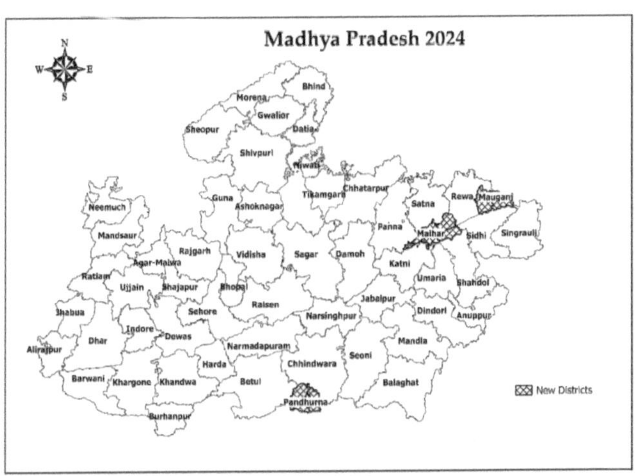

Figure 11: Map of India and Madhya Pradesh 2024

Madhya Pradesh 2024: Madhya Pradesh is the second largest State in India with ageographical area of 3,08,252 sq km which accountsfor 9.98 percent of the country's total geographical area. The State lies between 21°17'N to 26°52'N latitude and 74° 08' E to 82°49'E longitude. It is bounded by Gujarat in the west, on the northwest by Rajasthan, on the northeast by Uttar Pradesh, on the east by Chhattisgarh, and the south by Maharashtra. For administrative convenience, the State is divided into ten divisions and fifty-five districts namely., Bhopal division (Bhopal, Raisen, Rajgarh, Sehore, Vidisha), Chambal division (Morena, Sheopur, Bhind), Gwalior division (Gwalior, Ashoknagar, Shivpuri, Datia, Guna), Indore division (Alirajpur, Barwani, Burhanpur, Indore, Dhar, Jhabua, Khandwa, Khargone), Jabalpur division (Balaghat, Chhindwara, Jabalpur, Katni, Mandla, Narsinghapur, Seoni, Dindori, Pandhurna), Narmadapuram division (Betul, Harda, Narmadapuram), Rewa division (Rewa, Satna, Sidhi, Singrauli, Mauganj, Maihar), Sagar division (Panna, Sagar, Tikamgarh, Niwari, Damoh, Chhatarpur) Shahdol division (Anuppur, Shahdol, Umaria) Ujjain division (Agar Malwa, Dewas, Mandsaur, Neemuch, Ratlam, Shajapur, Ujjain).

Reference

1. A.K. Pandya(1974) Census of India 1971. Series 10., Madhya Pradesh, Part II-A. General Population Tables.
    https://new.census.gov.in/nada/index.php/catalog/30726/download/3390

2. C.E. Luard (1923). Central India Agency, Census of India, 1921. Volume XVIII
    http://lsi.gov.in/library/handle/123456789/1591

3. C.S. Venkatachar (1931) Central India Agency, Part I- Report. Volume XX. Census of India, 1931.

4. G.Jagathpathi (1974). Census of India 1961, Volume VIII, Madhya Pradesh, Part I-A, General report.
    http://lsi.gov.in/library/handle/123456789/1731

5. J.T. Marten (1912) Central Provinces and Berar, Part I (report). Census of India, 1911

6. N.K. Dube (1957) Vindhya Pradesh, Census of India, 1951. Volume XVI,

7. Part II. Adminstration Division Census 1951-2001.

8. P.K. Bhattacharyya (1977). Historical geography of Madhya Pradesh from early records, Motilal Banarsidass, Indological publishers and booksellers, Delhi

CHAPTER 2

PHYSIOGRAPHY

The physiography of a region plays a crucial role in climate, vegetation, agriculture, transportation, economic activities, cultural practices, natural resources,etc. Understanding the physiography of a region is important for effective planning and development, as it provides insights into the challengesand opportunities presented by the natural environment.

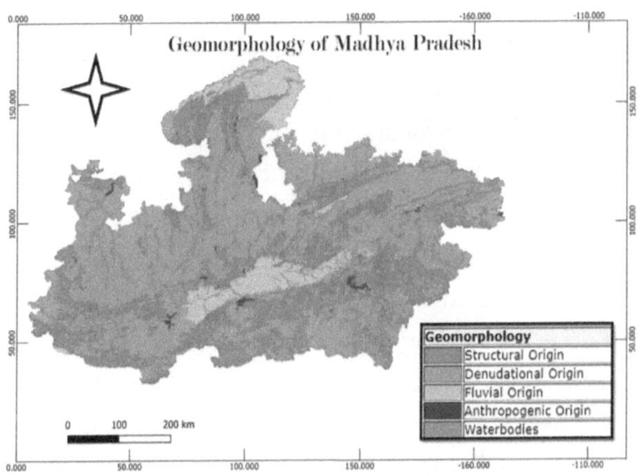

Figure 12: Geomorphology of Madhya Pradesh

The northern part of the Indian Peninsula is marked by the Madhya Pradesh plateau region, characterized by diverse lithology and geological structures that give rise to a wide range of landforms. Madhya Pradesh is physiographically divided into three major regions namely, Central Highlands, Satupura Maikal range, and Eastern Plateau/Banghelkhand plateau.

The Central Highland: The Central Highland is a part of the peninsular plateau situated the north of Narmada River and comprises a major part of the Malwa plateau. The Central highland is divided into five sub-physiography groups, (i) Plateau of Central India, (ii) Bundelkhand Plateau, (iii) Rewa-Panna plateau, (iv) Malwa plateau, and (v) Narmada –Son Valley. The Central Highland is mainly associated with basalt, granite, sandstone, quartzite, and alluvium.

(i) The Plateau of Central India: The Plateauof Centraltakes shape from the Vindhyan rock groups, coupled with the presence of the Deccan Trap in the southern part and the BundelkhandGneiss rocks in the east. The region has an average elevation of 150 to 300 meters above mean sea level (MSL). The plateau of Central India stretched over the districts of Bhind, Morena, Gwalior, Shivpuri, Sheopur, Guna, and Mandsaur. This region is traversed by rivers like Chambal, Kali, Sindh, and Parvati.

(ii) The Bundelkhand plateau: TheBundelkhand plateau is bounded by the Chambal in the northwest and the Rewa-Panna Ajaigarh range in the southeast. The region has an average elevation of 150 to 450 msl. Sidhababa hill (1172m) is the highest peak in the Bundelkhand plateau region. The plateau consists of granite rocks. The topography of this region is characterized by senile. The Bundelkhand plateau stretched over the districts of Tikamgarh, Chhatarpur, Datia, Gwalior, and Shivpuri. Noteworthy river like the Betwa, Dhasan, Ken, and Sindh have sculpted steep gorges, rapids, cataracts, and waterfalls across the landscape. (iii) The Rewa-Panna Plateau: The Rewa-Panna Plateau is also known as the Vindhyan Plateau and lies to the southeast of the Bundelkahnd Plateau. The Vindhyan range runs in an east-west direction, roughly parallel to the Narmada valley. Comprising predominantly horizontally bedded sedimentary rocks of ancient origin, the western segment of the range is overlaid with lava. As the Vindhyas extends eastward, it transforms into the Bharner and Kaimur/Kymore hills. The average elevation is between 630 to 750 msl.

 GEOGRAPHY OF MADHYA PRADESH

The Great Boundary Fault (GBF) serves as the demarcation between the Aravallis ranges and the Vindhyan Mountain. The Bhander hills and the Kymore/Kaimur range have several waterfalls and rapids created by swift-flowing Tons and Sonar rivers. Some important waterfalls are Odda Falls/Bahuti Falls (145 m) on the Odda River (a tributary of Belah River), Chachai Falls (127 m) on the Bhind River (a tributary of Tons), Keoti Falls (98 m) on the Mahana river (a tributary of Tons), Purwa/Tons Falls (70 m) on the Tons, etc. The famous diamond mine is located in this region. The Rewa-Panna plateau stretched over the districts of Damoh, Satna, Rewa, Panna, and Sagar.

(iv) The Malwa Plateau: The Malwa plateau is bounded by the Aravallis in the north, the Vindhyan range in the south, and the Bundelkhand plateau in the east. Its elevation gradually decreases from 600 meters in the south to 500 meters in the north. The plateau is drained by two main river systems: the Narmada and Mahi Rivers flowing towards the Arabia Sea, and the Chambal, Sindh, Betwa, and Ken Rivers (a tributary of Yamuna) flowing towards the Bay of Bengal. The plateau is composed of extensive lava flow and covered by black soils. The Malwa upland stretches over the districts of Raisen, Shajapur, Rajgarh, Ujjain, Dewas, Sehore, Vidisha, Ratlam, Dhar, Jhabua, Mandsor and some parts of Guna and Sagar. Sigar (881m), Dhgari(810m), and Janapav (854m) are some of the important peaks in this region.

(v) The Narmada-Son Valley: The Narmada-Son Valley is a narrow valley bounded by Vindhyan, Kaimur, and Bhander in the north, Satpura Maikal hill in the south, and the Baghelkhan highlands in the east. The Narmada valley is an example of Graben (a block of land bounded by parallel faults in which the block has been relatively downthrown, producing a distinctive structural valley with straight, steep-sided fault scraps on both sides). Two normal faults, the Narmada North Fault and Narmada South Fault run parallel to the river's course separating the Narmada block from the Vindhya and Satpura blocks/horst, which rose relative to the Narmada Graben. The Narmada-Son valley stretches over the districts of Mandla, Jabalpur, Hoshangabad, Raisen, East Nimar, West Nimar, Barwani, Harda, Dhar, and Dewas part of Rewa, Shahdol, Umaria and Sidhi districts forms the part of Son valley. The valley is the lowest landmass of Madhya Pradesh with an average elevation of 300 msl. The valley is composed of the Deccan Trap, Vindhyan, and Cuddapah rock systems. The watershed of the Narmada includes the northern slopes of the Satpuras and the steep southern slope of the Vindhyas but not the Vindhyan tableland, from where the Ganga and Yamuna receive their water.

The Satpura and Maikal ranges: The name Satpura comes from Sanskrit, 'Sat' means 'Seven', and 'Pura' means 'Mountain'. Parallel to the Vindhyas between the Narmada and the Tapi rivers is the Satpura range. This range consists of Rajpipla Hills, Mahadev Hills, and the Maikal range. These hills appear to be affected by tectonic disturbances. There is evidence that parts of the Satpuras have been folded and upheaval. They are regarded as structural uplift or 'horst'. Dhupgarh(1350m) near Panchmarhi (on Mahadev) is the highest peak of Satpura. Astamba Dongar(1325m) and Amarkantak (1,12m) are other important peak of the Satpura. These ranges are mostly composed of granite and basalt rocks. The Deccan Trap and Dharwar group of rocks constitute this region. The Narmada and Son rivers originate from the Amarkantak plateau in Satpura range. The ranges stretch over the districts of Chhindwara, Burhanpur, Khandwa, Seoni, Betul, Mandla, Balaghat, and Jabhua. River Narmada, Tapi, Wainganga, and Tawa drained this region.

The Eastern / Baghelkhand plateau: The Baghelkhand plateau is the smallest in Madhya Pradesh in terms of area coverage. The average elevation varies between 150 to 1200msl

　　　　GEOGRAPHY OF MADHYA PRADESH

with uneven relief. To the south lies the Narmada-Son trough (rift valley) characterized by the Archaeans and Bijwar series. South of this trough is the eastward extension of the Satpura which is an area of radial drainage. Among the basin, Singrauli and Dudhi (150-300m) are upper Gondwana basins, which are rich in coal deposits. Besides the Narmada and Son, this region is drained by the Karmanasa, Tons, Ken, and Belandare rivers. Baghelkhan plateau stretches over the districts of Rewa, Satna, Shahdol, Umaria, Sidhi, Singruali, and Anuppur. This region is rich in coal, bauxite, limestone, etc. The second largest coalfield of Madhya Pradesh is located in the Singrauli district in Baghelkhand plateau. Other important coalfieldsare Sohagpur, Korar, and Johila.

Geology

Madhya Pradesh is part of the Central Indian Shield with rocks ranging from Archaean to Phanerozoic age. This Shield is divided into two broad domains namely., the Northern Crustal Province (NCP) and the Southern Crustal Province (SCP), separated by the extensive Central Indian Shear Zone (CIS). The majority of the state falls within the Northern Crustal Province. The generalized lithostratigraphic sequence is plotted in Table 4.

Table 4: The Generalized Lithostratigraphic Sequence

Cenozoic	Quaternary Cainozoic Mio-Pliocene	Alluvium Laterite, bauxite Katni formation
Paleozoic-Mesozoic	Upper Cretaceous to Palaeogene Upper Carboniferous to Lower Cretaceaous	Deccan trap/ lameta Formation Gondwana Supergroup

Proterozoic	Meso- Neoproterozoic Palaeo – Mesoproterozoic	Vindhyan Supergroup – Godhra Granite Bijawar Group/Barwah – Handia area Gwalior Group, Khairanarh Group, Chilpi Group
	Palaeoproterozoic	Dongargarh Supergroup: (nandgaon Group, malanjhkhand Granite and Granites of Narmada valley). Aravalli Supergroup (Lunavada Group) Metamorphites of Bilaspur- Raigarh – Surguja and Betul- Chindwara belt.
Archaean- Palaeoproterozoic		Mahakoshal Group, Sausar group. Chotanagar Gneissic Complex
Archaean		Bundelkhand Granitoid Complex (BGC)Gneissic Complexes with Supeacrustals:
		Tirodi, Amgaon, Sidhi, Jhabua, Harda, Betul, and Mehroni/ Kuraicha Group(Supracrustals and Gneissic enclaves within BGC)

Source: Geology and Mineral Resources of Madhya Pradesh

Archaean

The term 'Archaean', coined by J.D. Dana in 1782, refers to the oldest rocks of the earth's crust. The rocks of the Archaean system lack any signs of life; they are entirely devoid of fossils or azoic. Characterized by a crystalline nature, extensive contortions, and faulting, these rocks exhibit minimal sediment are predominantly intruded by plutonic intrusions, and generally have a well-defined foliated structure.

Archaean formation in Madhya Pradesh comprises Tirodi Biotite Gneiss (TBC), Amgaon Gneiss, Sidhi Gneiss (Son valley), Jhabua Gneiss complex, Gneisses of Harda Inlier, Betul Gneissic complex, Kuraicha/Mehroni Groups (enclaves within Bundelkhand Granite Complex).

Tirodi Biotite Gneiss (TBG): The gneiss found in the Sausar belt, particularly in Seoni, Balaghat, and Chhindwara districts, is identified as Tirodi Biotite Gneiss. This rock formation extends to the base of the Amarkantak Plateau in the Dindori district. The Tirodi Biotete Gneiss is characterised by its coarse to medium-grained texture, ranging from light to dark grey. It exhibits distinct banding and is often porphyroblastic. The foliation and banding are due to alternating quartzo-feldspathic and micaceous layers and are exposed in narrow, parallel, tightly folded formations. folds.

Amgaon Gneiss-Supracrustal: The higher-grade gneiss-migmatite-supracrustal association, found south of the Central Indian Shear (CIS) in the southeast Balaghat district, specifically in the Lanji area, is categorized as the Amagoan Gneiss Complex (AGC). Within the Amagoan Group, both meta-sedimentary and meta-igneous suites are present, consisting of metapelite, quartzite, banded magnetite quartzite, calc-silicate rock, amphibolite and meta- ultramafites.

Sidhi Gneiss-Supracrustal (Son Valley): The Sidhi Gneiss is exposed near Sidhi town, forming a slender band situated between the Mahakoshal Group and Vindhyan Supergroup. This geological formation comprises melanocratic gneisses, banded gneiss, feldspathic mica schist, and associated grey to pink granite gneiss with enclaves of quartz-mica schist, and quartzose phyllite, talc-chlorite schist, quartz-sericite schist, sillimanite schist, and crystalline limestone.

Jhabua Gneiss Complex: Jhabua Gneiss Complex, also known as the Alirajpur Gneissic Complex, forms the basement of the Aravalli Supergroup. The gneisses in this region exhibit migmatitic features and commonly include enclaves of quartz-hornblende gneiss, amphibolite gneiss, and ultrabasic rocks.

Gneisses of Harda Inlier: Archaean rocks inliers are scattered in patches between Barwah-Bain-Newar. In the eastern region, these inliers are primarily composed of granitoids. On the western side, they are predominantly characterized by meta-sediments, like chlorite-sericite phyllite, phyllitic conglomerate, and quartzite. Notably, there is a significant presence of a large pyroxene–hornblendite body near Semli in this geological area.

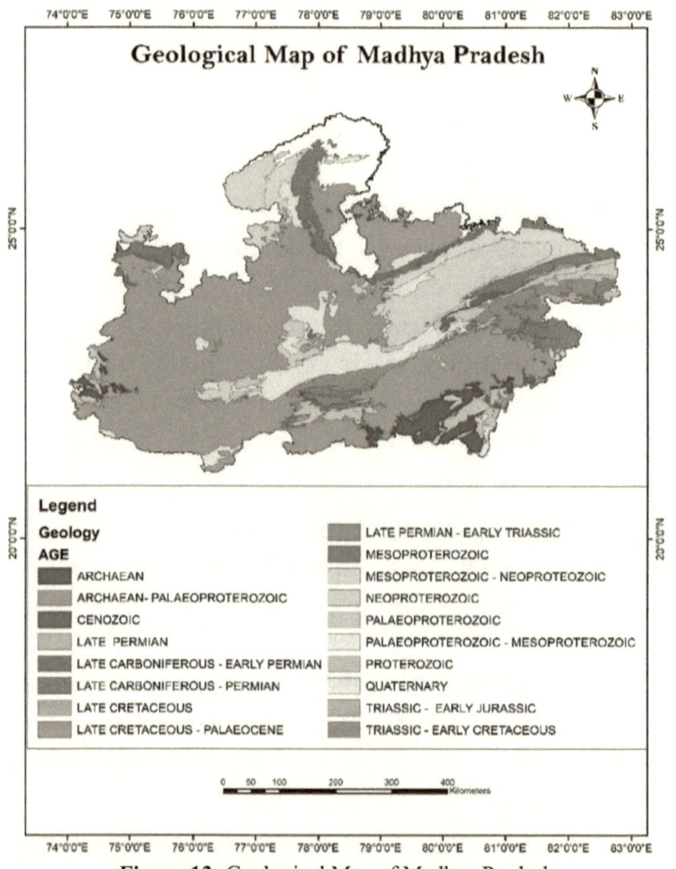

Figure 13: Geological Map of Madhya Pradesh

Betul Gneissic Complex: Betul Gneissic Complex represents the reworked basement, encompassing high-grade banded gneiss, granitic gneiss, and amphibolite. These basement rocks are exposed as patches at different locations, exhibiting varying degrees of ductile deformation. The most extensive exposure is observed near Amla and Betul, featuring granite gneiss, injection gneiss, and banded gneiss. Additionally, associated intercalated bands of tremolite-actinolite schist and amphibolite are present within this complex.

Kuraicha/Mehroni Groups (Enclaves within Bundelkhand Granite Complex): Bundelkhand Granite Complex (BGC) incorporates enclaves of older gneiss and supracrustals. The Complex extends from a few centimetres to large linear belts, reaching widths of approximately 8 km and lengths ranging from tens of kilometres to 200 km. The supracrustal component is characterized by a volcano-sedimentary sequence, comprising basaltic, andesitic, and dacitic flows, quartzite (occasionally bearing fuchsite), argillites, Banded Iron Formation (BIF), and calc-silicate.

Archaean – Paleoproterozoic

This formation consists of Bundelkhand Granite Complex, Mohar Cauldron, Chotanagpur Gneissic Complex (CGC).

Bundelkhand Granite Complex: Shivpuri – Tikamgarh – Chhatarpur region of north Madhya Pradesh is occupied by the Bundelkhand Granite Complex. This batholithic mass primarily consists of multiphase granitic intrusion with relicts of Tonalite – Trondhjemite Gneiss (TTG) and supracrustals. Three distinct granitic phases have been identified: (i) porphyritic to non-porphyritic medium-grained granite, forming main batholithic mass in Gwalior and Shivpuri districts (ii) aplitic granite occurring as small plutons and dykes and (iii) pink porphyritic coarse-grained granite constituting the batholithic mass in Tikamgarh and Chhatarpur districts.

Mohar Cauldron: The cauldron is located around Mohar village in the east of Shivpuri district, spans an area of approximately 50 sq km. this unique geological structure us characterized by a circular outcrop pattern consisting of granite collapse breccia, measuring around 7.5 km in diameter. The Mohar Cauldron structure is composed collapse breccia, felsic volcanics, and intra filled up Vindhyan sediments.

Chotanagpur Gneissic Complex (CGC): In the Sidhi (Son Valley) area, a linear belt exposes older metamorphics and granite gneiss located to the south of the Mahakoshal Belt and bordering Mirapur district of Uttar Pradesh in Rihand reservoir area. The gneissic complex is associated with high-grade meta-sediments and meta- volcanics, encompassing mafic and ultramafic schist. Notable formations within this complex include sillimanite – garnet gneiss, garnet – sillimanite – corundum schist, staurolite – garnet – biotite schist, garnetiferous grunerite – magnetite quartzite, quartz – sericite schist, quartzite, marble and calc-silicate rocks, talc – chlorite schist and amphibolite and hornblende granulite. In specific locations, such as west of Makrohar, northeast of Mahadeva, and southeast of Pipra, there are discontinuous bodies of gabbroic anorthosite, gabbro and norite embedded within migmatitic gneiss.

These intrusive bodies exhibit distinct contacts with the surrounding rocks, showing no significant impact on the gneiss. Enclaves of gneiss and restites of basic rock are observed within anorthosites. The region also features numerous syenite, pegmatite and quartz veins traverse the gneiss. Syenite is exposed northwest and west of Sidhi. Additionally, there are post - Gondwana basic dykes present in the area.

Palaeoproterozoic

Palaeoproterozoic formation consists of Mahakoshal Group, Sausar Group, Metamorphites of Bilaspur – Taigarh – Surguja (BRS) Belt, Betul – Chhindwara Belt, Aravalli supergroup, Dongargarh supergroup.

Mahakoshal Group: The Mahakoshal Belt, trending ENE – WSW to E-W, stretches fro more than 500 km from Barmanghat (southwest of Jabalpur) in the west to Palamau in Jharkhand in the east, exhibiting an average width of 20 km and covering an expansive area exceeding 9000 sq km. The Mahakoshal Group is distinguished by the presence of basic meta-volcanics, pyroclastics, clastics and chemical precipitates, complemented by numerous post-tectonic granite plugs, syenite bodies, ultramafic plugs and a wide variety of alkaline intrusives.

Sausar group: Sausar Group occurs engulfed within the Tirodi Gneiss along the southern fringe of Satpura Province, with the Central Indian Suture (CIS) delineating its southern limit. This group manifests as a 75 km wide arc-shaped fold belt, displaying a predominant ENE-WSW trend with a southerly convexity. The rock of Sausar Group spand from Kachidhana in Chhindwara district to Baihar in Balaghat district, covering a distance of approximately 210 km across Seoni and Balaghat districts in Madhya Pradesh, as well as Nagpur and Bhandara districts in Maharashtra.

Metamorphites of Bilaspur – Raigarh – Surguja (BRS) Belt: A section of the gneiss- supracrustal belt occurs occurs on the eastern fringe of Dindori district, adjascent to the Koria district of Chhattisgarh. The Bilaspur – Raigarh – Surguja Belt encompassess high grade gneiss, supracrustal rocks and a series of low to medium grade meta-sedimentary rocks, occasionally accompanied by metabasic intrusions. The lithologic and tectonic characterists observed in the Bilaspur-Raigarh – Surguja belt closely resemble those of the Sausar Mobile belt.

Betul- Chhindwara belt: The Betul- Chhindwara Belt occurs in the western part of Satpura Province and is situated between the Mahakoshal Belt in the northeast and Sausar belt to the southeast. Extending approximately 20 to 30 km in width and spanning a length of about 150 km, this belt follows an ENE-WSW trend from Chicholi in the west to Chhindwara in the east. In the Kanhan valley, a barrier of deformed granitoid rocks act as a dividing line between the Betul- Chhindwara belt and the Sausar belt.

Aravalli supergroup: In the Jhabua area, the metasedimentary – metavolcanics sequence that overlays the gneiss – supracrustal assemblage has been linked to the Aravalli Supergroup found in the neighbouring states of Rajasthan and Gujarat. Specifically, in the Jhabua region, the Aravalli supergroup has been divided into three groups: Badi Sardi, Hathni and Meghnagar groups.

Badi Sardi group: The volcano-sedimentary rocks occurring to the south of Hathni lineament have been classified under the Badi Sardi group. This group includes various rock types such as quartzite, dolomitic marble and mica-schist with bands of BHQ, calc-silicate, calc-gneiss, talc-tremolite schist, phyllite, graphite schist etc. the rocks are co-folded with the Alirajpur Gneissic Complex.

Hathni group: The low - grade volcano sedimentary rocks, specifically chlorite schist and Phyllite, which are exposed within the Hathni lineament zone, have been categorised under the Hathni group.

Meghnagar group: The low-grade sedimentary sequence, which encompasses quartzite, phyllite and dolomitic limestone and phosphorite and is located to the north of Hathni lineament, is designated as part of the Meghnagar group. Additionally, small isolated bodies of manganese ore have been observed in association with calc phyllite, chert and quartzite of Anas Formation within the Meghnagar group at various locations such as Kajlidongri, Rambhapur, Tumdia, Parnali, Jamli and Palsa.

Dongargarh supergroup: In the Rajnandgaon – Dongargarh area of western Chhattisgarh, a distinctive sequence of late Archaean – Mesoproterozoic age, consisting of volcanics and low-grade metasedimentary rocks, is exposed and is classified as part of the Dongargarh supergroup. This supergroup includes three main components: (i) the Nandgaon group, (ii) Chilpi group and (iii) Khairagarh group.

Nandgaon group: The Nandgaon group encompasses two main formations: The Bijli Rhyolite and the Pitepani basic volcanics.

The Bijli Rhyolite is primarily composed of rhyolite, featuring interbanded rhyolite conglomerate, welded rhyolite tuffs, rhyolitic agglomerate, ignimbrite and sandstone. Pitepani volcanics mainly include massive to porphyritc basalt with rare pillow structure.

Malanjkhand granite: The Malanjkhand granite spans an area of approximately 1000 sq km in the eastern part of Balaghat district in Madhya Pradesh. It extends into the adjacent Rajnandgaon district of Chhattisgarh and host the famous Malanjkhand copper deposit. Malanjkhand batholith comprises various rock types, including tonalite, granodiorite and granite.

Palaeo- Mesoproterozoic

This formation consists of Bijawar group, Barwah-Handia area, Narmada valley (Harda Inlier), Gwalior group, Khairagarh group.

Bijawar group: In 1859, Medlicott, H.B. coined the term "Bijawar" formation for the metamorphics found in the linear east-west trending narrow basin near Bijawar town, emphaasing their resistance to grouping into stages. The Bijawar group comprises predominantly unmetamorphosed and very little deformed sedimentary rocks such as, dolomite, shale, sandstone, etc. Metasediments and metavolcanics of Sidhi (Son valley) and upper Narmada valley, earlier considered as Bijawars have been included in Mahakoshal group.

Bijawar group hosts several economic minerals like phosphorite and low silica dolomite. Iron ore is however pocket in nature. Minor occurrences of base metals are also reported from Bajno Dolomite.

Barwah-Handia area, Narmada valley (Harda Inlier):In the Narmada valley, specifically in Dewas and Hoshangabad districts between Barwah and Handia, a set of rock closely resembling the sedimentary rocks found in the Bijawar region is observed. This rock assemblage primarily includes chert breccia, quartzite, cherty limestone, dolomitic limestone with stromatolitic features, clay, and contemporaneous lava flows.

Gwalior group: Gwalior group primarily comprises sandstone, shale, and traps, forming hill ranges in an east-west direction across Gwalior, Datia, and the southern part of Bhind districts. The Vindhyan rocks of the Kaimur group, dipping north-west, overlay these formations in a conformable manner. The rocks are practically unmetamorphosed and very similar to the Gijawar group of Bundelkhand.

Khairagarh group: To the east of Lanji in Balaghat district, the Khairagarh group is observed, unconformably overlying the Nandgaon group. This geological formation includes a volcano sedimentary sequence, commencing with the basal conglomerate, sandstone, and shale of Bortalao formation. Subsequently, it features the Sitagota volcanics, karutola formation (sandstone), Mangikuta volcanics, Ghogra formation (sandstone and shale) and Kotima basic volcanics.

Meso-Neoproterozoic

Vindhyan supergroup: The Vindhyan Basin spreads over an area of 1,00,000 sq km, with 60,000 sq km exposed in Central India between Hoshangabad in the west, Sasaram in the east, Chittorgarh in the south and Dholpur in the north. The remaining potion lies beneath the Deccan Traps and Quaternary alluvium.

The Vindhyan Basin represents one of the spectacular Proterozic basins developed in the shadow of the Bundelkhand Granite massif and the Aravalli – Delhi and Satpura orogenic belts. In Madhya Pradesh, the Vindhyans are found in the western Son valley, Sagar, Panna, Guna, Shivpuri, Mandsaur, Gandhisagar, Harda and Bhopal regions, separated by Deccan Trap and alluvium cover. The Son-Narmada North Fault, active since early Proterozoic times, demarcates the southern boundary of the Vindhyan basin. The Jabera dome stands out as one the most remarkable structures on the southern margin.

Semri group: The Semri group is exposed along the peripheries of the basin and is well developed in the Son valley, Rewa , Sidhi,

Katni, and Jabalpur districts. It is also well- developed along the norther limit of the Vindhyan terrain in the Bundelkhand region in parts of Satna, Panna, Chhattarpur and Damoh districts. The group mainly consists on conglomerate, sandstone, dolomitic limestone, porcellanitic shale, olive shale, glauconitic sandstone, as well as alternating layers of limestone and shale.

Kaimur group: The Kaimur sandstone extends beyond the Semri rocks in a northward and westward direction, directly overlaying the Bundelkhand granite and Bijawar rocks. The Kaimur group is distinguished by the notable escarpment and magnificent waterfalls sculpted within the sandstone.

Rewa group: Rewa group represents a fairly thick alternating sequence of argillaceous litho units with interbedded diamondiferous conglomerate horizons conformably overlying the Kaimur rocks with a gradational contact. This group is ddistinguished by the lateral facies variation and is most prominently observed along the Satna-Chitrakoot section, showcasing a sequence that includes shale, sandstone, limestone, bedded chert and thin conglomerate. Bhander group: Bhander group occupies the central part of the basin in Rewa, Satna, Damoh, Sagar and Bhopal.

Volcanics and Intrusives: Synsedimentry volcanism had taken place on the eastern (Son valley) as well as western (Chittorgarh area) margins of the Vindhyan basin during early Semri period.

Palaeozoic – Mesozoic

This group comprises of Gondwana supergroup, late carboniferous – early Permian (Talchir formation), early Permian (Barakar formation), Late Permian (Rewa basin, Barren measures, Raniganj formation, Satpura basin, Motur formation, Bijori formation).

Gondwana supregroup: Gondwana supregroup is mainly developed in two regions, Satpura basin, which includes portions of Betul, Chhindwara, Hoshangabad, Narsinghpur and Jabalpur districts and the south Rewa basin, covering parts of Katni, Umaria, Shahdol, Anuppur and Sidhi districts. Within these basins, the Gondwana sequence from the Late Carboniferous to the early Cretaceous period is well-preserved.

Late Carboniferous – early Permian:

Talchir formation: The Talchir formation includes diamictite, fine to medium-grained sandstone, grey and olive-green needle shale, along with varves and rhythmites. The presence of striated pavements in the Popas nala near Chordingri beneath the basal tillite corroborate Talchir glaciation. Plant fossils found in the upper part of the Talchir formation show an assemblage of Glossopteris indica, Neoggreratheopsis hislopi and Samaropsis sp.

Early Permian: Barakar formation: The Barakar formation is predominantly composed of coarse to medium-grained feldspathic sandstone, along with grey shale, carbonaceous shale and coal seams. Within the Satpura region, it is mainly divided into arenaceaous lower member with thin impersistent coal seams and more argillanceous upper member, which contains all the economically viable regional seams.

Mesozoic – Cretaceous

Mesozoic – Cretaceous consists of Early Traissic, Middle-Late Traiassic, Jurassic, Upper Cretaceous, Late Cretaceous.

The Deccan Trap comprises basaltic lava flows from the Cretaceous – Eocene age, accompanied by subordinate inter-trappean sediments. In Madhya Pradesh, the Deccan Trap covers over half of the total area of the State, extending across almost the entirety of east and west Nimar, Dhar, Indore, Ujjain, Ratlam, Shahapur, Raigarh, Vidisha districts and a significant portion of Jhabua, Dewas, Sehore, Bhopal, Guna, Shivpuri, Sagar, Betul, Chhindwara, Seoni, Mandla and Shahdol districts. Isolated exposures of the Deccan Trap are also present in Hoshangabad, Narsinghpur and Jabalpur.

In Madhya Pradesh, the Deccan lava flows have been classified into three groups, namely., the Malwa group, the Satpura group, and the Amarkantak group.

Cenozoic

Cenozoic consists of Mio-pliocene, Pleistocene(recent), Quaternary alluvial deposits.

The Katni formation of Mio-Pliocene is exposed at an elevation of 300 m above msl over the entire Katni valley. On the Amarkantak plateau, primarily high-level laterite, accompanied by bauxite, has developed on the Deccan basalt. In the Bilaspur-Raigarh-Surguja belt, there are four distinct tyeps of laterite assemblages. Additionally, between Hoshangabad and Narsinghpur, within Narmada river terrace, Pleistocene lateritic lumps containing haematitic iron ore and pieces of Deccan trap are observed deposited.

Approximately 12 percent of the regions total area is covered by Quaternary deposits, and sedimentation is predominantly confined to river basins. The major Quaternary basins are namely., Narmada valley, Tapti valley and Chambal Basin.

The Quaternary deposits span from the Lower Pleistocene to Holocene. Seven lithostratigraphic formations have been identified on the basis of (i) order of superposition (ii) erosional unconformity (iii) degree of oxidation and calcification (iv) pedogenic characters (v) fossil assemblage (vi) presence of rhyolitic tephra and (vii) palaeomagnetic signatures.

The Quaternary sediments of Narmada valley have yielded an extensive collection of mammalian vertebrate fossil ranging from Middle to Upper Pleistocene. Notably, the skull of the globally renowned Homo erectus was discovered in the Surajkund formation on the right bank of Narmada river in the village Hathnora. Other Quaternary deposits in the region include the Pilikarar formation(along the left bank section of Kaliadoh nala, a tributary of Narmada river), Dhansi formation (on the left bank of Narmada river), Baneta formation (along the right bank section of Narmada river), Hirdepur formation (found in the right bank section of Shakker river at Hirdepur), Bauras formation (on the right bank of Narmada river) and Ramnagar formation(the youngest formation of the central Narmada alluvial complex, located downstream of Ramnagar on the northern (right) bank of Narmada river.

Tectonism

The movement of lithospheric plates in different directions induces stress and strain on the brittle rocks of the earth's surface. When these rocks ultimately break and move in different directions, they cause a fracture in the crust called a fault. Major fractures in the earth's crust can be observed for many kilometers on the ground and several kilometers extending down into the crust.

Important faults and earthquakes in the State are;

(i) Son-Narmada-North Fault (SNNF): This fault marks the southern margin of the Vindhyan Supergroup.

(ii) Son-Narmada-South Fault (SNSF): This fault marks the southern boundary of the Palaeoproterozoic Mahakoshal Supercrustal Belt.

(iii) Balrampur Fault (BF): This fault stretches in an ENE-WSW direction from southeast of Shahdol to Tattapani in Chhattisgarh, spanning over 200 km across the Mahanadi-Gondwana Basin. There is no geological evidence indicating post- Mesozoic reactivation along this fault, except the emplacement of mafic dykes, possibly of Upper Cretaceous origin.

(iv) Gavilgarh – Tan Shear (GTS): The Gavilgarh-Tan Shear extends over more than 400 km with width ranging from 50 m to 1.5 km from Gavilgarh to east of Amarkantak.

(v) Central Indian Shear Zone (CIS): The Central Indian Shear Zone (CIS) is traceable from southeast of Nagpur

                    GEOGRAPHY OF MADHYA PRADESH

in Maharashtra to northwest of Raigarh in Chhattisgarh, passing through Balaghat in Madhya Pradesh, covering a distance of over 500 km. There is no geological evidence indicating post- Precambrain reactivation along the CIS.

Earthquakes are usually (not exclusively) associated with faulting. Large sections of the Bundelkhand Craton have not experienced major earthquake in recent years. On December 31, 1926, an earthquake with a magnitude of 6.0 was recorded in the northwestern part of Bundelkhand Craton, specifically in the Guna district. Subsequently, on April 11, 1929, the same area witnessed another earthquake of similar magnitude.

The Son Valley earthquake (Umaria earthquake), registering a magnitude 6.5 took place on 2nd June, 1927. The earthquake was felt up to Ranchi and Allahabad. The epicenter of the earthquake was in close proximity to the Son-Narmada-South Fault.

The Satpura earthquake occurred on 14th March, 1938, with a magnitude of 5.5. Its impact was felt in most parts of central and western India and parts of Rajasthan and Andhra Pradesh. This earthquake was considered as a dep-focus earthquake with the hypo-central depth of about 40 km. the Balaghat earthquake of 25th August, 1957 with a magnitude of 5.5 was felt at Nagpur and Jabalpur.

The Jabalpur earthquake which occurred on May 22, 1997 with a magnitude of 6.0 was the first earthquake recorded on the newly set up Broad Band Seismic network of India Meteorological Department (IMD). The seismic event was ascribed to the reverse reactivation of the crustal scale fault of Son-Narmada-South Fault (SNSF) at a focal depth of 35 km by a slip of 37 cm.

Soil

Madhya Pradesh's soil varies from region to region depending on the types of rocks/minerals found. The soil of Madhya Pradesh is influenced by its location (peninsular plateau) and geologic formation. The soil classification of the State (as per the US Soil Taxonomy) belongs to 5 Orders, 6 Suborders, 11 Greatgroups, 26 subgroups, and 130 Soil families. The Inceptisols (Latin inceptum, "beginning"; young soils at the beginning of their "life") are the most dominant covering about 40.5 percent of the total geographical area of the State, followed by Vertisols (Latin verto, "turn"; soils in which material from O and A horizons falls through surface cracks and ends up below deeper horizons; the usual horizon order is inverted) covering about 20.7 percent, Alfisol("al" for aluminum, "f" for iron (chemical symbol Fe), two prominent elements in these soils) covering about 19.1 percent, Entisols (last three letters in "recent"; these are recently formed soils) covering about 19.0 percent, Mollisols (Latin mollis, "soft"; soft soils) covering about 0.6 percent, and rockout cropscover about 0.03 percent.

The State has 4 soil types based on their formation, colors, and thickness namely, Shallow and Medium black soil, Deep medium black soil, alluvial soil, and mixed red and black soil. Shallow and Medium black soil covered about 3.06 percent of the total geographical area of the state. This soil is mostly found in the Betul, Chhindwara, and Seoni districtsof the State. Deep medium black soil covered about 36.53 percent of the total geographical area of the State. This soil is mostly found in Narsinghpur, Hoshangabad, Harda, Shahdol, Umaria, Jabalpur, Katni, Sagar, Damoh, Vidhisha, Raisen, Bhopal, Sehore, Rajgarh, Ujjain, Dewas, Shajapur, Agar (Malwa) Mandsaur, Neemuch, Ratlam, Jhabua, Dhar, Indore, Khargone, Barwani, Khandwa, Guna(partly), Shivpuri(partly), Datia(partly) and Sidhi(partly), Anuppur, Ashoknagar, Burhanpur, Alirajpur, Singroli.

Alluvial soil covered about 7.57 percent of the total geographical area of the State. This soil is mostly found in Gwalior, Morena, Sheopurkala, Bhind, and Shivpuri(partly).

The Mixed Red and Black soil covered about 18.30 percent of the total geographical area of the State. This soil is mostly found in Mandla, Dindori, Balaghat, Rewa, Satna, Panna, Chhatarpur, Tikamgarh, Shivpuri(partly), Guna(partly), Datia(partly) and Sidhi (partly).

Reference

1. Briefing book, June 2014. Geological Survey of India (Central Region), Ministry of Mines, Government of India. https:// www.gsi.gov.in/webcenterShowProperty;jsessionid=0Z55efYJ_ BESqyoTUVmGW1xLxCw-v2tcVblEs3RAfnoIcg8zvPf2!- 107032927!-68022989?nodeId=/UCM/DC

2. D.B. Tamgadge, S.T. Gaikawad, S.R. Naga Bhushana, K.S. Gajbhiye, S.N. Deshmuk and J. Sehgal (1996), "Soil of Madhya Pradesh (Their kinds, distributions, characterisations, and interpretations) for Optimising Land Use". NBSS Publ.59b(Soils of India Series 6). National Bureau of Soil Survey and Land Use Planning, Nagpur, India. P.182+9 sheet soil map (I:500,000 scale).

3. Geology and Mineral Resources of Madhya Pradesh (2014) Geological Survey of India Miscellaneous publication No. 30, Part XI, 3 rd revised edition, Govt. of India. ISSN 0579-4706

4. Hess, D (2015). Physical geography, A landscape appreciation. Pearson Idna Education services Pvt. Ltd. ISBN 978-93-3255- 190-9

5. Thematic Services - Bhuvan. https://bhuvan.nrsc.gov.in/home/ index.php

CHAPTER 3

DRAINAGE SYSTEM AND CLIMATE

Drainage systems also known as the river system is an integrated systems of river tributaries that collect and funnel surface water to the sea, lake, and other water bodies. The entire area drained by rivers and streams that contribute water to a single drainage system is known as a drainage basin. Madhya Pradesh is blessed with a number of large and small rivers which drain the length and breadth of the State. The drainage system of

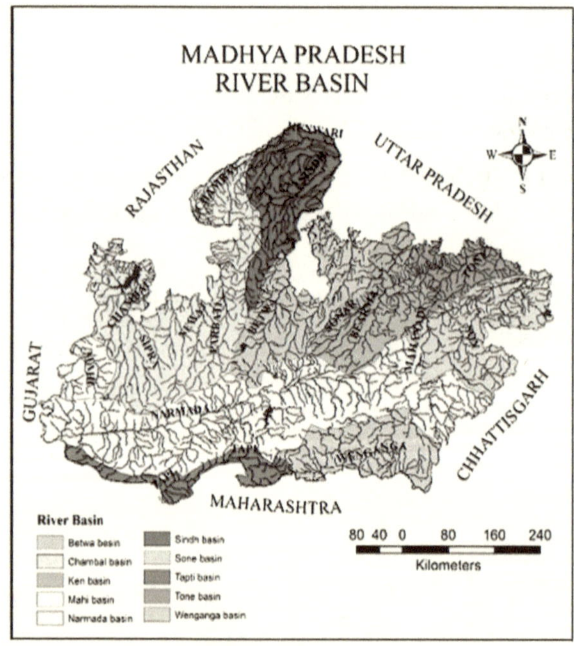

Figure 14: River Basin

the State can be broadly classified as; the Ganga River basin (Chambal, Betwa, Son, Ken, Sindh etc), The Narmada River basin, The Tapti River basin, The Mahi basin, and the Godavari basin (Wainganga, Pench, and Wardha).

Ganga River Basin: The Ganga River basin spreads over India, Tibet (China), Nepal, and Bangladesh with a total area of 10,86,000 sq. km. The major part of the Ganga River basin lies in India and is the largest river basin in the country draining an area of 861452 sq km which is approximately one-fourth (26.3 %) of the total geographical area of the country. The Ganga River is the 20th longest river in Asia and the 41st longest in the world.

In India the Ganga River Basin spreads over 11 (Eleven) states namely, Uttar Pradesh (241392 sq. km (28.02%), Madhya Pradesh (181065.5 sq. km (21.02%), Rajasthan (112496.26 sq. km (13.06%), Bihar (93579.8 sq. km (10.86%), West Bengal (71489 sq. km (8.30%), Uttarakhand (52988.5 sq. km (6.15%), Jharkhand (50389.14 sq. km (5.85%), Haryana (34343 sq. km(3.99%), Chhattisgarh (17907.60 sq. km(5.85%), Himachal Pradesh (4317 sq. km (0.50%), and Delhi (1484.2 sq. km(0.17%). The basin lies between 73°2' to 89°5' E Longitudes and 21° 6' to 31° 21' N Latitudes.

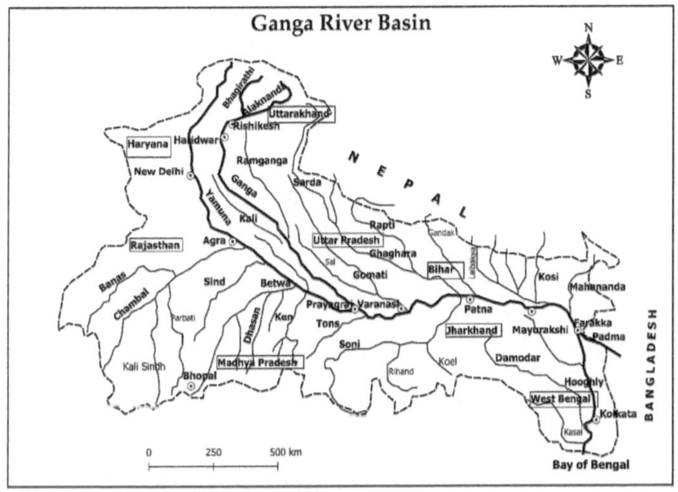

Figure 15: Ganga River Basin

The Chambal River and the Betwa River are two important sub-tributaries that join the Ganga River the from left.

Chambal River is a tributary of the Yamuna River which was known as Charmanvati in ancient times. The river rises in the Malwa plateau of the Vindhya range near Mhow Cantt., south-west of Indore district at an elevation of about 854 m above sea level. It has a total basin area of 143,219 sq km, out of which 76,854 sq km lies in Madhya Pradesh, 65,264 sq km lies in Rajasthan, and 1,101 sq km lies in Uttar Pradesh. The total length of the river is 938 km, out of which 320 km lies in Madhya Pradesh, 226 lies in Rajasthan, 216 km flows in the boundary between Madhya Pradesh and Rajasthan, 112 km flows in the boundary between Madhya Pradesh and Uttar Pradesh and 64 km in Uttar Pradesh. The river is mainly a rainfed river. The river flows north in a gorge up to the city of Kota. Below Kota, the river turns to the northeast and after passing Bundi, Sawai, Madhopur, and Dholpur in Rajasthan it finally joins the Yamuna River about 40 km to the west of Etawah district of Uttar Pradesh.

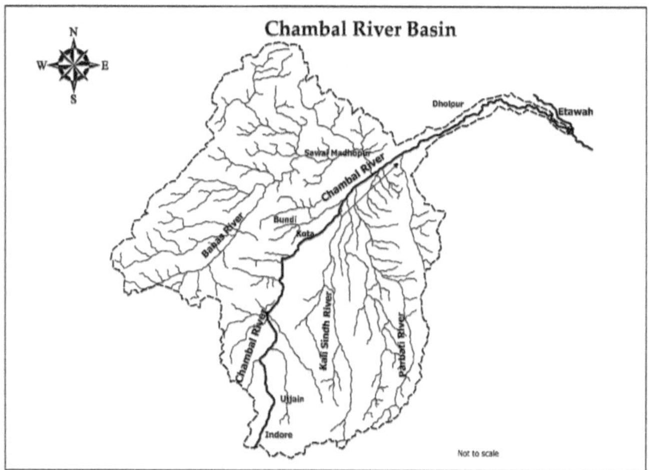

Figure 16: Chambal River Basin

The Banas River which rises from the Khamnor hills of the Aravalli range is the main left bank tributary of the Chambal River. The Sind River originates from the Vidisha district and joins the

Chambal River near Nonera village in the Kota district. The Ken River which originates from the Barner range joins Yamuna Near Chila. The Chambal River is well known for its extensive ravines which it has craved all along in the lower Chambal valley. The ravines formation of the Chambal basin is attributed to a slight uplift during the recent geological times.

Son/Sone River (Swarna Nadi) is a major right-bank tributary of the Ganga River. The river rises at Sonbhadra in the Maikala range at an elevation of 600 m above sea level in the Amarkantak plateau not far from the source of the Narmada River. Sone River leaves the plateau in a series of waterfalls and meets the Kaimur range which turns its course to the north-east. This river joins the Ganga River about 16 km upstream of Danapur in the Patna district of Bihar after flowing for a distance of 780 km from the source. The drainage basin of Sone is spread over 71,900 sq. km. The major tributaries are, Mahanadi, Banas, Johilla, Gopat, Rihand, Kanhar and North Koel.

Betwa River/Betravati also known as Vetravati (containing reeds) in Sanskrit rises in the Vindhya range north of Hoshangabad in Madhya Pradesh at an elevation of 475 m above sea level. The total catchment area of the Betwa River is 46,580 sq km of which 68.6% lies in Madhya Pradesh and 31.3 % lies in Uttar Pradesh. Betwa River flows northeast through Madhya Pradesh and Uttar Pradesh. After traversing a distance of 590 km, the river joins the Yamuna River near Hamirpur in Uttar Pradesh. Nearly half of its course is not navigable and runs over the Malwa plateau before it reaches the upland of Bundelkhand. The main tributaries of the Betwa River are, Halali (Thal River) and Dhasan River. Halali is the largest tributary with a length of 180 km. Betwa River has 14 major tributaries out of which 11 are in Madhya Pradesh. Rajghat Dam (an inter-sate dam project of Madhya Pradesh and Uttar Pradesh) is located in the Betwa River. The Betwa River is linked with the Ken River as part of the river linking project.

Ken River is one of the tributaries of the Yamuna River. The river rises from Ahirgawan village on the north-west slopes of the Barner range and flows through Madhya Pradesh and Uttar Pradesh. The total river basin of Ken River is 28,058 sq km out of which 87% lies in Madhya Pradesh and 13% lies in Uttar Pradesh. Ken River passes through the Panna district, where it makes a gorge at Gangau. Ken River has a total length of 357 km and forms a state boundary between the Chhattarpur district of Madhya Pradesh and the Banda district of Uttar Pradesh. Sonar and Beawar rivers are the main tributaries of the Ken River. Other tributaries are, Kopra, Bewas, Urmil, Mirhasan, Kutni, Kail, Gurne, Patan, Siameri, Chandrawal, Banne, etc. The longest tributary is the Sonar River with 227 km in length and wholly lies in Madhya Pradesh. Ken River joins the Yamuna River in the Banda district in Uttar Pradesh.

Sindh River is one of the longest rivers in central India to join the Yamuna River on its right bank. The river rises in the Malwa plateau in the Vidisha district of Madhya Pradesh. The total length of the river is 470 km, out of which 461 km lies in Madhya Pradesh and 9 km lies in Uttar Pradesh. Sindh River flows north-northeast through the districts of Guna, Ashoknagar, Shivpuri, Datia, Gwalior, and Bhind and joins the Yamuna River in the Jalaun district of Uttar Pradesh, just after the confluence of the Chambal River with Yamuna River. Major tributaries of the Sindh River are, Parbati, Pahuj, Kwari/Kunwari, and Mahuar. Madikheda Dam, a multi-purpose dam is located on the Sindh River in the Shivpuri district of Madhya Pradesh.

The Narmada River basin: The Narmada River originates from the Amarkantak hill in the Anuppur district and is the largest west-flowing river in peninsular India. The Narmada River Basin covers an area of 92,672.42 Sq.km and lies between 72°38' to 81° 43' E Longitude and 21° 27' to 23° 37' N Latitude which is approximately 3 percent of the total geographical area of the country.

 GEOGRAPHY OF MADHYA PRADESH

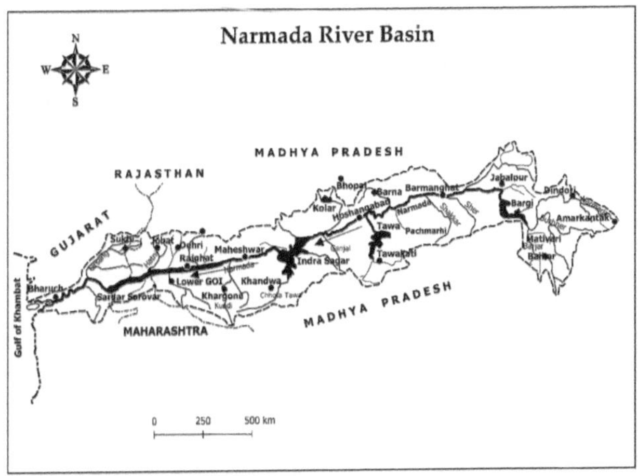

Figure 17: Narmada River Basin

The river basin is bounded by Vindhyas in the north, Maikala range in the east, Satpuras, and the Arabian Sea in the west. The basin covers large areas of Madhya Pradesh (82094.94 Sq. Km (88.58%), Gujarat (8326.34 Sq.km (8.98%), Maharashtra (1580.07 Sq. km (1.7%) and Chhattisgarh (675.7 sq. km (0.73). The basin is divided into 3 (three) sub-basins namely, Narmada Upper, Narmada Middle, and Narmada Lower. The drainage network of Narmada River consists of 41 tributaries out of which 19 are major tributaries.

The total length of the river from its source to the estuary in the Gulf of Khambhat is about 1310 km. The river drained the State for 1,078 km, 32 km flows in the boundary of Madhya Pradesh and Maharashtra, 40 km between Maharashtra and Gujarat, and about 160 km in Gujarat. The river after flowing for about 400 km from its sources, slopes down in Jabalpur where it cascades into a marble gorge to form the world-famous Dhuandhar Falls. Flowing westward from Jabalpur, the river flows through a rift valley between the Vidhyan and the Satpura ranges. Emerging from the hills near Gardeshwar, it meanders through an alluvial plain past Bharuch and makes a 27 km wide estuary to enter the Gulf of Khambat/Arabian Sea.

Narmada River does not form the delta. In Madhya Pradesh, the Narmada River flows through the districts of Mandla, Jabalpur, Narsinghpur, Hoshangabad, Khandwa, and Khargone. The right bank tributaries of the Naramada rivers are, Hiran, Orsang, Barna, Kolar, Tendoni, Man, Uri, and Hatni. The left bank tributaries are, Burhner, Banjar, Shar, Shakkar, Tawa, Kundi, Dudhi, Ganjal, Chhota Tawa, Kundi, Goi, and Karjan.

Narmada River basin is divided into five physiographic zones, (i) The Upper hilly areas, (ii) The Upper Plains (iii) The Middle Plains (iv) The Lower hilly areas, and (v) The Lower plains.

The upper hilly areas and plains come under the Vindhyanchal Baghelkhand region. The region is a hill-valley complex covering Annupur, Shahdol, Dindori, Mandla, Balaghat, Jabalpur, Narsimhapur, and Chhindwara.

The Narmada valley has a youthful appearance with falls, rapids, and gorges in its course. The Dhuandhar Falls (Bheraghat, 15m) followed by a 3 km long marble gorge is an example. The Middle plains and the lower hilly areas come under the Malwa region. The region covers Hoshangabad, Betul, East Nimar, West Nimar, Barwani, Dhar, Dewas, Sehore, and Jhabua districts. The basin has well-marked physiographic units, (i) West Vidhyas, (ii) West Narmada Trough, and (iii) West Satpuras.

The lower plains fall in the Gujarat region. The Gujarat Alluvial Plain is the outcome of an extensive Pleistocene sedimentation known as Coastal Alluvium. The elevation of this region ranges from 5-10 m or even less.

Godavari Basin: The Godavari River basin spreads over the States of Maharashtra, Andhra Pradesh, Chhattisgarh, Odisha, Madhya Pradesh, Karnataka, and the Union Territory of Puducherry having a total area of 3,12,812 Sq.km out of which

31,821 sq. km lies in Madhya Pradesh. The basin lies between 73°24' to 83°4' E longitudes and 16°19' to 22°34' N latitudes. Wainganga, Wardha and Pench rivers of Madhya Pradesh flow south and joins Godavari River. The river Wainganga rises in the Mahadeo hills in Mundara near Gopalganj village in Seoni district of Madhya Pradesh. Wainganga River is the main tributary of the Godavari River (the largest river system of peninsular India). This river develops an extensive floodplain characterized by meanders, low alluvial flats, and slip-off slopes. The river flows south in a winding course through Madhya Pradesh and Maharashtra for about 579 km. The Penganga which rises from the Buldana range joins the Wardha river near Ghughus. Wardha River later joins the Wainganga and becomes the Pranhita River which joins the Godavari River below Sironcha.

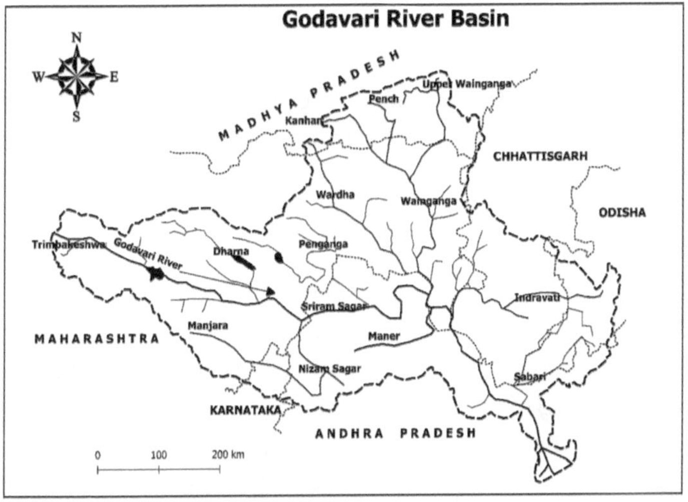

Figure 18: Godavari River Basin

The main tributaries of the Wainganga River are, Thel, Thanwar, Bagh, Garhavi, Khobragadi, and Kathani (Left bank) and Hirri, Chandan, Bawanthari, Kanhan and Mul (Right bank). Wardha River also known as Varada River rises at an altitude of 777m in the Betul district of Madhya Pradesh. This river enters Maharashtra about 32 km from its source. Wardha

River is one of the main right-bank tributaries of Pranhita (The largest tributary of Godavari with about 34.87% of the drainage area). After flowing for 528 km, the Wardha River joins the Wainganga River. Major left bank tributaries are, Kar, Wena, Jam, and Erai, and the right bank tributaries are Madu, Bembla, and Penganga.

Pench River rises from the Chhindwara district of Madhya Pradesh. The river flows from north to south through Pench National Park. It separates the National Park into two halves, east and west Pench. Pench River joins Kanhan River near Bina village and Kanhan River after flowing for 40 km joins Wainganga River as a right bank tributary.

Tapti Basin: Tapti River (Tapi) is known as 'the twin' or 'the handmaid' of the Narmada River. The basin spreads over the States of Madhya Pradesh, Maharashtra, and Gujarat with a total area of 65,145 sq. km out of which 51,504 sq. km lies in Maharashtra, 9804 sq. km lies in Madhya Pradesh and 3837 sq. km lies in Gujarat. The basin lies between 72°33' to 78°17' E longitudes and 20°9' to 21° 50' N latitudes. The Tapti River rises from Multai on Satpura range in Betul district of Madhya Pradesh at an elevation of 752 m above sea level. The total length of the river from origin to outfall into the Arabian Sea is 724 km and it is the peninsular India's second largest west flowing river. Tapti River flows westward almost parallel to Satpura range. It traverses a plain area and then pugs into a rocky gorge of the Satpra hills between the Kalibhit range in Nimar and Chikalda in Berar. At a distance of 192 km from its source, the river enters the Nimar region in Madhya Pradesh and enters the Khandesh plain of Maharashtra. Tapti River has many tributaries; important right bank tributaries are, Vaki, Gomai, Arunavati, Aner (Maharashtra), Important left bank tributaries are, Purna, Girna, Nesu, Amravati, Buray, Panjhra, Bori, Waghur, Mona and Sipna.

                    GEOGRAPHY OF MADHYA PRADESH

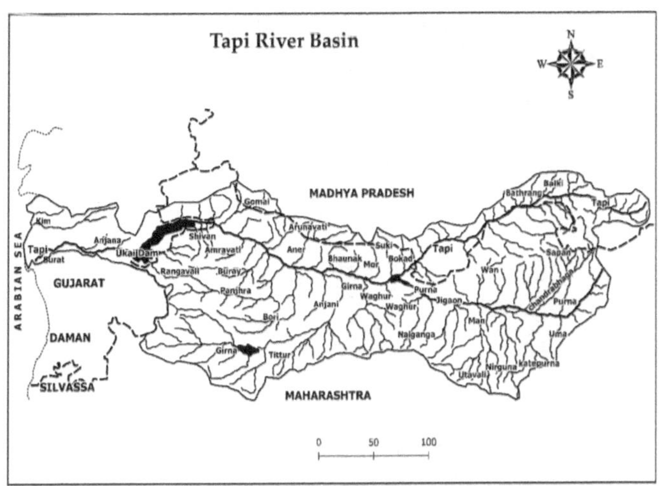

Figure 19: Tapi River Basin

At the Khandwa-Burhanpur gap, the Narmada and Tapti come close to each other. Below the city of Surat (Gujarat), the Tapti River makes an estuary and merges into the Gulf of Khambat.

Mahi Basin: The Mahi Basin spreads over the state of Madhya Pradesh, Rajasthan, and Gujarat with a total drainage area of 34,842 sq. km out of which 16453 sq. km lies in Rajasthan, 11694 sq. km lies in Gujarat, and 6695 sq. km lies in Madhya Pradesh. The basin lies between 72°21' to 75° 19' E longitudes and 21°46' to 24°30' N Latitudes. The basin is bounded by Aravalli hills on the north and northwest, the Malwa plateau on the east, the Vindhyas on the south, and the Gulf of Khambhat on the west. Mahi River rises in the Vindhyan hills in Madhya Pradesh at an elevation of 500 m above sea level near Bhopawar village, Sardarpur tehsil in Dhar district of Madhya Pradesh. The river flows northward through the Dhar and Jhabua districts, turns left, and passes through the Ratlam district of Madhya Pradesh and turns north-west, it enters the Banswara district of Rajasthan and flows south-west directions and enters the Panchmahal district of Gujarat. The river flows in the same direction through the Kheda district of Gujarat and empties itself into the Gulf of Khambhat in the Arabian Sea. The total length of the Mahi River is 583 km. The major tributaries of the Mahi River are, Som, Jakham, Moran, Anas, and Bhador. Important projects such as Jakham Reservoir, Panam Dam, Mahi Bajaj Sagar Project, and Kadana Project are being constructed in this river.

Figure 20: Mahi River Basin

Climate

The geographical location and orographic features have a profound influence on the climate system of the State which is virtually free from maritime influence. The State falls under the sub-tropical climatic region. The Tropic of Cancer (Kark Rekha) passes through 14(fourteen) districts which are located in the center of the State viz., Ratlam, Ujjain, Shajapur, Rajgarh, Sehore, Bhopal, Vidisha, Raisen, Sagar, Damoh, Katni, Jabalpur, Umariya and Shahdol. The climatic system can be further broadly classified into three categories viz., Semi-Arid, Warm temperate rainy, and tropical wet and dry climate. The semi-arid climatic conditions influence the north-western districts of the State. Warm temperate with dry winter and hot summer influence plateaus of Vindhyas and Satpura range and adjoining northern plains. Tropical wet and dry climatic conditions with distinct dry winter seasons influence southern parts of the State.

The maximum and minimum temperature and mean monthly rainfall recorded (Normal climate data) in different stations in the State are plotted in figures.

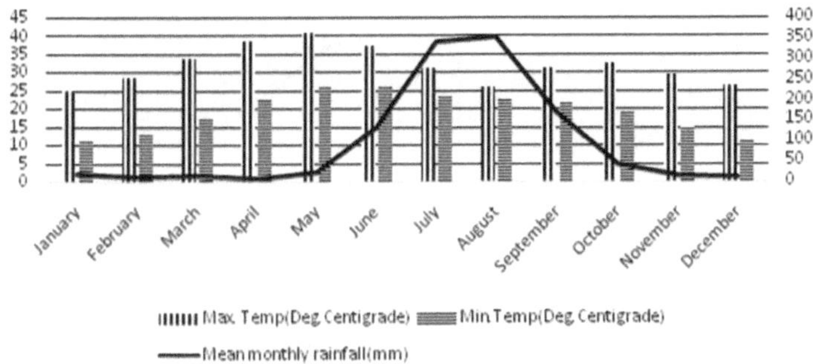

Figure 21: Station-Bhopal, Max and Min. Temperature and Rainfall

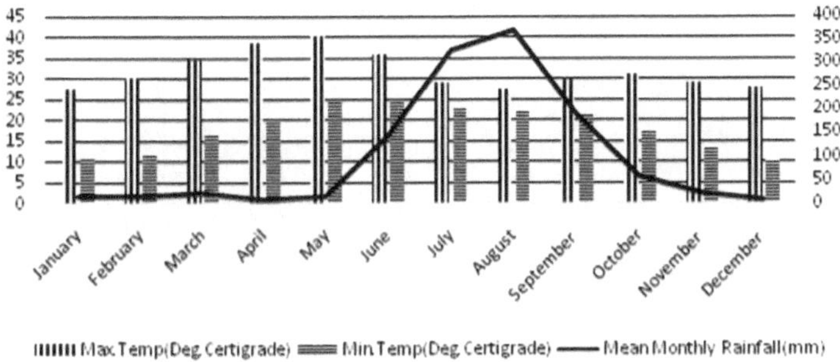

Figure 22: Station-Betul, Max and Min. Temperature and Rainfall

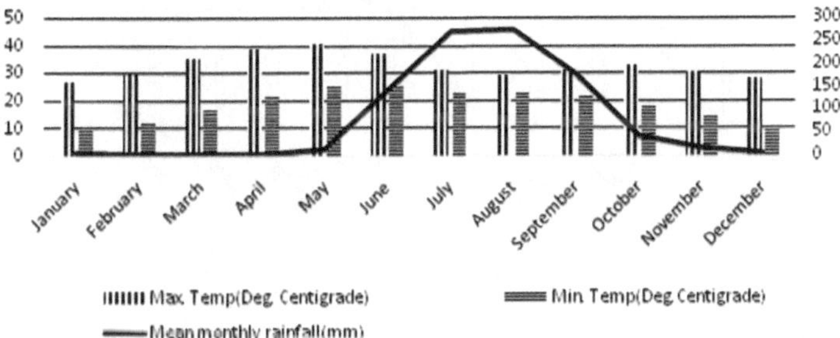

Figure 23: Station-Indore, Max and Min. Temperature and Rainfall

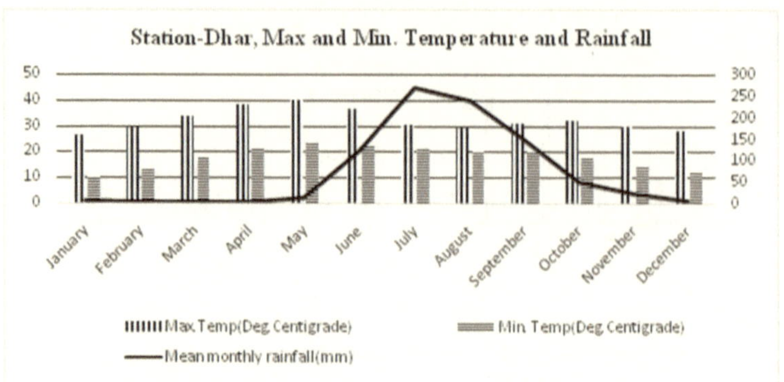

Figure 24: Station-Dhar, Max and Min. Temperature and Rainfall.

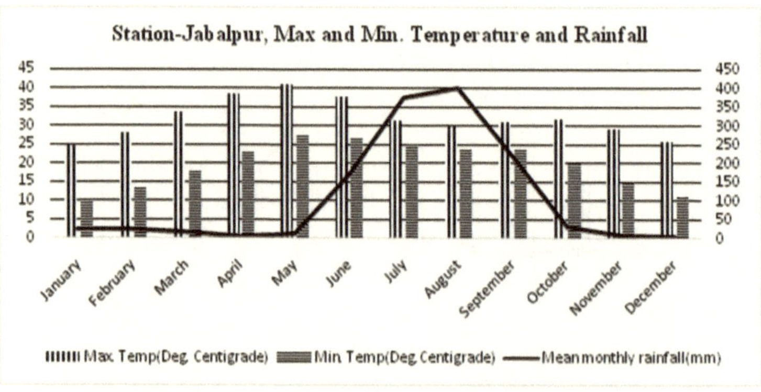

Figure 25: Station-Jabalpur, Max and Min. Temperature and Rainfall

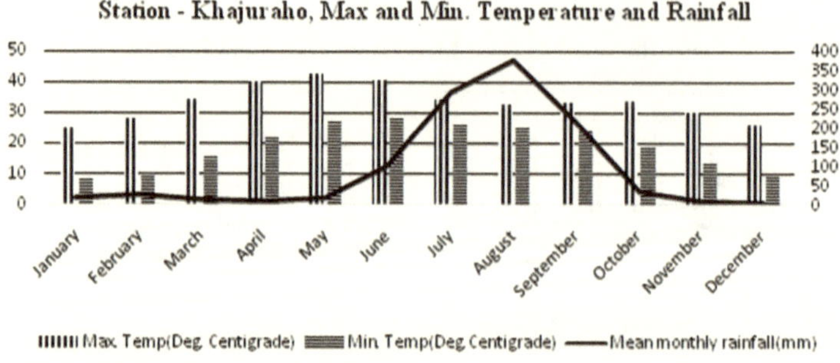

Figure 26: Station-Khajuraho, Max and Min. Temperature and Rainfall

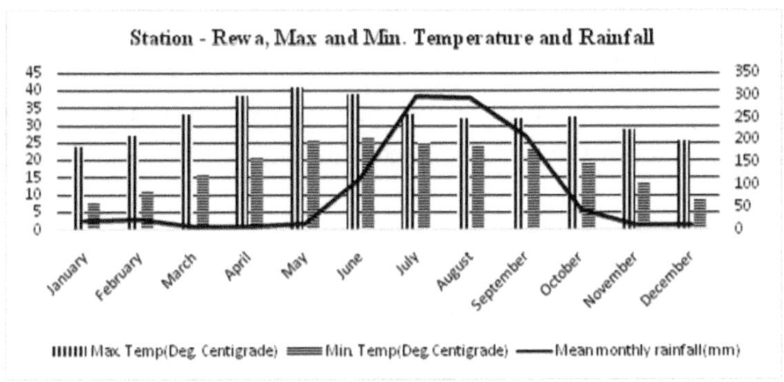

Figure 27: Station-Rewa, Max and Min. Temperature and Rainfall

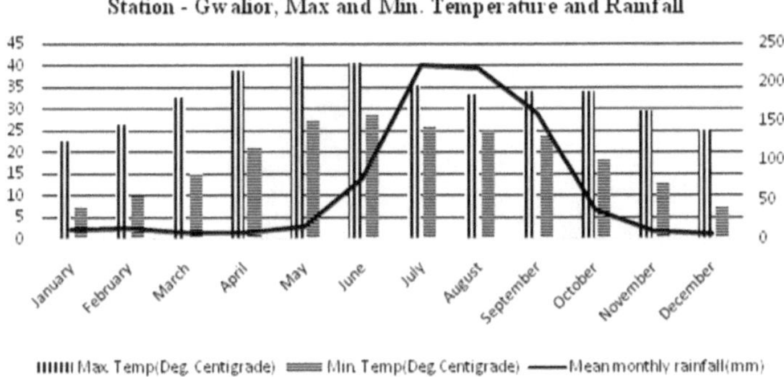

Figure 28: Station-Gwalior, Max and Min. Temperature and Rainfall

The data from the figures 21 to 28 of different stations indicates the State experienced maximum temperature in May, soaring to 41°C in the plains, plateau region, and elevated areas recording 2° to 5 °C lower. December and January are the coldest months when the mean minimum temperature for the State is 10°C, varying from 7°C in the northwest to about 14°C in the South.

Generally, the weather conditions from November to Marchare pleasant over the entire State except few spells when severe cold waves associated with western disturbancesaffect northern parts of the State in the winter season. The period from April to May is hot, very dry, and uncomfortable. Because of the lower temperature, the plateau regions are comparatively less uncomfortable in summer. June is usually uncomfortable due to high humidity and temperature. Generally, July to September is fairly comfortable due to lower temperatures and precipitation but the humidity remains high.

District-wise rainfall normal between 1971 to 2020 (Annual) is plotted in the figure.

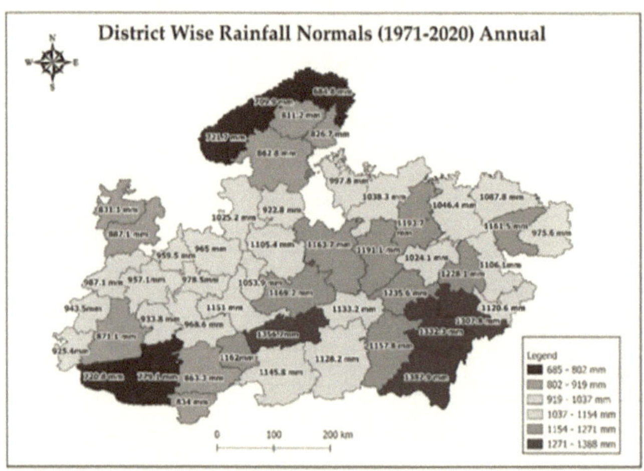

Figure 29: District wise rainfall normal (1971 – 2020) Annual

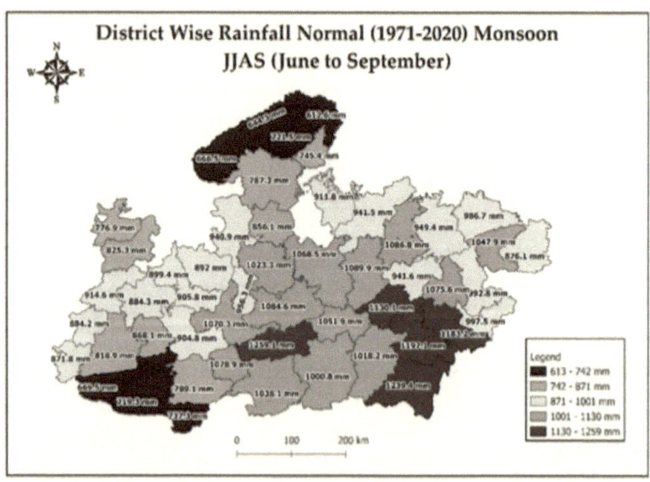

Figure 30: District wise rainfall normal (1971 – 2020) Monsoon JJAS (June to September)

Table 5: District wise rainfall normal (1971-2020) annual and Monsoon JJAS (June to September)

Sl.No	Districts	Annual	Monsoon(June to September)
1	Agar-Malwa	959.5mm	899.4mm
2	Alirajpur	925.4mm	871.8mm
3	Anuppur	1120.6mm	997.5mm
4	Ashoknagar	922.8mm	856.1mm
5	Balaghat	1387.9mm	1239.4mm
6	Barwani	720.8mm	669.5mm
7	Betul	1145.8mm	1038.1mm
8	Bhind	684.8mm	612.6mm
9	Bhopal	1053.9mm	956.3mm
10	Burhampur	834mm	737.3mm
11	Chhatarpur	1038.3mm	941.5mm
12	Chhindwara	1128.2mm	1000.8mm
13	Damoh	1191.1mm	1089.9mm
14	Datia	826.7mm	745.4mm
15	Dewas	968.6mm	904.8mm
16	Dhar	871.1mm	818.9mm
17	Dindori	1307mm	1183.2mm
18	Gwalior	811.2mm	721.5 mm
19	Guna	1025.2mm	940.9mm
20	Harda	1162.mm	1078.9mm
21	Hoshangabad	1356.7mm	1259.1mm
22	Indore	933.8mm	868.1 mm
23	Jabalpur	1235.6mm	1130mm
24	Jhabua	943.5mm	884.2mm
25	Katni	1024.1mm	941.6mm
26	Khandwa	863.3mm	789.1mm
27	Khargone	779.1mm	719.3mm

28	Mandla	1332.3mm	1197.1mm
29	Mandsaur	887.1mm	825.3mm
30	Morena	709.9mm	644.3mm
31	Narshimapur	1133.2mm	1051.9mm
32	Nimach	831.1mm	776.9mm
33	Panna	1193.7mm	1086.8mm
34	Raisen	1169.2mm	1084.6mm
35	Rajgarh	965mm	892mm
36	Ratlam	987.1mm	914.6mm
37	Rewa	1087.8mm	986.7mm
38	Sagar	1163.mm	1068.5mm
39	Satna	1046.4mm	949.4mm
40	Sehore	1151mm	1070.3mm
41	Seoni	1157.8mm	1018.2mm
42	Shahdol	1106.1mm	992.8mm
43	Shajapur	978.5mm	905.8mm
44	Shivpuri	862.8 mm	787.3mm
45	Sheopur	721. mm	666.5 mm
46	Sidhi	1161.5mm	1047.9mm
47	Singrauli	975.6mm	876.1mm
48	Tikamgarh	997.8mm	911.8mm
49	Ujjain	957.1mm	884.3mm
50	Umaria	1228.1mm	1075.6mm
51	Vidisha	1105.4mm	1023.3mm

Source:

The above data in the figures and table indicated that maximum rainfall in the State is received from June to September (southwest monsoon). Among the districts, Hoshangabad/Narmadapuram, Balaghat, Mandla, Dindori, and Jabalpur received the highest rainfall while Bhind, Morena, Barwani, and Sheopur received lesser rainfall.

The State can be broadly divided intofour seasons, the Winter season from Januaryand February, the summer season/pre-monsoonfrom March to May, the Southwest monsoon season from June to September, and the post-monsoon season from October to December.

The Summer season/pre-monsoon: The months after the December solstice the earth experiences the March equinox (Vernal equinox) approximately on March 21. It is commonly called the first day of spring" in the Northern Hemisphere. Following the March equinox, the vertical rays of the sun migrate from the equator northward and strike the Tropic of Cancer on the June solstice (June 21). These geographical phenomena lead to a rise in mercury and a fall in air pressure in Madhya Pradesh which results in severe heat in the month of April-May. Nowgoan in Chattarpur district recorded 4°9C in mid-June 2019. Gwalior recorded 48°C as the second hottest city. Damoh, Guna, Rewa, and Satna recorded 47°C. In Madhya Pradesh, the summer season is locally known as Unala.

The Southwest Monsoon Season: The southwest monsoon is the principal rainy season (June to September) when the State receives more than 80 percent of its annual rainfall. The total annual rainfall varies from 700 mm over extreme northwestern parts, to 1600 mm over the southern parts of the State. This season is locally known as Chaumasa. In 2021, the State received 943.9 mm of rain from June to September while normal rainfall for the period is 938.9 mm. East Madhya Pradesh received a 15% rain deficit. A total of 1046.2 mm of rain is considered normal but it has received only 8921.1 mm. West Madhya Pradesh received a 15% rain surplus. A total of 855.8 mm of rain rainfall is considered normal for west Madhya Pradesh but it received 983.8 mm of rain. Balaghat, Chhatarpur, Damoh, and Jabalpur received deficit rain while Bhopal, Indore, and Gwalior received slightly above the normal.

The Winter season: The rainy season comes to an end in September or around the first week of October. In September, the earth experiences the September equinox or autumnal equinox around September 22/23 in the Northern Hemisphere. It is commonly called the "first day of fall". After the September equinox, the vertical rays of the sun migrate to the southernmost latitude on the December solstice (the December solstice marks the day of the year when the sun is lowest in the sky in the Northern Hemisphere). These geographical phenomena led to a fall in mercury and an increase in air pressure in Madhya Pradesh. This season is locally known as Siyala. In 2020, Umaria recorded 3.2^{0}C (the coldest place in the State). Nowgoan, Daita, Umaria, Rewa, Gwalior, Guna, Raisen, Khajuraho, Shajapur, Satna, Damoh, and Jabalpur recorded between 3^{0} to 5^{0} C. Mercury levels fall in various parts of the State due to northerly winds that sweep across the State.

Reference

1. Crop weather calendars, Madhya Pradesh, The Director General of Meteorology, India Meteorological Department. Govt. Of India.

2. Climate Research and Services, Pune. India Meteorological Department, Ministry of Earth Science, Govt. of India. www.imdpune.gov.in/climinform.php

3. Ganga Basin (2014). Central Water Commission, Ministry of Water Resources. National Remote Sensing Centre, Department of Space, Govt. Of India. indiawris.gov.in was first indexed by Google in July 2019

4. Guhathakurta. P, Et al. Observed rainfall variability and changes over Madhya Pradesh State. Climate research and services, India Meteorological Department, Ministry of Earth Sciences, Pune. https://www.imdpune.gov.in/reports.php

5. Mahi Basin (2014). Central Water Commission, Ministry of Water Resources. National Remote Sensing Centre, Department of Space, Govt. Of India. indiawris.gov.in was first indexed by Google in July 2019 Narmada River Basin. Central Water Commission, Ministry of Water Resources.

6. National Remote Sensing Centre, Department of Space, Govt. Of India. www.india-wris.nrsc.gov.in

7. Tapi-INDIA WRIS WIKI indiawris.gov.in was first indexed by Google in July 2019

CHAPTER **4**

NATURAL VEGETATION AND PROTECTED AREA

The concept of Land Use and Land Cover holds significant importance in geographical studies. It is crucial to comprehend the changes in land use and land cover within a region for effective management and monitoring of natural resources like forests, minerals, fauna, etc., as well as for promoting sustainable development. According to NRSC "Land cover is what covers the surface of the earth and land use describes how the land is used. Examples of land cover classes include Water, snow, grassland, deciduous forest, and bare soil. Land use examples include wildlife management area, agricultural land, urban, recreational area, etc."

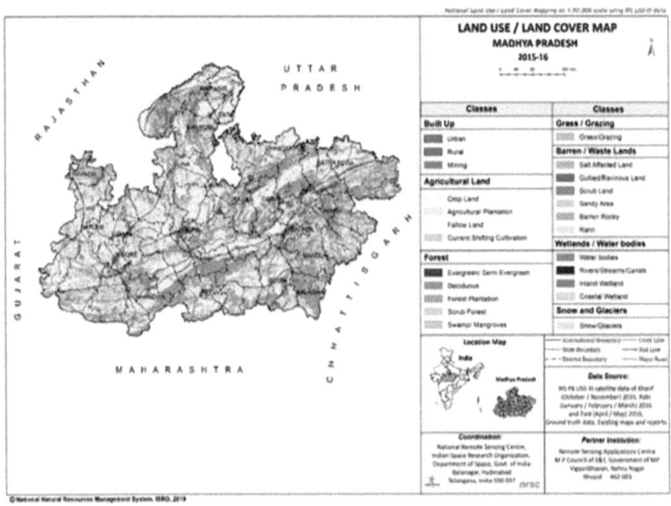

Figure 31: Land Use/Land Cover Map

As per the NRSC Land Use/Land Cover of Madhya Pradesh (2015-16), Agriculture land covers 188,138.6 sq. km, out of which 183563.24sq. km falls under Crop Land, 4173.49 sq. km falls under Fallow and 401.87 sq. km falls under plantation. Barren/ unculturable/wastelands cover 24,854.27 sq. km, out of which Barren rocky covers 380.01 sq. km, Gullied/Ravinous land covers 1491.30 sq. km, and scrubland covers 22982.96 sq. km.

The forest covers about 80,616.74 sq. km. out of which Deciduous covers 67922.22 sq. km, Evergreen/semi-evergreen covers 0.10 sq. km, forest plantation 87.61 sq. km, and scrub forest covers 12606.81 sq. km.

Grass/Grazing covers 1.61 sq. km. Wetlands/water bodies cover 8,919.17 sq. km. out of which River/Stream/Canals covers 3204.74 sq. km and water bodies cover 5714.43 sq. km.

Forest

The National Forest Policy of India 1988 envisages a goal of achieving 33 percent of the geographical area of the country under forest and tree cover. The total forest cover of the country as per the India State of Forest Report 2021 is 7,13,789 sq. km which is 21.71 percent of the total geographical area of the country.

Madhya Pradesh is a forest-rich State and is ranked first among the States in terms of Recorded Forest Area (RFA). The Recorded Forest Area (RFA) in the State is 94,689 sq. km which accounts for 30.72 percent of the total geographical area of the State. Out of the total 94,689 sq. km of RFA, 61886 sq. km is Reserved Forests, 31,098 sq. km is Protected Forests and 1,705 sq. km is unclassed forests.

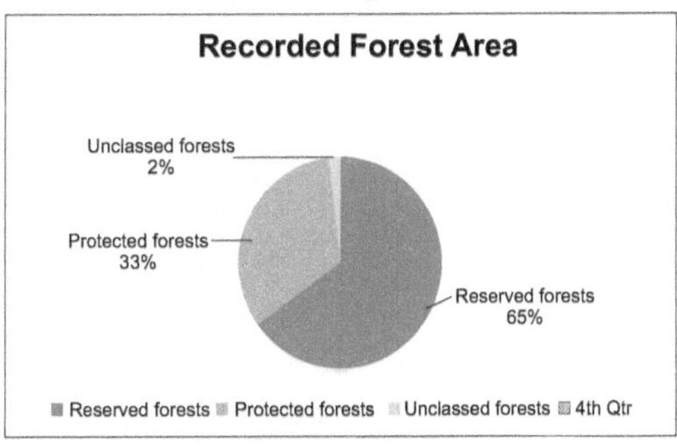

Figure 32: Recorded Forest Area of Madhya Pradesh
Source: India State of Forest Report 2021

The State has 77,492.60 sq. km which accounts for 25.14 percent of the total geographical area of the State. The forest cover of the State in terms of forest canopy density classes is plotted in table 6.

Table 6: Forest cover of Madhya Pradesh and India (in terms of forest canopy density classes)

Class	Madhya Pradesh		India	
	Area (in sq. km)	% of geographical area	Area (in sq. km)	% of geographical area
VDF	6,664.95	2.16	99,779	3.04
MDF	34,209.02	11.10	3,06,890	9.33
OF	36,618.63	11.88	3,07,120	9.34
Total	77,492.60	25.14	7,13,789	21.71
Scrub	5,456.55	1.77	46,539	1.42

Source: India State of Forest Report 2021

Very Dense Forest (VDF): All lands with tree canopy density of 70 percent and above

Moderately Dense Forest (MDF): All lands with tree canopy density of 40 percent and more but less than 70 percent

Open Forest (OF): All lands with tree canopy density of 10 percent and more but less than 40 percent

Scrub: Forest lands with a canopy density of less than 10 percent

Non-forest: Lands not included in any of the above classes (including water)

As per the Champion and Seth classification of forest types (1968), the forests of Madhya Pradesh belong to five forest type groups viz., tropical moist deciduous, Littoral and swamp forest, tropical dry deciduous forests, tropical thorn forests, and subtropical broad-leaved hill forest which are further divided into 21 forest types.

The percentage under different forest types of the State as per the Champion and Seth classification (1968) are plotted in the following table7.

Table 7: Area statistics of the forest types found in the State

Sl.No	Forest type	Area (in sq. km)	% of forest cover
1.	3B/C1c Slightly moist teak forest	1,889.89	2.26
2.	3B/C2 Southern moist mixed deciduous forest	1,909.35	2.28
3.	3C/C2e (i) Moist peninsular high level sal	2,746.69	3.29
4.	4E/RS1 Riparian fringing forest	15.07	0.02
5.	5A/C1a Very dry teak forest	712.34	0.85
6.	5A/C1b Dry teak forest	22,283.27	26.68
7.	5A/C3 Southern dry mixed deciduous forest	20,147.88	24.12
8.	5B/C1c Dry peninsular sal forest	4,152.12	4.97
9.	5B/C2 Northern dry mixed deciduous forest	15,752.36	18.86
10.	5/DS1 Dry deciduous scrub	5,468.47	6.55
11.	5/DS2 Dry Savannah Forest	1.15	0.00
12.	5/E1 Anogeissus pendula forest	2,813.01	3.37
13.	5/E1/DS1 Anogeissus pendula scrub	368.80	0.44
14.	5/E2 Boswellia forest	388.48	0.46
15.	5/E5 Butea forest	194.38	0.23
16.	5/E9 Dry bamboo brakes	734.60	0.88
17.	5/1S2 Khair-sissu Forest	1,370.77	1.64
18.	6B/C2 Ravine thorn forest	882.97	1.06
19.	8A/C3 Central Indian subtropical hill forest	1.35	0.00
	Subtotal	**81,832.95**	**97.96**
20.	TOF/Plantation	1,651.45	1.98
	Total (forest cover and Scrub)	**83,484.40**	

Grassland forest types (outside forest cover)			
21.	3C/C2/DS1 Moist sal savannah	40.41	0.05
22.	5/DS4 Dry grassland	6.83	0.01
	Total	**47.24**	**0.06**
	Grand total	**83,531.64**	**100.00**

Source: India State of Forest Report(ISFR) 2021

According to the ISFR 2021, the Dry teak forest of type 5A/C1b constitutes 26.68 percent of the overall forest cover, while the Southern dry mixed deciduous forest of type 5A/C3 accounts for 24.12 percent. The Northern dry mixed deciduous forest of type 5B/C2follows, among others. Tree Outside Forest (TOF) and plantation areas comprise approximately 1.98 percent, while Grassland Forest types (outside forest cover) i.e., Moist sal savannah and dry grasslandcover 0.05 percent and 0.01 percent respectively.

Table 8: Districts with the highest forest cover

District	Geograph-ical Area (GA)	Very Dense Forest	Mod. Dense Forest	Open Forest	Total	% of GA	Scrub
Balaghat	9,229	1,407.64	2,630.88	884.26	4,922.8	53.34	28.06
Sheopur	6,606	6.00	1,394.25	2,043.66	3,443.91	52.13	130.51
Umaria	4,076	377.98	1,092.66	530.60	2,001.24	49.10	22.90
Mandla	5,800	691.78	1,092.55	792.65	2,576.98	44.43	36.93
Sidhi	4,851	315.96	881.29	805.27	2,002.52	41.28	47.02
Dindori	7,470	1,084.98	1,271.24	666.21	3,022.43	40.46	123.13
Chhindwara	11,815	575.68	2,021.61	2,010.84	4,608.13	39.00	284.14
Panna	7,135	82.95	1,476.06	1,189.59	2,748.60	38.52	190.67
Singrauli	5,675	393.73	992.29	776.84	2,162.86	38.11	54.41
Burhanpur	3,427	57.92	625.89	603.75	1,287.56	37.57	37.74

Source: India State of Forest Report 2021

                    GEOGRAPHY OF MADHYA PRADESH

Table 9: Districts with the lowest forest cover

District	Geographical Area (GA)	Very Dense Forest	Mod. Dense Forest	Open Forest	Total	% of GA	Scrub
Ujjain	6,091	0.00	2.60	34.10	36.70	0.60	55.83
Shajapur	6,195	0.00	2.44	59.47	61.91	1.00	64.90
Ratlam	4,861	0.00	2.53	72.63	75.16	1.55	111.54
Rajgarh	6,153	0.00	37.86	133.94	171.80	2.79	78.14
Mandsaur	5,535	0.00	42.01	198.67	240.68	4.35	108.31
Bhind	4,459	0.00	28.08	198.48	226.56	5.08	283.24
Jhabua	3,600	0.00	30.69	189.52	220.21	6.12	160.07
Datia	2,902	0.00	91.13	121.65	212.78	7.33	68.07

Source: India State of Forest Report 2021

Balaghat district has the highest forest cover with 4,922.8 sq. km which accounts for 53.34 percent of the total geographical area of the district followed by Sheopur district with 52.13 percent forest cover, Umaria district with 49.10 percent forest cover, Mandla district with 44.43 percent forest cover etc. The lowest forest cover is recorded in Ujjain district with 36.70 sq. km of forest cover which account for 0.60 percent of the total geographical area of the district followed by Shajapur district with 1.00 percent, Ratlam district with 1.55 percent, etc.

Forests of the State classified on the basis of composition species are viz., teak forest, sal tree/sal forest, and miscellaneous forest.

Teak forest (tectonagrandis) is widely distributed in the State. This forest is found mainly where average rainfall is between 5 -125 cm. It is found in the districts of Indore, Khandwa, Harda, Dewas, Sehore, Bhopal, Raisen, Vidisha, Betul, Hoshangabad, Chhindwara, Seoni, Balaghat, Mandla, Dindori, Shahdol, Umaria, Jabalpur, Damoh, Panna, Chhattarpur, Sagar, Satna, Rewa and Sindhi.

Sal forest (Shorearobusta) is a large evergreen tree belonging to the family dipterocarpaceae. Sal forests are found in the eastern part of the State while teak forests are mainly found in the western part. In between these forests lies the transition belt of mixed miscellaneous forests. Sal forests occupy an area of 7244 sq. km which is about 7.6 percent of the total forest area of the State. This forest is confined to the eastern part of the State in the districts of Rewa, Sidhi, Umaria, Anuppur, and southwards districts of Balaghat, Mandla, Dindori, and Sabalpur. Sal forests are distributed in and around Panchmarhi in Hoshangabad and Chhindwara districts. The Mixed Forest covers the maximum area of the forest cover in the State. The mixed forest includes teak(Tectonagrandis) and Sal (Shorearobusta) mixed with other species like soja(Terminalia tomentosa), Bija (Pterocarpus Marsupium), Lendia (Lager stroemiaparvi flora), Haldu (Haldinacordifolia), Dhaora (Anogeissuslatifolia), Salai (Boswellia Serrata), Aonla (Emblica officinalis), Amaltas (Cassia fistula), Gamhar (Gmelina arborea) etc. Dendrocalamusstrctus (Bamboo) is found in the districts of Balaghat, Seoni, Chhindwara, Betul, Mandla, and Shahdol.

Tropical Moist Deciduous Forest covers about 8.9 percent of the total geographical area of the State. It is found mainly in the districts of Sidhi, Mandla, Balaghat, Seoni, Umaria, Anuppur, and Shahdol. This forest isa typical monsoon forest with teak (Tectonagrandis) and Sal (Shorearobusta) as the dominant species. Other species found in this forest are Peepal, Rosewood, Bamboo, etc. Tropical moist deciduous grow in the area where average rainfall ranges between 100-200 cm.

Tropical Dry Deciduous Forest covers an area of 88.65 percent of the total geographical area of the State. It is found in the districts of Chhatarpur, Parma, Chhindwara, Damoh, Seoni, Sagar, Jabalpur, Betul, Hoshangabad, Gwalior and Bhopal. This forest grows in an area where average rainfall ranges between 50 to 100 cm. In this forest trees shed their leaves during summer due to lack of water. Teak, Rosewood, Neem, Peepal,etc are major trees in this forest.

Tropical Thorn Forest covers about 0.26 percent of the total geographical area of the State. This type of forest is found in the districts of Sheopur, Nimar, Ratlam, Mandsaur, Tikamgarh, Datia, Gwalior, and Shivpuri. Tropical thorn forest grows in the area where average rainfall range between 25 to 75 cm. Major species are babool, Sheesham, tendu, keekar, teak, neem etc.

Subtropical broad leaves hills forest is found in high peaks of Satpura and Vindhya ranges.

Joint Forest Management (JFM): Madhya Pradesh is a pioneering State in the implementation of the Joint Forest Management (JFM) movement in the country. The State has a strong JFM network through 15,228/JFMC/VSS/EDCs covering an area of 66,84 sq. km.

Forest fire

Forest fires have long been an integral part of the forest environment and have played an important role in shaping the forest ecosystems, their conservation, and management. Although fire has benefits in terms of clearing the forest floor and paving the way for the regeneration of new grass, herds, and saplings, these are marginal when compared to the huge losses linked to it. Controlled forest fires are often used as important resources and management tools for enhancing ecological conditions and eliminating excessive fuel build- up in forest areas.

In India, severe fires are prevalent across various forest types, particularly affecting dry deciduous forests, whereas evergreen, semi-evergreen, and montane temperate forests exhibit relatively lower susceptibility, as indicated by the India State of Forest Report 2015.It is estimated that over 36 percent of the country's forest cover is susceptible to frequent forest fires. Nearly 4 percent of the country's forest cover is extremely prone to fire, whereas 6 percent of forest cover is found to be very highly fire-prone (ISFR 2019).

In Madhya Pradesh, 0.43 percent of the forest falls in the extremely fire-prone category, 6.11 percent of the forest under

Very highly fire-prone, 14.05 percent of the forest under Highly fire-prone, 19.66 percent of forest under Moderately fire-prone, and 59.75 percent of forest under Less fire-prone.

Protected Area

Protected Areas are designated areas where human habitation or resource utilization is limited. There are several kinds of protected areas, which vary by level of protection depending on the enabling and regulations of the country. The term "protected area" also includes Marine Protected Areas, the boundaries of which will include some areas of ocean. The Wild Life (Protection) Act, 1972 defines protected areas as Sanctuaries, National Parks, Tiger Reserves, Conservation Reserves, and Community Reserves (MoEF&CC (Comp.)2021).

Madhya Pradesh is blessed with diverse wildlife and its national parks, wildlife sanctuary, and biosphere reserves are home to many endangered wildlife species.

National Park

The national park is an area notified by the State or Central government for its ecological, faunal, floral, geomorphological, or zoological importance, intending to protect and propagate or develop wildlife and its environment. A National Park is the highest level of protection that can be given to an area under the Wildlife (Protection), Act, 1972 (MoEF&CC(Comp.) 2021) is a relatively large area of one or more ecosystems that are not materially altered by human exploitation and occupation. The National Park provides the foundation for the environment and culture-compatible spiritual, scientific, educational, and recreational activity. There are 11(eleven) National Parks in the State namely., Kanha National Park, Bandhavgarh National Park,Kuno National Park, PannaNational Park, PenchNational Park, SatpuraNational Park, Sanjay-DubriNational Park, Madhav National Park, Van Vihar National Park, GhughwaFossil National Park, and DinosaurFossilNational Park.

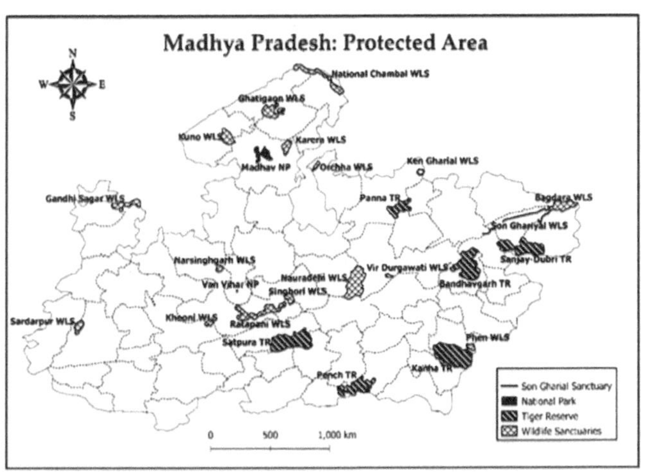

Figure 33: Protected Areas in Madhya Pradesh

Kanha National Park was notified in the year 1955 and spreads over 940 sq. km. This park stands as one of India's most meticulously preserved wildlife sanctuaries. Its lushlandscapes provide the backdrop for Rudyard Kipling's masterpiece "The Jungle Book". The park boasts a diverse array of fauna, featuring notable species such as gaur, hyena, leopard, sloth bear, tiger, wild boar, wild dog, etc. as well as a variety of avian species including the woolly-necked stork, changeable hawk-eagle, flycatcher, etc. the National Park showcases a wealth of diverse flora, contributing to its ecological richness.

Bandhavgarh National Park was notified in the year 1968. According to legend, Bandhavgarh was reportedly gifted by Lord Rama to his younger brother Lakshmana. This historical tale imbuesBandhavgarh with profound spiritual significance, complemented by its remarkable ecological importance. This National Park is a sanctuary for various iconic species such as tigers, leopards, sambar deer, Indian bison, Barking deer, wild boar, and other mammal,birds, and reptiles. Renowned as the "Land of Tigers," Bandhavgarh boasts the highest density of tigers in the world.

Kuno National Park was notified on December 10th, 2018, spread over 748.7618 sq. km, nestled within the Central Indian Vindhyan hills. Initially established as the Kuno Wildlife Sanctuary in 1981, later designated as a National Park in 2018. The park boasts a remarkable richness and diversity of indigenous flora and fauna, offering a representative glimpse into the dry deciduous forest of Central India. Furthermore, KunoNational Park has been identified as a potential location for the re-introduction of Asiatic Lions and the Cheetah. Panna National Park notified in the year 1981, is spread over an area of 542.67 sq. km. the park is endowed with a rich diversity of fauna, avian, and flora. Among the notable fauna inhabiting the park are Tigers, leopards, wild dogs, wolves, hyenas, caracals, sambar, etc. The park also hostsa variety of bird species including white-necked storks, bar-headed geese, oriental honey buzzards, king vultures, etc. The diverse flora of the park includes teakwood, coromandel ebony, mahua, chirony trees, axlewood trees, etc.

Pench National Park was notified in the year 1975 and spreads over 757.85 sq. km. Pench National Park is named after the entrancing river Pench that flows through the park. This Park served as an inspiration for Rudyard Kipling's iconic masterpiece "The Jungle Book". This park is inhabited by a myriad of wildlife species including tigers, spotted deer, Sabar, bluebell, wild boar, Jackal, Indian Leopard, sloth bear, Indian wolf, fox, hyena, gaur, four- horned antelope, and a plethora of bird species such as India peafowl, jungle fowl, Indian roller, magpie robin, egrets, herons, and common kingfisher. The park also boasts with abundant array of flora, including bamboo, teak, saja, bijiayasal, lendia, haldu, etc.

Satpura National Park was notified on October 13th, 1981, spanning an area of 585.17 sq. km. This National Park stands as a precious jewel in the crown of the Gangetic plains' rich biodiversity. Home to a complex and tremendous diversity of species and habitats, characterized by rugged terrain, including narrow gorges, sandstone peaks, challenging ravines, and dense forest, the park offers a captivating landscape. Within the park lies the Tiger Reserve, which also serves as an important archaeological site. Over 50 rock shelters within the reserve have revealed ancient rock paintingsdepicting various animals, such as elephants, tigers, deer, and porcupines, dating back as far as 1500 to 10000 years.

Sanjay National Park notified in the year 1981 spreads over 466.88 sq. km. The National Park is known for its rich biodiversity and is home to a diverse range of flora and fauna. Among the notable inhabitants are tigers, Indian leopards, spotted deer, sambar, wild boars, blue bulls, chinkaras and porcupines. The park is also home to a variety of bird species such as black-hooded oriole, racket-tailed drongo, Indian pitta, rufous treepie, lesser adjutant, red- headedvulture, cinereous vulture, white-rumped vulture, and Egyptian vulture. Reptiles such as monitor lizards, Cobras, kraits, rock pythons, rat snakes, and saw-scaled vipers also thrive here. The diverse flora of the park includes sal, bamboo, palas, salai, dhawada, gurajan, mahua, semal, harra, ber, and tendu.

Madhav National Park, notified in the year 1959, is spread over 375 sq. km and is situated near Shivpuri town. Originally the private game preserve of the Sindhi rulers of the former princely state of Gwalior. This national park is endowed with a rich diversity of fauna, avian, and flora. Among the notable fauna inhabiting the park are chinkara, spotted deer, sambar, chausingha, and leopard, along with a variety of bird species such as common pochard, northern pintail, mallad, gadwell, as well as predators like mugger crocodiles, Indian pythons, monitor lizards, etc. the noteworthy plants species includes Khair (Acacia Catechu), dhawda(Anogeissuslatifolia), tendu (Diospyros melanoxycon), and Palash (Butea monosperma). Adding to its allure are two lakes named after Maharani SakhyaRajeScindia and Madho Rao Scindia – Sakhya Sagar and Madhav Sagar, respectively.

Van Vihar National Park was notified in the year 1979. The park spanning over 4.45 sq. km is one of the most revered national parks of Central India. It is one of the most important tourist destinations in Bhopal. The park boasts diverse landscapes including lush wetlands, sprawling meadows, serene water bodies, rugged slopes, mixed bamboo vegetation along with grass-covered plateau and mixed plantations, fostering a thriving array of flora and fauna.

Ghughwa National Fossil Park was notified in the year 1983. The park sprawls over 75 acres of land, showcasing an array of attractive and rare fossilization leaves and trees. This National Park boasts fossilized plants that date back between 40 million and 150 million years offering a glimpse into India's ancient flora. Among the discoveries are petrified trunks of gymnosperms, angiosperms, monocotyledons, palms, and even Bryophytes.

Dinosaur Fossil National Park was notified in 2011 spanning an area of 375 sq. km. The park is home to a wide range of fossils such as dinosaur eggs, and wood fossils.

Tiger reserve

The project Tiger was launched in 1973 in line with the Wildlife Protection Act of 1972 (Amended 2006). The Act called for the conservation of tigers in-situ in the country. A tiger reserve is made up of a core area, which is kept as inviolate for tiger conservation and the peripheral area constitutes the buffer, which is a multiple-use area, with a preference for conservation over other land uses, thereby, maintaining an equilibrium between wildlife and human activities for livelihood, developmental, social and cultural rights of the local people. Madhya Pradesh and Maharashtra State have the highest number of Tiger Reserves in the country with six tiger reserves each. Madhya Pradesh has 6 (six) Tiger Reserves (Core Area and Buffer Area) viz., Bandhavgarh Tiger Reserve, Kanha Tiger Reserve, Panna Tiger Reserve, Pench Tiger Reserve, Sanjay-Dubri Tiger Reserves, and Satpura Tiger Reserve. The Core Area remainsuntouched, whereas, the Buffer Area, surrounding the core, is aimed to facilitate harmonious interaction between wildlife and human activity.

                    GEOGRAPHY OF MADHYA PRADESH

Bandhavgarh Tiger Reserve was notified in December 2007 (Core Area) and October 2020 (Buffer Area). It covers an area of 1536.93 sq. km with a 716.90 sq. km core zone and 820.03 sq. km buffer zone. This reserve is known for its healthy population of tigers and variety of herbivores. Apart from the tiger, there are about 345 species of mammals, 260 species of birds, and 70 species of butterflies. The reserve is located in the eastern Satpura hill range of the Umaria and Katni districts. Bandhavgarh Tiger Reserve is known for its evergreen Sal Forest and mixed forest with about 515 species of plants. The reserve is home to about 242 species of birds and many species of reptiles, and insects.

The Smooth-costed Otter listed as 'Vulnerable' in the International Union for Conservation of Nature Red list of threatened species and legally protected in India under Schedule II of the Wildlife (Protection) Act, 1972 is found in Bandhavgarh Tiger Reserve, which was previously unreported in the reserve.

Kanha Tiger Reservespread over Mandla and Balaghat districts was notifiedin December 2007 (Core Area) and October 2010 (Buffer Area). It covers an area of 2051.79 sq. km with 917.43 sq. km core zone and 1134.36 sq. km buffer zone. It is the largest National Park in the State. Hard Ground Barasingh "the State animal of Madhya Pradesh" is found exclusively in Kanha Tiger Reserve. The reserve is home to about 300 species of birds, 43 species of mammals, 26 species of reptiles, and more than 500 species of insects. Kanha Tiger Reserve is best known for its evergreen Sal forests.

Panna Tiger Reservewas habitat notified in December 2007 (Core Area) and July 2014 (Buffer Area). It is located in Vindhya Hill in Northern Madhya Pradesh. The reserve spreads over the Panna and Chhatarpur districts. It covers an area of 1598.1 sq. km with 576.13 sq. km core zone and 1021.97 sq. km buffer zone. the area is characterized by extensive plateaus and gorges. Apart from the tiger, it is home to leopards, wild dogs, wolves, hyenas, sloth bears, sambar, chital, chowsingba, blue bull, chinkara, etc. The avifauna comprises more than 200 species including migratory birds. The dry and hot climate associated with shallow Vindhyan soils has given rise to dry teak and dry mixed forests. The dominating vegetation type is miscellaneous Dry deciduous forest interspread with grassland areas. Other major forest types are riverine, open grasslands, open woodlands with tall grasses, and thorny woodlands. Floral species including tree species found are, Tectonagrandis, diospyros melanoxylon, madhucaindicia, buchnanialatifolia, anogeissus pendula, lanneacoromandelica, bosswelia serrata, etc. the dominant grass species are Apludamutica, themedaquadrivalvis, meteropogoncontortus, arishtidasp, etc Pench Tiger Reserve was notified in December 2007 (Core Area) and October 2010 (Buffer Area). It is located in the Seoni district. The reserve covers an area of 1179.632 sq. km with 411.33 sq. km core zone and 768.30 sq. km buffer zone. Pench tiger reserve and its surrounding area is well known for Rudyard Kipling's "The Jungle Book." The idea of Mongali was inspired by Sir William Henry Sliman's pamphlet "An account of wolves nurturing children in their dens." In 1831 there was a report that a child who had grown up with wolves was arrested in the village of Satbavadi near Seoni. The Vainganga river, its valley where Sher Khan was killed, the mountain ranges of hamlet Kannivara and Sivani, and other locations mentioned in "The Jungle Book" are all actual places in the Seoni district. This reserve is home to tiger, leopard, wildcat, wild dog, hyena, jackal, fox, wolf, weasel, gaur, nilgai, sambar, chital, chasinga, chinkara, wild pig,etc, and about 325 species of birds. The forest found in Pench tiger reserve is divided into viz., (i) southern tropical wet deciduous forest, (ii) southern tropical dry deciduous teak forest, (iii) southern tropical dry deciduous mixed forest. The dry mixed forest spreads in about one-third area of the protected area. The main species are salai, pickle, moyan, tendu, etc. Kahua (Aryuna), jamuna, guular and saja are found along the backs of river streams. Trees of mahua, palash, plum,etc are found scattered around the open forests of displaced areas of old villages. Teak forests are

                    GEOGRAPHY OF MADHYA PRADESH

found in about one-quarter area. There are about 82 types of grass species and bamboo found in this forest area. PenchTiger Reserve was awarded the "Best maintain tourist friendly National Park" award under the National Tourism Prize 2006-07.

Sanjay-DubriTiger Reserve notifiedin February 2011 (Core Area) and May 2014 (Buffer Area) is located in Sidhi district. This tiger reserve is well known for the world-famous white tiger 'Mohan'. Sanjay- Dubri tiger reserve forms the wildlife corridor of Bandhavgarh and Palamau tiger reserve. It covers an area of 1674.502 sq. km with 812.57 sq. km core zone and 861.93 sq. km buffer zone. Sanjay-Dubri is known for its evergreen sal forests and is home to about 152 species of birds 32 species of mammals, 11 species of reptiles, 03 species of amphibians, and 34 species of freshwater fishes. The major species found in this biosphere reserve are viz., tiger, sloth bear, chital, nilgai, chinkara, sambar, leopard, dhole (wild dog), jungle cat, hyaena, porcupine, jackal, fox, Indian wolf, Indian python, four-horned antelope and barking dear.

Satpura Tiger Reserve was notified in December 2007 (Core Area) and January 2011 (Buffer Area) and is located in the south of Narmada River. It covers an area of 2133.3 sq. km with 1339.26 sq. km core zone and 794.04 sq. km buffer zone. the reserve is inhabited by 52 species of mammals, 31 reptiles, and 300 species of birds, out of which 14 are endangered. Satpura tiger reserves were declared as the first biosphere reserve of the State in 1999. The high range of the Panchmarhi plateau is covered by Sal forests, while dense teak forests spread over its lower hill ranges. The reserve is home to 26 species of the Himalayan region and 42 species of Nilgiri areas, because of this SatpuraTiger Reserve is also known as the northern extremity of the Western Ghats.

Wildlife Corridors

The National Tiger Conservation Authority and the Wildlife Institute of India identified Tiger Corridors in 2014 between the Protected Area of Madhya Pradesh on one side and Chhattisgarh,

Maharashtra, and Rajasthan on the other side. Tiger Corridor aims to maintain genetic diversity and provide dispersal for young tigers. Seven corridors are plotted in Table10.

Table10: Wildlife corridors in the State as per the Wildlife Institute of India

Sl.No	Corridor	Protected areas	States involved
1.	Kanha-Pench	Kanha Tiger Reserve-Pench Tiger Reserve	Madhya Pradesh
2.	Kanha-Navegaon-Nagzira-Tadoba-Indravati	Kanha Tiger Reserve, Bhoramdev Wildlife Sanctuary, Navegaon- Nagzira Tiger Reserve, Tadoba- Andhari Tiger Reserve and Indravati	Madhya Pradesh, Chhattisgarh, Maharashtra and Andhra Pradesh
		Tiger Reserve	(Now Telangana)
3.	Kanha-Achanakmar	Kanha Tiger Reserve, Phen Wildlife Sanctuary, Achanakmar Tiger Reserve, Bhoramdev Wildlife Sanctuary	Madhya Pradesh and Chhattisgarh
4.	Pench-Satpura-Melghat	Pench Tiger Reserve, Satpura Tiger Reserve, Melghat Tiger Reserve	Madhya Pradesh and Maharashtra
5.	Ranthambore-Kuno-Madhav	Ranthambore Tiger Reserve, Kuno National Park, Madhav National Park	Madhya Pradesh and Rajasthan
6.	Bandhavgarh-Sanjay-Dubri-Guru Ghasidas	Bandhavgarh Tiger Reserve, Sanjay Tiger Reserve, Guru Ghasidas National Park	Madhya Pradesh and Chhattisgarh
7.	Bandhavgarh-Achanakmar	Bandhavgarh Tiger Reserve, Achanakmar Tiger Reserve	Madhya Pradesh and Chhattisgarh

Source: Wildlife conservation and sustainable management of wildlife habitats in Madhya Pradesh. Govt. of Madhya Pradesh

 GEOGRAPHY OF MADHYA PRADESH

Wildlife sanctuaries

"An Area having adequate ecological, faunal, floral, geomorphological, natural or zoological significance, notified by the State/Central Government to protect, propagate or developing wildlife or its environment" (MoEF & CC (Comp.) 2021). Madhya Pradesh has 25 Wildlife Sanctuaries.

Table 11: Wildlife sanctuaries in Madhya Pradesh

Sl.No.	Wildlife Sanctuaries	Location
1.	Bori Wildlife Sanctuaries	Hoshangabad
2.	Phen Wildlife Sanctuaries	Mandla
3.	Gandhi Sagar Wildlife Sanctuaries	Mandsaur
4.	Ken Gharial Wildlife Sanctuaries	Chhatarpur
5.	Narsinghgarh Wildlife Sanctuaries	Rajgarh
6.	Nauradehi Wildlife Sanctuaries	Sagar, Damoh, Narsinghpur, and Raisen
7.	Panpatha Wildlife Sanctuaries	Umaria
8.	Pench Mowgli Wildlife Sanctuaries	Seoni&Chhindwara
9.	Sanjay-Dubri Wildlife Sanctuaries	Sidhi
10.	Son GhariyalWildlife Sanctuaries	Sidhi
11.	SailanaWildlife Sanctuaries	Ratlam
12.	Orchha Wildlife Sanctuaries	Tikamgarh
13.	VirDurgawatiWildlife Sanctuaries	Damoh
14.	BagdaraWildlife Sanctuaries	Sidhi
15.	GhatigaonWildlife Sanctuaries	Gwalior
16.	KareraWildlife Sanctuaries	Shivpuri
17.	KheoniWildlife Sanctuaries	Dewas and Sehore
18.	National Chambal Wildlife Sanctuaries	Morena
19.	PachmariWildlife Sanctuaries	Hoshangabad
20.	KunoPalpurWildlife Sanctuaries	Morena

21.	RatapaniWildlife Sanctuaries	Raisen
22.	SinghoriWildlife Sanctuaries	Raisen
23.	SardarpurWildlife Sanctuaries	Dhar
24.	RalamandalWildlife Sanctuaries	Indore
25.	GangauWildlife Sanctuaries	Chhatarpur

Source: Forest Department, Government of Madhya Pradesh.
mpforest.gov.in/HO_Outer/Forest_Visit_NationalPark.aspx

Bori Wildlife Sanctuary, notified on June 1st, 1977, covers an area of 518 sq. km and is located in Hoshangabad. Adjacent to both the PachmarhiSanctuary and the Satpura National Park, these three collectively form the Pachmarhi Biosphere Reserve. The Sanctuary boasts a rich diversity of flora and fauna, including leopard, blackbuck, dhole, Indian gaur, Malabar giant squirrel, sloth bear, woolly-necked stork, painted stork, Indian roller, Malabar whistling thrush, paradise flycatcher, honey buzzard, and Malabar pied hornbill. The sanctuary is also home to a variety of vegetation such as teak, bamboo, dhaora, tendu, kusum, kanakchampa, ber, karanj, kaim, kadamb, lendia, mahua, saptparni, baans,lasura,dhaman, shisham, palash, amaltas, bahera, and goolar.

Phen Wildlife Sanctuary, notified on March 10th, 1983 spans an area of 111sq. km and is located in Mandla district. This sanctuary is located in the buffer zone of the KanhaNational Park, Mukkit Gate. The sanctuary features diverselandscapes and scenic forests. Commonly spotted wildlife species include Tigers, Leopards, wild boar, spotted Deer, and Sambar.

Gandhi Sagar Wildlife Sanctuary, notified in the year 1974 spans an area of 368.62 sq. km and is situated on the northern boundary of Mandsaur and Nimachdistricts. The sanctuary presents ample opportunities for observing a diverse range of wildlife, including the Indian gazelle, blue bull, sambar, Indian leopard, langur, Indian wild dog, otter, bar-headed goose, common

  GEOGRAPHY OF MADHYA PRADESH

sandpiper, migratory waterbirds, vultures, mugger crocodile, and various flora suchas khair (Acacia catechu), salai, kardhai, dhawda, tendu, palash, kusum, kanakChampa, etc.

Ken Gharial Wildlife Sanctuary, notified in the year 1981 spans an area of 45.201 sq. km. It is situated at the confluence of the Ken and Khudar rivers. Sanctuary derives its name from the rare six-meter-long fish-eating Gharial Crocodile. Among its notable features are vultures, mugger crocodiles, chinkaras, spotted deer, wild boars, blue bulls, sambar deer, peafowl, and the breathtaking spectacle of waterfalls, vibrant rocks, and dramatic canyons. Narsinghgarh / Chidikho Wildlife Sanctuary, notified in the year 1978 spans an area of 59 sq.kmand is located in Rajgarh. The sanctuary is home to both local and migratory birds, with over 164 species spotted. The name "Chidikho" signifies its role as a birding destination, with "Chidi" meaning birds and "Kho" meaning nesting site. Notable fauna includes Spotted Deer, Sambar, Bluebull, Leopard, and Wild Boar, alongside migratory ducks, waterbirds, crocodiles, and various reptiles such as lizards, chameleons, Indian Pythons, and snakes. The sanctuary's flora includes Teak, Saja, Dhawda, Khair, Bhaeda, Kronda, Lendia, Arjun, and Chandan trees. Apart from biodiversity, the sanctuary also boasts historical and archaeological significance, housing rock shelters adorned with red and white wall paintings.

Nauradehi Wildlife Sanctuary, notified in the year 1984 spans an area of 119.67 sq. km in the districts of Sagar, Damoh, Narsinghpur, and Raisen. It is the largest wildlife sanctuary in Madhya Pradesh and is the single largest forest block in the area.The two major river basins of India namely., the Ganga and the Narmada are part of this sanctuary, making it an extremely unique protected area. This sanctuary is a potential site for the cheetah reintroduction in India. The important animals found in this sanctuary are the Indian wolf, Bengal tiger, leopard, striped hyena, wild dog (Dhole), Bengal fox, Muggar crocodile, golden jackal, and bears.

Panpatha Wildlife Sanctuary, notified on June24th,1983 spans an area of 245.84 sq.km and is situated in Umaria district. The sanctuary forms an integral part of the Bandhavgarh Tiger Reserve. The name "Bandhavgarh" means "Fort of Brother" in Hindi, symbolizing its historical significance. Nestled amidst the Vindhya ranges and the eastern slopes of the Satpuraranges within the Central Indian Highlands, the sanctuary boasts a diverse array of fauna, avifauna, and flora. Notable species include Tiger, Leopard, Sambar, Barking deer, Gaur, and Sloth Bear, among others. Avian species such as the woolly-necked stork and Barred Button Quail, reptiles like Krait, viper, and python, alongside a variety of vegetation including sal, bamboo, tendu, and Mango add to its ecological richness.

Pench Wildlife Sanctuary notified on August 21st, August 1998 spans an area of 118.47 sq.km and is located in Seoni and Chhindwara districts. The sanctuary comprises a mixture of various kinds of forests and houses abundant fauna and flora diversity. Notable species include the tiger, sloth Bear, Wolf, Leopard, Wild Dog, Jackal, Striped Hyaena, Small Indian Civet, and Palm, alongside a variety of plant species such as Madhucaindica, Buchananialanzan, Lagerstroemiaparviflora, Ougeiniadalbergioides, Miliusavelutina, Lanneacoromandelica, Boswellia serrata, Anogeissuslatifolia.

Sanjay-Dubri Wildlife Sanctuary, notified on August 30th,1975 spans an area of 364 sq.km is located in Sidhi district. The sanctuary boasts a rich diversity fauna and avian including Tiger, Indian Leopard, Spotted Deer, Sambar, Wild boar, Bluebull, Chinkara, Civet, Porcupine, as well as avian species like Black-hooded Oriole, Racket-Tailed Drongo, Indian Pitta, Rufous Treepie, Lesser Adjutant, Red-headed vulture, Cinereous vulture, White- Rumped vulture, Egyptian Vulture. It is also home to reptilessuch as Monitor Lizard, Cobra, Krait, Rocky python, Rat Snake,etc.

Son Ghariyal Wildlife Sanctuary, notified in the year 1981 spans an area of 41.80 sq.km. it is located in Sidhi district. The Son Gharial Sanctuary is characterized by riverine islands, sand banks, etcwhich are crucial habitats to many endangered species like the Indian Soft- Shell Turtle,Gharial, etc. About 101 species of birds have been recorded in the sanctuary. Thesanctuary was established under Project Crocodile.

Sailana Wildlife Sanctuary, notified on June 04th, 1983 spans an area of 12.96 sq.kmand is located in Ratlam district. The sanctuary is known for bird species. Notable fauna and avian species inhabiting the sanctuary include the bluebull, golden jackal, Indian Fox, Jungle cat, Lesser Florican, Sarus Crane, Lesser Whistling Duck, Sykes Crested Lark, European Roller, Blue- Cheeked Bee-eater, Blue-tailed Bee-eater.

Orchha Wildlife Sanctuary, notified on September 22nd,1994 spans an area of 44.91 sq.km and is situated in Tikamgarh district. The sanctuary is nestled between the Betwa and Jamni rivers in the Bundelkhand region and boasts a spectacular array of flora and fauna. Among the notable fauna are Deer, Bluebull, monkey, wild boar, jackal, and sloth bear, while avian species include kingfisher, woodpecker, spotted Owlet, jungle bush Quail, and Geese.

Reptiles such as lizards, chameleons, Indian Pythons, cobras, and kraits also inhabit the sanctuary. Teak and kardhai trees dominate the forest cover.

VirDurgawati Wildlife Sanctuary or Rani Durgavati Sanctuary, notified on January 06th, 1997 spans an area of 23.97 sq.km. It is located in Damoh district. This protected area is known for both biologicaldiversity and historical-cultural value. The sanctuary is home to Singourgarh Fort. It isalso home to trees of Palash, Mahua, etc. typical of the local vegetation, as well as toendangered fauna like the leopard, wolf, Indian fox, sloth bear, etc.

Bagdara Wildlife Sanctuarynotified on February 15, 1978, spreads over 478 sq. km and is situated in Sidhi district. The name Bagdara originates from two Hindi words, "Bagh," meaning tiger, and "Dara, meaning home, collectively translating to "home of tigers." Characterized by dry deciduous forests, this sanctuary boasts a diverse range of fauna and flora. Among the notable wildlife species found here are tigers, chinkara, leopards, blackbucks, wild deer, blue bulls, wild boars, hyenas, sambars, and spotted deer.

Ghatigaon Wildlife Sanctuaries, notified on May 21st, 1981 spans an area of 511 sq. km and is located near Gwalior city. The sanctuary was established primarily to safeguard the natural habitat of the Great Indian Bustard and numerous other bird species. The sanctuary boasts a diverse avian population, with 73 bird species representing 42 families and 67 genera. Besides these avian inhabitants, wild animals such as wild boars, blackbucks, chital, and striped hyenas etc are sighted. Predominated tree species within the sanctuary include khair (Senegalia catechu), Tendu (Diospyros melanoxylon), and dhawara (Anogeissus, Acacia).

Karera Wildlife Sanctuaries, notified on 21stMay 1981 spans an area of 202 sq. km is situated in the Shivpuri district. The sanctuary is a haven for bird enthusiasts, boasting approximately 245 species of birds, with its most renowned resident being the Indian bustard. Besides the avian population, the sanctuary also supports a diverse array of wildlife.

Kheoni Wildlife Sanctuaries notified on December 4th,1982 span an area of 122 sq.kmand is situated in Dewas and Sehore districts. Renowned as the emerging hotspot for tiger and leopard sightings, the KheoniWildlife Sanctuary is interconnected with the Ratapani Tiger Reserve through corridors. Its vegetation comprises dry deciduous forests rich in teak, tendu, and bamboo. The sanctuary hosts a diverse range of wildlife, including jackals, palm civets, sambar deer, and avian species like little brown dove.

National Chambal Wildlife Sanctuary/National Chambal Gharial Wildlife Sanctuary, notified on December 20th, 1978 spans an area of 5,400 sq. km tri-state. The sanctuary located on the Chambal River has a unique geographical position, being situated near the tri-point of Rajasthan, Madhya Pradesh, and Uttar Pradesh. This sanctuary is home to some of the most endangered species of wildlife such as the Gharial, Muggar, Otter, the red-crowned roof turtle, and the endangered Ganges River dolphin.

Pachmari Wildlife Sanctuary, notified on 01st June 1977 spans an area of 477 sq.kmand is an integral part of the Pachmarhi Biosphere Reserve and the Satpura Tiger Reserve. Known for its rich biological diversity, this sanctuary holds significant cultural and historical importance. The region is adorned with numerous caves and cave paintings, some of which date back over 10,000 years. Among the notable fauna are Tiger, Leopard, Blackbuck, Dhole, Indian Gaur, and Malabar giant, etc. avian species include Eagles, owls, woolly-necked storks, painted storks, etc. Thesanctuary's lush flora comprises Teak, Saal, Tendu, Mahua (Indian butter tree), Bel (stone apple), and various species of bamboo.

Kuno Wildlife Sanctuary, notified on December 20th, 1978 spans an area of 5,400 sq.km tri-State. the sanctuary boasts a vast array of indigenous flora and fauna, showcasing the characteristic dry deciduous forest ecosystem of Central India. It has been earmarked as a potential site for the reintroduction of Asiatic Lions and Cheetahs. Notable fauna species include the Gangetic River Dolphin, Hedgehog, Small Indian Otter, and Smooth-coated Indian Oter, alongside avian species like the Great Horned Owl, Sarus Crane, and Black-bellied Tern. The sanctuary also hosts reptiles such as the Gharial, Marsh Crocodile, and various turtle species. Rich vegetation comprises trees like Khair, Palash, and teak, among others.

Ratapani Wildlife Sanctuary, notified in the year 1978 spans an area of 907.7 sq.km and is located in Raisen district. This untamed expanse, characterized by teak and bamboo forests interspersed with crocodile bark and tendu trees, gained sanctuary status in 1976. Featuring a varied terrain of hills, plains, seasonal streams, and rocky outcrops, the sanctuary offers diverse habitats that support a rich array of wildlife. Dominating this ecosystem as the apex predator is the Tiger, with approximately 40 of these striped cats roaming the forests alongside leopards, sloth bears, jackals,and hyenas.

Singhori Wildlife Sanctuary, notified on April 15th,1976 spans an area of 288 sq.km. It is located in Raisendistrict. The sanctuary stands out as one of Madhya Pradesh's top wildlife destinations. The sanctuary is characterized by a diverse landscape encompassing hills, plateaus, valleys, gorges, and plains. It is thehome to Tiger, Leopard, Sambhar, Spotted Deer, and Wild Boar as well as historicalmonuments like Choukigarh Fort, Bhandariya Temple, and the archaeological caves ofJamgarh.

Sardarpur Wildlife Sanctuary, notified in the year 1983 spans an area of 348 sq.km. it is located in Dhar district. The sanctuary is inhabited by numerous fauna and avian species, including the Golden Jackel, Indian Fox, Common Langur, Lesser Florican, Montagu's Pallid Harrier, Paradise Flycatcher, Pond Heron, partridges, Quails, Peafowls, Parakeets, Egret, Mynas, Bulbul, Cuckoo, Jungle Crow, as well as various reptiles like lizards, chameleons, Indian Pythons, cobras, and Kraits.

Ralamandal Wildlife Sanctuary located in Indore district was established in the year 1989. This sanctuary is the smallest in the State with a total area of 5 sq. km. The sanctuary is the home of leopards, black bucks, cheetahs, blue bulls, hyenas, barking dears, peacocks, palm civets, porcupines, and hares.

Ralamandal Wildlife Sanctuary, notified in the year 1989 spans an area of 2.34 sq.km and is located in the Indore district. This sanctuary is one of the oldest protected areas of Madhya Pradesh, with the mighty riverNarmada flowing through the sanctuary and adding to the serenity of the area. The sanctuary is home to wildlife species such as deer, wild hare, and tigers together with a richdiversity of birds.

Gangau Wildlife Sanctuary, established in the year 1975 spans an area of 68 sq.kmand is a mini wildlife sanctuary on the banks of Jen River, in Chhatarpur district. The sanctuary serves as a crucial buffer zone for the Panna National Park and is situated 38 KM southwest of Khajuraho. Its diverse ecosystem supports a plethora of flora and fauna, with notable animal species including the striped hyena, spotted deer, sambar, langurs, bluebull deer, Indian hare, and wild boar.

Biosphere reserves

Biodiversity reserves are sites established under UNESCO's Man and the Biosphere (MAB) programme to promote sustainable development based on local community efforts and sound science. The programme was initiated by UNESCO in 1971 to conserve all forms of life in situ, along with its support system, in its totality, so that it could serve as a referral system for monitoring and evaluating changes in a natural ecosystem. The first biosphere reserve in the world was established in 1979.

There are 18 Biosphere reserves in India, among which 12 biosphere reserves are listed in UNESCO's List of Man and Biosphere reserves programme. Madhya Pradesh has three Biosphere reserves viz., Pachmarhi biosphere reserves, Achanakmar-Amarkantak biosphere reserve, and Panna biosphere reserve.

Panchmarhi Biosphere Reserve was established in the year 1999. It covers the parks of Hoshangabad, Chhindwara, and Betul districts of Madhya Pradesh. The total area covered by Panchmarhi biosphere reserve is 4981.72 sq. km. The reserve falls almost in the northern part of the biogeographical zone (6) and biogeographic province (6A) viz., Deccan peninsula central highlands. Panchmarhi biosphere reserve is recognized as the "Genetic Express Highway" as it links two biodiversity hot spots of the country viz., Eastern Himalaya and Western Ghats, and also as a confluence of northern and southern types of vegetation. The total reported species of angiosperms belongs to 633 genera under 127 families.

Achanakmar-Amarkantak Biosphere Reserve is an interstate biosphere reserve established in 2005. Achanakmar-Amarkantak is the 14th biosphere reserve of the country and the 2nd biosphere reserve of Madhya Pradesh. This biosphere reserve extends across the State of Madhya Pradesh and Chhattisgarh covering a total area of 3835.51 sq. Km. It is located in the northern part of Bio-Geographic Zone 6 and Bio-geographic Province 6A (Deccan peninsula and central highlands). The region provides shelter to various thallophytes, bryophytes, pteridophytes, and gymnosperm and angiosperm species.

Panna Biosphere Reserve is the third biosphere reserve in the State, established in the year 2011. It is located within the narrow belt of tabletop mountains of the Vindhyan hill range and part of the Bundelkhand region in the Panna and Chhatarpur districts. Panna biosphere reserve includes the traditional Agroecosystems, dry deciduous forests of teak, salai, kardhai, bamboo, and mixed types of forests. This biosphere reserve falls under the bio-geographic zones of the Deccan peninsula 6 and covers the biotic province of Central Highlands 6(A). This biosphere falls under the Bundelkhand and Kymore plateau of the Satpura hill ranges agro-climatic zone.

Wetland

Wetlands are ecologically diverse and highly productive ecosystems that improve water quality, regulate erosion, sustain stream flows, store carbon and offer habitat for at least one- third of all threatened and endangered species, provide recreational and educational exposure. The Ramsar Convention, the world's oldest environmental treaty, was signed in Ramsar in 1971, Iran. The convention brings together 168 countries with a common goal of ensuring the sensible use of wetlands. The convention came into force in India on 1st February 1982. At present India has 75 sites designated as wetlands of international importance (Ramsar sites), with a surface area of 1,326,677 hectares. Madhya Pradesh has three designated wetlands of international importance viz., Bhoj Wetland, Yashwant Sagar, and Sirpur Wetland.

Bhoj wetland with an area of 3,201 ha is situated at 23°13'59"N and 77°19'59"E and is surrounded by Bhopal city. The Ramsar Convention recognized the upper and lower lakes of Bhopal as wetlands of international importance and designated them as Ramsar sites in 2002. The lakes are extremely diverse in terms of macrophytes, phytoplankton, zooplankton, natural and cultural fish species, resident and migratory birds, insects, reptiles, and amphibians, among other species.

                    GEOGRAPHY OF MADHYA PRADESH

Yaswant Sagar with an area of 822.9 ha is situated between 22°48'14"N and 75°41'44"E in the Indore district. The Yaswant Sagar is designated as an Important Birds and Biodiversity Area (IBA). This wetland is one of the most significant places for birdwatching sites in the region. In the winter, the wetland provides nesting, breeding, and foraging habitats for many migratory birds including the vulnerable sqrus crane (Grus Antigone).

Sirpur wetland, commonly known as PakshiVihar (bird sanctuary) is a human-made wetland that has stabilized and acquired near-natural characteristics in the last two centuries. The site covers an area of 161 ha and is situated between 22°41'58" and 75° 48'44"E in the Indore district. The site supports 175 terrestrial plant species, 6 macrophytes, 30 natural and cultural fish species, 8 reptiles, and amphibians. In the winter season, the site supports 130 bird species (resident and migrants) such as the common pochard (Aythyaferina), Egyptian vulture (Neophron percnopterus), and Indian river tern (sterna aurantia).

Reference

1. Bhuvan, Thematic services.
    https://bhuvan-app1.nrsc.gov.in/thematic/thematic/index.php

2. Environmental Planning and Coordination Organization (EPCO) www.epco.mp.gov.in/biosphere-reserve

3. ENVIS Centre on Wildlife and Protected Areas, Wildlife Institute of India, Dehradun, Ministry of Environment Forests and Climate Change, Govt. of India. www.wiienvis.nic.in/Database.br_8225.aspx

4. Jena J., Yogesh J., Harsh S., Dave C. and Borah J (2014). Large carnivore and prey status in Phen Wildlife Sanctuary., Madhya Pradesh, India Technical report, WWF- India

5. Mathur,V.B, A.K. Nayak, N.A. Ansari (2019). Fourth cycle of Management Effectiveness Evaluation (MEE) of Tiger Reserve in India, 2018. National Tiger Conservation Authority and

Wildlife Initiative of India, Ministry of Environment, Forest and Climate Change, Govt. Of India

6. MoEF&CC(Comp.) 2021. National Parks and Wildlife Sanctuaries in India. Ministry of Environment, Forest and Climate Change, Government of India.

7. National Fossil Park, Ghughwa. District Dindori. https://dindori.nic.in/en/tourist- place/national-fossil-park-ghughwa/

8. Ramsar. www.ramsar.org/wetland/india

9. Remote Sensing Application, National Remote Sensing Central(NRSC). https://www.nrsc.gov.in/Aboutus_NRSC_RSA/page_1?language_content_entity=en

10. Report No.1 of 2022 – Performance Audit on Wildlife Conservation and Sustainable Management for the year ended 31 March 2019 https://cag.gov.in/en/audit-report/details/117199

11. Wildlife, safari reservation portal, forest department of Madhya Pradesh. Forest.mponline.govt.in

12. Yadav, S.P., Tiwari, V.R., Mallick, A., Garawad, R., Taludar, G., Sultan, S., Ansari, N.A., Banerjee, K. & Das, A.(2023). Management Effectiveness Evaluation of Tiger Reserves in India, 2022 (Fifth cycle). Summary report Wildlife Institute of India, Dehradun and National Tiger Conservation Authority, Govt. Of India, New Delhi.

CHAPTER 5

MINERAL AND ENERGY RESOURCES

Minerals are valuable natural resources. Mineral is a naturally formed solid, inorganic substance with a characteristic crystal structure and chemical composition. The majority of known minerals are found in the crust and a more limited number of minerals are found within the mantle. Mineral nomenclature is very unsystematic. Some names reflect the mineral's chemical composition or physical property, some names are based on a person or a place and some appear to have been simply chosen at random. Minerals,both metallic and non-metallic are the most important raw materials for industrial development. It provides a strong base for the development of the metallurgical industry and helps industrialization and urbanization.

Madhya Pradesh is endowed with huge resources of metallic and non-metallic minerals. In terms of mineral availability, Madhya Pradesh is the fourth mineral-prosperous State in the country. The State is the only diamond-producingState in the country and a leading producer of copper concentrate, pyrophyllite, manganese ore, diaspora, and clay. Madhya Pradesh hosts the country's 90% diamond, 74% diaspore, 55% laterite, 48% pyrophyllite, 41% molybdenum, 27% dolomite, 91% copper ore, 18% fire clay, 12% manganese, and 8% rock phosphate ore resource. According to the Ministry of Mines, during 2020-21, Madhya Pradesh in terms of estimated value of mineral production in the country had a share of 6.16% in the national output.

Coal, bauxite, limestone, dolomite, rock phosphate, copper, manganese, iron ore, diaspore, pyrophyllite, and diamond are some of the major minerals produced in the State. More than half of the country's manganese production comes from the State. The second thickest coal seam in Asia is located at Singrauli in the Sidhi district. Presently, the only diamond- producing mines in the country are located in the Panna district.

मध्यप्रदेश का भूविज्ञान तथा खनिज मानचित्र
GEOLOGICAL AND MINERAL MAP OF MADHYA PRADESH

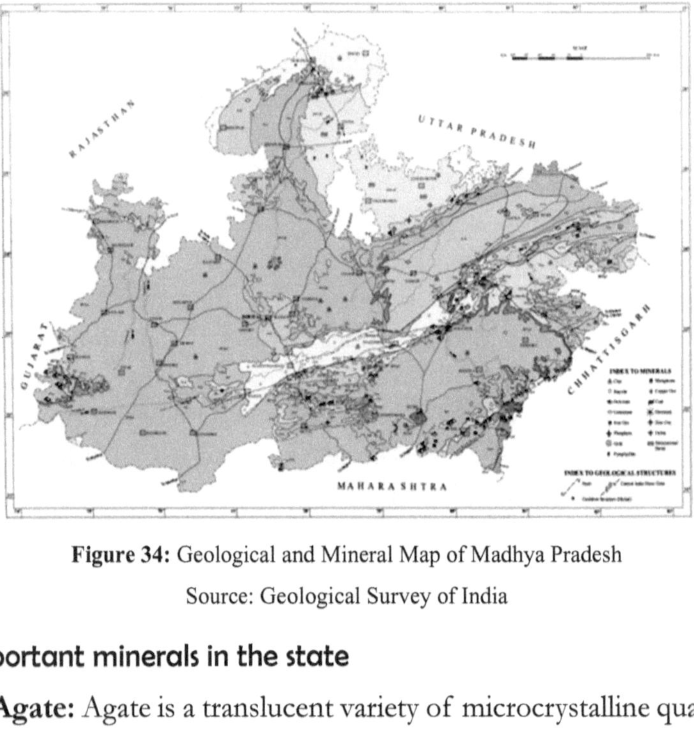

Figure 34: Geological and Mineral Map of Madhya Pradesh

Source: Geological Survey of India

Important minerals in the state

Agate: Agate is a translucent variety of microcrystalline quartz. In Madhya Pradesh, pockets and veins of semi-precious stones like agate, chalcedony, and other crypto-crystalline forms of silica are abundant in Deccan basalt at Bhatikhobra in Dhar district. Agate occurs in a wide range of colors viz., brown, white, red, gray, pink, black, and yellow.

Amethyst: Amethyst is a transparent variety of quartz that comes in shades of purple. Amethyst mineral is found in the

 GEOGRAPHY OF MADHYA PRADESH

quartz reefs in Bundelkhand granite at Andar in Shivpuri district. Amethyst has a Mohs hardness of 7 and does not break by cleavage.

Asbestos: Asbestos is a group of six naturally occurring silicate minerals made up of thin, microscopic fibers. It is resistant to heat and corrosion and is used in products such as insulation for pipes, floor tiles, building materials, vehicle brakes, and clutches. In Madhya Pradesh Asbestos is found in Goreghat (Balaghat district), Badagaon and Khamra (Betul district), Dhantalab near Sonkatch (Dewas district), Abdia (Hoshangabad district), Jobat, Morghisna, Bhilkeri, Dhadhla and Khanbi (Jhabua district), Neemuch (Mandsaur district), Barai (Narsinghpur district), Unantalav (Sehore district), Jamrapani (Seoni district), Gerui (Sidhi district), Jalandarpur (Tikamgarh district).

Barytes: Barytes/Barite is a mineral composed of barium sulfate ($BaSO_4$). Barytes, often being converted to barium carbonate is used to make ceramics and glass. Approximately, 85 percent of barites produced worldwide is used for oil and gas drilling as a weighting agent in drilling mud because of its unique physical and chemical properties and magnetic neutrality. It is also used as a feedstock for the production of various barium compounds and is also utilized as filler, extender, and aggregate. In Madhya Pradesh Barytes/Barite occurs in Gairi, Rehti, Andar and Pipalkota (Dewas district), Dhar area, Sunehra, Manehra, Mohania, Khirsua and Imalia (Jabalpur district), Kerua, Amola (Shivpuri district), Sidhi, Andheri Kho, Bari, Dhan Kho, Parkhuri, Kusilhawha, Khirkhori and Chhindanwa (Sidhi district), Bhoiron and Chakrada hill near Surajpura village (Tikamgarh district).

Bauxite: Bauxite is a naturally occurring heterogeneous material composed of one or more aluminum hydroxide minerals and various mixtures of silica, iron oxide, titania, aluminosilicate, and other impurities in minor or trace amounts. It is also used for making heat-resistant bricks (refractory bricks) and the high-grade variety is used in chemical industries.

In Madhya Pradesh, Bauxite deposits are located in Mundi Dadar, Touri Dadar, Kauwajhar Dadar, Warjiri Dadar, Bear Hill, Kot Pahar, and Gad Dadar in Balaghat district, Tantar and Tainchi blocks in Dindori district, Guna district, Bakarwara, Sleemanabad and Dundi area in Jabalpur district, Tikuri, Tikaria, Bargawan and Padarwana, Kusmi, Baghai, etc in Katni district, Rakti Dadar, Nanhu Dadar, Jamuna Dadar, Umargaon, Hazari Dadar, Daikribanda pahar, Pondibahra pahar, Bangla Dadar and Chikmi Dadar in Mandla district, Jhamar, Bilwani and Bamnor hill in Raisen district, Dhankhania, Kumarian, Dhuar, Teekar and Katai village in Rewa district, Adhi hill, southwest of Ranipur, Rajabara hill, Nongama, Naru hill, Chui hill and Khonda hill in Satna district, in Shadol district, bauxite occurrences are reported within Deccan Trap from Amarkantak, Khapri Pani, Ridge south Saraha and Kunaha, Pondit Pahara, Daiki banda Pahara, Dhodo tola, Chita pahar, and Chhindi Pani area. Hirapur, Mada, Ganeshkhera, Akhai, Mahadeo, Barkhera and Harhapura in Shipuri district, Basoda, Dabar, Mule, Isharwar and Kotra in Vidisha district and Sidhi district.

Bauxite in Katni district is the most developed and exploited bauxite area of Madhya Pradesh. Katni bauxite has a good reserve of refractory grade. The most important occurrences of bauxite in the State are located in the Amarkantak area, which covers part of the Shahdol, Mandla, and Bilaspur districts.

Bentonite: Bentonite is a clay consisting mainly of smectite minerals, commonly formed by decomposition of volcanic ash or tuff, or sometimes from other igneous or sedimentary rocks. Bentonite deposit is recorded in Chhan, Jodma, and Jiran in the Mandsaur district.

Beryl: Beryl is a silicate mineral with the chemical composition of $Be_3Al_2Si_6O_{18}$. It is found in igneous and metamorphic rocks. In Madhya Pradesh, the Beryl deposit is found in Tirodi, Kosamba, and Koylari in Balaghat district and Temni and Chunaloma in Betul district. Building stones: Madhya Pradesh has rich deposits of building materials stone such as Slate, Sandstone, Granite, Dolerite, Limestone, Marble, and Quartzite.

     GEOGRAPHY OF MADHYA PRADESH

Slate: Slate is a fine-grained, very low to low metamorphic rock possessing a well-developed fissility parallel to the planes of slaty cleavage. The production of slate in 2008-09 from Madhya Pradesh was 8,920 tonnes. There was no production of slate during 2009-10 and 2010-11. (IMY Book 2011). Slate deposit in Madhya Pradesh is found in the Dhar district (Udaipur and Wandha) and Mandsaur district. Slate production mainly comes from the Mandsaur district. Slate occurs in association with the shale of Semri Group (Vindhyan). Sandstone: Sandstone is a sedimentary rock composed of sand-size grains of mineral, rock, or organic material. The Vindhyan and Satpura mountains in Madhya Pradesh have vast resources of sandstone. Sandstone deposits are found in Gwalior, Hoshangabad, Jhabua, Khargone, Khandwa, Mandsaur, Raisen, Rewa, Vidisha, Satna, and Shivpuri districts. The flagstone and red sandstone of Rewa and Hoshangabad districts are famous for roofing and decorative building stones. The Par sandstone, found at the base of the Gwalior Group, and Kaimur sandstone of the Vindhyan supergroup are extensively used in building construction, flooring, roofing slabs, and beams.

Granite: Granite is a light-colored igneous rock composed of felspars, plagioclase, and quartz with minor amounts of mica, amphiboles, and other minerals. Madhya Pradesh accounts for 4 percent of granite resources with total resource accounting for 19,94,084 thousand cubic metres (IMY Book 2010). Granite occurs in Gwalior, Betul, Chhatarpur, Datia, Jhabua, Panna, Tikamgarh, Sidhi, Jabalpur, Shahdol, Dhar, Dewas and Shivpuri.

The Bundelkhand granite exposed in Chhatarpur, Panna, and Tikamgarh districts has been used as building stone and road metal for centuries. During the Chandella period, long pillars and blocks of pink and grey granite from these areas were used for the construction of temples and dams. Chhatarpur is the main producer of granite blocks used as dimension stones.

Dolerite: Dolerite/Diabase is a dark igneous rock intermediate in grain size between basalt and gabbro. In Madhya Pradesh, some jet-blackfine-grained and compact dolerite dykes traverse the Deccan Trap all along the Satpura hill ranges and Bundelkhand granite terrain may provide good decorative and ornamental building stone.

Limestone: Limestone is a sedimentary rock composed mainly of Calcium Carbonate ($CaCO_3$) in the form of the mineral Calcite. Calcite and dolomite are two important constituents of limestone. In Madhya Pradesh, deposits of limestone are found in Katni, Rewa, Satna, Jabalpur, Morena, Damoh, Jhabua, Mandsaur, Balaghat, Chhindwara, Damoh, Dhar, Hoshangabad, Khargone, Nasinghpur, Neemach, Sagar, Sehore, Shahdol and Sidhi districts.

Marble: Marble is a metamorphic rock that forms when limestone is subjected to the heat and pressure of metamorphism. It is composed primarily of the mineral calcite (CaCO3) and usually contains other minerals such as clay minerals, micas, quartz, pyrite, iron oxides, and graphite. In Madhya Pradesh, dolomitic marble is found in the districts of Jhabua, Jabalpur, Balaghat, Betul, and Chhindwara. The dolomitic marble of the Aravalli Supergroup occurs as parallel folded bands in the Jhabua district. Marble in Jabalpur, Sidhi, Shahdol, and Surguja area belongs to the Mahakoshal Group. Marbles in the Balaghat and Chhindwara areasare associated with the Sausar Group. Minor occurrences of marble have also been reported from Majhagawan village of Shahdol district within the Bijawar Group of rock (Directorate of Geology and Mines, Madhya Pradesh).

Quartz/Silica sand: The term 'Quartz' is often referred as synonym for 'silica'. Quartz consists of one part silicon and two parts oxygen (SiO_2). It is the most common mineral found on the earth's surface. Silica minerals include quartz, quartz crystals, quartzite, silica sand, sand (others), and moulding sand. Quartzite is used in some industries such as glass, foundry, sodium silicate, silicon alloys, iron and steel, refractory and ceramic industries. The total resource of quartzite in Madhya Pradesh is less than 1 million tonnes (National Mineral Inventory 2010, IBM).

　GEOGRAPHY OF MADHYA PRADESH

In Madhya Pradesh, quartzites are associated with the Aravalli, Bijawar, Vindhyan, and Chhattisgarh rocks. Aravalli quartzites are found in the Mandsaur, Ratlam, Jhabua, and Dhar districts. Bijawar quartzites are mainly found in the Hoshangabad, Dewas, Khandwa, and Sagar districts. Vindhyan quartzites are found in Rewa, Satna, Panna, Chhatarpur, Shivpuri, Morena, Gwalior, Dewas, Hoshangabad, and Mandsaur districts.

Calcareous shales: Calcareous shales used in slate pencilsoccur in the Mandsaur district of Madhya Pradesh.

Calcite: Calcite is a rock-forming mineral with a chemical formula of $(CaCO_3)$, containing 56% CaO and 44% CO_2. It is commonly found in igneous, sedimentary, and metamorphic rocks. A pure crystallized transparent variety of calcite known as 'Iceland spar' is used for optical purposes. In Madhya Pradesh calcite is found in the districts of Betul, Barwani, Jhabua, Dhar, Khandwa, and Khargone. Madhya Pradesh hosts 5% of the total calcite mineral of the country.

Calc-Tuffa: Calc-Tuffa is a soft porous rock consisting of calcium carbonate deposited from springs rich in lime. Calc-tuffa is found in the Betul and Shivpuri districts of Madhya Pradesh.

China clay: China clay/Kaolin in its natural form is a white, soft powder consisting predominantly of the mineral Kaolinite $(Al_2Si_2O_5(OH)_4)$, associated with other clay minerals like dickite, halloysite, nacrite, and anauxite. The name Kaolin is associated with the village of Gaoling in Jiangxi province of China where the white clay was mined. Three types of clay are found in Madhya Pradesh viz., China clay, fire clay, and red clay. This is one of the essential raw materials in the ceramic industry for the production of insulators, spark plugs, ceramic switches, whiteware, sanitaryware, glazed tiles, stoneware, pipe, and jars. The supply of China clay in Madhya Pradesh comes mainly from Betul, Chhatarpur, Chhindwara, Gwalior, Hoshangabad, Jabalpur, Khargone, Narsinghpur, Raisen, Satna, Shahdol and Sidhi districts. It is also found in Datia, Dewas, Gwalior, Katni, Mandsaur and Rewa. The total resource of China clay/Kaolin as of 1.4.2010 is 13161000 tonnes (National Mineral Inventory, 2010, IBM).

Coal: Coal is an organic sedimentary rock that forms from the accumulation of ancient vegetation which has been consolidated between the rock strata and transformed by the combined effects of microbial action, pressure, and heat over a considerable period. It is an important fossil fuel that not only powers the nation but is also used in various industries for producing coke for metal extraction, fertilizer, cement, and raw material for various chemicals like naphtha, wax, tar, etc. Madhya Pradesh is endowed with bountiful coal deposits in different Gondwana basins. The coalfields located in Betul, Chhindwara, and Hoshangabad districts belong to the Satpura Gondwana basin and the coalfields located in Sidhi, Shahdol, and Bandhavgarh (Umaria) districts belong to Rewa Gondwana basin. The coalfields in the State are designated as Pench-Kanhan-Tawa Valley, Mohpani, Sohagpur, Singruli, Umaria, Johila, and Korar coalfields. Apart from Damodar-Koel Valley, Pench- Kanha in Satpura and Sohagpur Coalfield are the only known areas with coking coal resources. Jhingurdah top seam in the Singrauli coalfield is the thickest coal seam in India with thickness varying from 131 m to 138 m. Coal reserves/resources in the State are shown in Table12.

Table12: Reserves/Resources of Coal as of 1.4.2019: Madhya Pradesh

Coalfield	Proved	Indicated	Inferred	Total (In million tonnes)
Total	12182.45	12735.98	3874.67	28793.10
Johilla	185.08	104.09	32.83	322.00
Umaria	17.70	3.59	-	181.29
Pench-Kanhan	1515.71	991.93	982.21	3489.85
Pathakhera	290.80	88.13	68.00	446.93
Gurgunda	-	84.92	53.39	138.31
Mohpani	7.83	-	-	7.83
Sohagpur	2129.18	5659.25	293.47	8081.90
Singruali	7876.15	5804.07	2444.77	16124.99

Source: Coal Directory of India, 2018-19

     GEOGRAPHY OF MADHYA PRADESH

Copper: Native copper is an element and a mineral. It is a soft, malleable, and ductile metal with very high thermal and electrical conductivity. It has a wide range of applications such as defense, space programme, railways, power cables, mint, telecommunication, etc. In Madhya Pradesh copper deposit is found in Balaghat, Betul, Chhatarpur, Chhindwara, Dewas, Gwalior, Jabalpur, Katni, Mandla, Narsinghpur, Panna, Sagar, Satna, Sidhi, Shahdol, and Tikamgarh. Madhya Pradesh with 283 million tonnes of reserves/resources of copper ore accounts for 18.75% of the total copper ore reserves/resources of the country. The State contributes substantially to the country's copper ore production through its Malanjkhand Copper Mine (Hindustan Copper Limited) in Balaghat district. Malanjkhand Copper Mine is the biggest copper-producing mine in the country. Chalcopyrite is the main copper ore and forms the main mineral with pyrite in the mineralized zone. Molybdenite and sphalerite are the associated minerals.

Corundum: Corundum is a rock-forming mineral that is found in Igneous, metamorphic and sedimentary rocks. It is an aluminum oxide with a chemical composition of AI2 O3 and a member of the trigonal crystal system (Geology.com). In Madhya Pradesh, corundum deposit is found in Morena and Sidhi districts.

Diamond: A diamond is a precious gem. It is composed of pure carbon and has a cubic crystal system and common form octahedron. Diamond occurs in two types of deposits, primarily in igneous rock of basic or ultrabasic composition and in alluvial deposits derived from the primary sources. India (as per the NMI data based on UNFC system 1.4.2015) has a diamond reserves/ resources of 31.83 million carats (0.95 million carats under the Reserve category and 30.87 million carats under the Remaining Resources category). In Madhya Pradesh diamond deposit occurs in Chhatarpur, Sagar, Tikamgarh, Panna, and Satna districts. The State accountsfor about 90.18 % resources of the country followed by Andhra Pradesh (5.72%) and Chhattisgarh (4.09%).

Panna district of Madhya Pradesh is the main diamond- producing district in the country. In the State, diamond occurs in three types of geological settings viz.,

(i) Kimberlite pipes, near Majhgawan and Hinota villages, intrusive into the Kaimur Group

(ii) Diamondiferous conglomerates associated with Itwa sandstone, Jhiri shale, and Gahadra sandstone of the Vindhyan supergroup

(iii) Laterite gravel on top of Baghain and Gahadra sandstone surfaces and alluvial gravel along streams draining the Panna Diamond Belt.

Dolomite: Dolomite is also known as dolostone and dolomite rock. It is a sedimentary rock composed primarily of the mineral dolomite ($CaMg(CO_3)_2$). In commercial parlance, the rock containing 40-45% $MgCO_3$ is usually called dolomite. Madhya Pradesh hosts 27% of the country's dolomite resource. Dolomite occurs in the districts of Balaghat, Chhindwara, Damoh, Dewas, Harda, Hoshangabad, Jabalpur, Jhabua, Katni, Mandla, Narsinghpur, Sagar, Betul, Chhatarpur, Khargone, Shahdol, Sindhi and Seoni. Madhya Pradesh has 2311395('000 tonnes) of dolomite resources (52557('000tonne) under Reserves category and 2258839 ('000tonne) under remaining resources).

Diaspore and Pyrophyllite: Diaspore also known as empholite, kayserite/Tanatarite is an aluminum oxide hydroxide mineral (A1O(OH). Diaspore occurs as thin veins, stringers, and geode-like bodies in association with pyrophyllite in Uttar Pradesh and Madhya Pradesh. The host rock mainly comprises granite, quartz, and pyrophyllite off Bundelkhand supergroup. India (As per the NMI database based on the UNFC system of resources classification) has 10.19 million tonnes of reserves/resources of which Madhya Pradesh hosts about 7.56 million tonnes (74%).

Pyrophyllite ($A1_2O_3. 4SiO_2.H_2O$) is a hydrous silicate of aluminum. Production of pyrophyllite is reported from the

Chhatarpur, Tikamgrah, Sagar, and Shivpuri districts of Madhya Pradesh. Madhya Pradesh hosts 48% of the total resources of the country.

Felspar: Felspar minerals are one of the most abundant rock-forming silicate minerals found in the earth's crust. The common feldspars are the potash feldspars called orthoclase and microcline ($K_2O.Al_2O_3.6SiO_2$), sodium feldspar called albite ($Na_2O.Al_2O_3.6SiO_2$), and Calcium feldspar called anorthite ($CaO.Al_2O_3.2SiO_2$). the total resource of feldspar in the State is 3,39,851 tonnes. Felspar occurs in commercial quantitiesin pegmatites, mainly in Chhatarpur, Betul, and also in Datia, Jabalpur, and Shahdol districts.

Fireclay: The name fireclay is given to a group of refractory clays that can withstand temperatures above the Pyrometric Cone Equivalent (PCE) value of 19. The best deposits occur in association with the coal seams in the lower Gondwana coal fields. Madhya Pradesh hosts 18% of the total reserves/resources of the country fireclay (Indian Minerals Yearbook 2020). The extensive deposits of fireclay in the State are mainly associated with the Gondwana rocks in the Narshighpur, Shahdol, Jabalpur, and Katni districts. Minor deposits are also found in the Betul, Panna, Chhindwara, Sidhi, and Chhatarpur districts.

Fluorite: Fluorite is composed of calcium and fluorine (CaF_2). It is used in a wide variety of chemical, metallurgical, and ceramic processes (Geology.com). In Madhya Pradesh, fluorite deposits are found in Jabalpur and Khargone districts. In Jabalpur, fluorite occurs in quartz- porphyry dykes traversing dolomite around Imalia and Sleemanabad. At Imalia, about 359 tonnes of fluorite ore, with 4 percent CaF_2 has been estimated up to a depth of 4.5 m. small lenses and pockets of fluorite are also seen in dolomite in association with galena, chalcopyrite, malachite, barytes, and calcite near Malban village. In Khargone, fluorite of purple and light blue color occurs as disseminations and crisscross veinlets in quartz porphyry dyke within the Bijawar Group at Sortipura and Koteswar in Barwah Tehsil.

Fuller's earth: Fuller's earth is a clay-like substance made largely of aluminum-magnesium silicate. It is a non-plastic clay that is used to decolorise, filter, and purify animal, mineral, and vegetable oils and greases. In Madhya Pradesh, fuller's earth deposit occurs in Mandla district. The total resource of Fuller's earth of Madhya Pradesh is 1,17,200 tonnes (National Mineral Inventory, 2010, IBM).

Garnet: Garnet is the name used for a large group of rock-forming minerals. These minerals are found in metamorphic, igneous, and sedimentary rocks. Most garnet found near earth's surface forms when a sedimentary rock with a high aluminum content, such as shale is subjected to heat and pressure intense enough to produce schist or gneiss (Geology.com). In Madhya Pradesh, garnet deposits are found in the Betul, Jhabua, Mandsaur, and Shahdol districts. In the Betul district, garnet occurrences have been recorded in Bisighat, Bhaldehi, Chunabhura, and Betul Nalasections. In the Jhabhua district, the mica-schist of the Aravalli Supergroup is widely garnetiferous. Almandine garnet is found near Jobat. In Mandsaur district, spessartite garnet occurs in association with manganese ores in the Aravalli Supergroup near Baghera in Gangpur and Udlia and Arnia in Neemuch. In Shahdol district, minor occurrences of garnet are reported from the Umaria area within the garnet schist (Directorate of Geology and Mines, Madhya Pradesh).

Glass sand and Silica sand: The deposit of glass sand and silica sand occurs in many localities in the State. Some weathered/leached orthoquartzites and white sandstone of Vindhyan Supergroup in Rewa, Panna, Satna, Damoh, Shipuri, Guna, Mandsaur, Bhopal, and Hoshangabad districts may become potential sources for silica and glass sand. The Bundelkhand granite/gneissic complex covering Gwalior, Shivpuri, Datia, Timkamgarh, Chhatarpur, and Panna districts is extensively traversed by quartz veins/reefs with quarts of high quality. The total resource of glass and silica sand in the State is 28,61,000 tonnes (all grades). This mineral is used in the manufacturing of glass, chemical, refractory and metallurgical industries.

Gold: Gold is a chemical element with the atomic number 79 and the symbol Au. Madhya Pradesh is endowed with some auriferous veins of primary origin but most of the occurrences fall under the residual and placer category. Gold is found as minute specks in river sand and in the colluvium at many places in Jabalpur, Sidhi, and Balaghat districts. It is being extracted locally by the Sonjharis community from the gravel and sands. Gold is also found in the Katni and Seoni districts. Gold occurs in the districts of Jabalpur and Sidhi.

Graphite: Graphite is a crystalline carbon that occurs naturally. Graphite is a native element mineral found in igneous and metamorphic rocks. It is generally used in industries like dry cell batteries, electrodes, foundries, crucibles, pencils, refractories, paints, lubricants, etc. In Madhya Pradesh, Graphite occurs in the Betul, Gwalior, Jhabua, and Sidhi districts. The total resource of graphite in the State as of 1.4.2010 is 10,06,660 tonnes (National Mineral Inventory, 2010, IBM).

Green earth: Green earth is a natural inorganic pigment derived from glauconite or celadonite minerals. A common feature of a Deccan Trap flow is the alternation of the basalt into a green mass known as green earth. Green earth is found frequently in western Madhya Pradesh. It is mostly used as a filling material in the paper and paint industries.

Gypsum: Gypsum ($CaSO_4.2H_2O$) is a hydrated calcium sulphate. Gypsum is used in various industries because of its special property of losing three-fourths of the combined water of crystallization when moderately heated (calcined) to about $°C1_3.0$ In Madhya Pradesh, gypsum occurs in Shahdol and Morena districts.

Iron Ore (Haematite): Iron ore deposits are found in sedimentary rocks. It is formed by the chemical reaction of iron and oxygen mixed in marine and freshwater. Haematite and magnetite are important iron ores in India. In Madhya Pradesh, minor deposits/occurrences of iron ore have been recorded in Sidhi, Mandsaur, Khargone, Narsinghpur, Jabalpur, Chhattarpur,

Khandwa, Gwalior, Jhabua, Dhar, Indore, Guna, Shivpuri, Shajapur and Ujjain districts. The grade of these occurrences varies from 35 % to 50% Fe, with a few rich pockets up to 60% Fe. The total resource of iron ore (Haematite) as of 1.4.2010 is 23,14,46,000 tonnes (National Mineral Inventory, 2010, IBM).

Lead-Zinc: Lead is a soft, heavy, toxic metal with a high malleability. Lead is a bluish-white when freshly cut, but when exposed to air, it tarnishes to dull grey. Galena (PbS) is the most important ore of lead. Other commonly occurring minerals are anglesite ($PbSO_4$) and cerussite ($PbCO_3$). Zinc is a silvery blue–grey metal with a relatively low melting and boiling point. Sphalerite (ZnS) is the principal ore of zinc. Other important minerals are calamine ($ZnCO_3$) and hemimorphite ($2ZnOSiO_2$). Both Lead and Zinc are found to occur together in ore along with other meals like silver and cadmium. Lead and zinc are strategic metals that are used in non-ferrous and ferrous industries. The battery sector is the main lead consumer while Galvanizing is the most important zinc consumer. In Madhya Pradesh, lead zinc occurs in Balaghat (Gidori and Dhorli), Betul (Muariya, Biskhan, Bhuyari etc), Chhatarpur, Chhindwara, Damoh, Dewas, Dhar, Gwalior, Hoshangabad, Jabalpur, Katni, Panna, Shivpuri, Sidhi, and Tikamgarh.

Manganese ore: Manganese is a chemical element with an atomic number of 25 and a chemical symbol Mn. It is not found as an element in nature. It occurs in many minerals such as manganite, sugilite, purpurite, rhodonite, rhodochrosite, and pyrolusite (Geology.com). In India, the highest concentration of Manganese is found in the Dharwar system of rocks. Manganese is an essential constituent of steel. The State-wise distribution of the resources in the country indicates that Odisha hosts 44% share followed by Karnataka (22%), Madhya Pradesh (13%), Maharashtra (8%), Andhra Pradesh (4%), and Jharkhand and Goa (3%) each (Indian Bureau of Mines).

The Madhya Pradesh- Maharashtra manganese belt stretches over about 200 km length from Balaghat district (Madhya Pradesh) in the east to Nagpur district (Maharashtra) in the west with a width of 25 km at its central part. The Precambrian Sausar Group metasediments host the manganese ore horizons. Madhya Pradesh has 56 million tonnes (13%) of resources mainly in Balaghat (40 million tonnes) and Jabalpur (11 million tonnes). Manganese deposit is also found in the Chhindwara, Dewas, Jhabua, Katni, Khargone, Seoni, and Sidhi districts.

Magnesite: Magnesite is a magnesium carbonate mineral with a chemical composition of $MgCO_3$. In Madhya Pradesh, a magnesite deposit is found in the Jhabua district. The green serpentinites of the Aravalli Supergroup are associated with thin magnesite veins. The thickness of these magnesite veins is up to 5 cm.

Mica: Muscovite is the most common mineral of the mica family. It is found in the form of flakes near Khandepapariya, Kacchar, Bisighat, Bhaldehi section, and Temni.

Molybdenum: Molybdenum (Mo) does not occur in nature in a free state. Molybdenite (MoS_2) is the principal ore of Molybdenum. Mo is used as an alloying agent in steel, cast iron, and superalloys to enhance strength and resistivity to wear and corrosion. In Madhya Pradesh Molybdenum occurs in the Balaghat, Chhatarpur, and Panna districts. Malanjkhand copper deposit in Balaghat district contains 0.04% recoverable molybdenum.

Ochre: Ochre is a natural mineral pigment known to humankind since ancient times. In the olden days, Ochre was used for coloring earthenware, household utensils, and decorative purposes. It occurs in variouscolors such as red ochre (mostly used in the cement industry), yellow ochre, and green earth. Ochre is essentially a mixture of haematite, limonite, and clay. In Madhya Pradesh, ochre mineral occurs in the districts of Betul, Dewas, Dhar, Gwalior, Jabalpur, Katni, Khargone, Mandla, Rewa, Raisen, Satna, Shahdol, Shivpuri and Umaria. The State hosts 11% of the country's ochre mineral reserves/resources. Madhya Pradesh produces 29,454 tonnes of ochre.

Rock phosphate: Rock phosphates also known as phosphorites are sedimentary phosphatic deposits comprising fine-grained mixtures of different Calcium phosphates, the most important of which being hydroxylapatite, carbonateapatite, fluorapatite as well as their solid solutions.

In Madhya Pradesh, phosphorite occurs in two different geological settings;

(i) Stromatolite-bearing rocks, belonging to the Aravalli Supergroup, in the Meghnagar area of Jhabua district.

(ii) Ferruginous shale in basal Bijawars, overlying the Bundelkhand granite, occurring in the Hirapur village of Sagar and Chhatarpur district.

Madhya Pradesh hosts 19% of the country's Rock Phosphate resources. Rock phosphate occurs in the Chhatarpur, Jhabua, Sagar, and Sidhi districts of Madhya Pradesh.

Potash: Potash is the common name for a group of minerals and chemicals that contain potassium carbonate and potassium (K), a key nutrient for plates and an important component of fertilizer. Potash is one of the three basic agricultural nutrients, with over 90% of it being utilized as fertilizer (N-P-K). Potasium-rich glauconitic sandstone occurs within the Vindhyan Supergroup and covers large areas in Vidisha, Bhopal, Guna, Shivpuri, Mandsaur, Dhar, Panna, Satna, and Rewa districts. The State hosts 5% of the country's potash resources.

Pyrite: Pyrite is an iron sulphide having chemical formula FeS_2. It is a brass-yellow mineral with a bright metallic luster. It is used for the manufacture of sulphuric acid and as direct feed for soil conditioning. Marcasite and pyrrhotite are the other iron sulphide minerals. After native Sulphur, pyrite is the common source of Sulphur. Minor occurrences of pyrite are found in Bajna at Bharar Pahar near Jata Shankar in Sagar district and Dilani in Chhatarpur district.

Scheelite: Scheelite is calcium tungstate $(CaWO_4)$. It is an important ore of wolfram. In Madhya Pradesh, Scheelite deposits occur in the Betul, Jhabua, and Raigarh districts. Sillimanite: Sillimanite has the chemical formula Al_2SiO_2. Theoretically, it contains 62.93% Al_2O_3 and 3.07% SiO_2. It is one of the three aluminosilicate polymorphs, with andalusite and kyanite. The decomposition of sillimanite occurs at a range of 1550°C to 1650°C. It is this property to withstand high temperaturesthat makes it suitable as a refractory in the form of high alumina refractory bricks. In Madhya Pradesh, the Sillimanite deposit occurs in the Sidhi district.

Talc/Steatite/soapstone: Talc is a hydrous magnesium silicate. In trade parlance, talc often includes (i) the mineral talc in the form of flakes and fibres (ii) steatite, the massive compact cryptocrystalline variety of high-grade talc (iii) Soapstone, the massive talcose rock containing variable talc, which is soft and soapy in nature. In Madhya Pradesh, Talc/Steatite/Soapstone occurs in the districts of Dhar, Jabalpur, Jhabua, Katni, Narsinghpur, and Sagar.

Thermal springs: Thermal springs are confined to the structurally controlled ENE-WSW trending Son-Narmada-Tapti Lineament Zone (SONATA Lineament). From ENE to WSW, the thermal spring localities occur in three different sectors viz., Son, Jhor, and Papreri.

Son valley sector: At Jhor and Paprei, the thermal springs are at a temperature of 40° to 43°C. The cumulative discharge of the thermal springs at Jhor is 40 litre/minute.

Narmada Valley sector: There are three thermal spring localities in Narmada Valley viz., Anhoni in Chhindwara district, Anhoni-Samoni (west of Anhoni) in Hoshangabad district, and Babeha to the SE of Chiraidongri in Mandla district. The temperature of thermal springs in these localities is 56° - 58° C at Anhoni, 40°–45° C at Anhoni – Samoni, and 38°C at Badeha.

Tapti – Satpura sector: There are two thermal spring localities in this sector;

(i)   **Salbardi area, Betul district:** There is a group of thermal springs in this area with feeble discharge and the temperature ranges between 38° and 42° C. The springs are located on either side of Salbardi's major fault zone trending N70°E-S70°W in the Maru River.

(ii)**Varla area, Khargone district:** The thermal springs in this area exhibit temperatures ranging between 39°C and 42°C and with a cumulative discharge of 30 litres/minute. Hot water springs are noted near Barwaki and they are known as Nageshwa Ka Kund, near Mohammadpur at Sagarnagar and Tajuddin Hill, Takiapani Springs.

Tin: Tin (Sn) is one of the earliest metals to be used by humans. Today, tin in cans and containers, construction materials, transportation materials, and solder. The predominant ore mineral of tin is cassiterite (SnO_2). In Jhabua district, sporadic occurrences of cassiterite have been noticed within the Aravalli Supergroup intruded by granitoid rocks. Colluvial aggregate of tin gravels has been noted near Kathiwara.

Titanium: Titanium occurs in the minerals namely., anatase, brookite, ilmenite, leucoxene, perovskite, rutile, and sphene. Most titanium is consumed in the form of titanium dioxide (TiO_2), a white pigment in paints, paper, and plastics (USGS). In Madhya Pradesh, titaniferous ore is associated with porphyritic granite as stringers, and discrete crystals occur in Imliadhana, Nishana nala section of Betul district.

Vermiculite: Vermiculite is formed by the alteration of biotite or phlogopite micas. In Madhya Pradesh, vermiculite mineral occurs in Kalikhetar and Pangola, Jhabua district. Vermiculite occurs in association with serpentinite and pyroxenite in juxtaposition with granitoids traversing ultramafic rocks as small clots and flakes.

Zeolite: Zeolite is found as scattered fillings in vugs, cavities, geodes, and fragmentary top and vesicular top of the Deccan basalts. The vesicular zones of lava flows may constitute up to

10% of the rock volume in rich zones. In Madhya Pradesh, zeolite occurs in the Dewas, Dhar, Khandwa, and Khargone districts.

Zeolite is used as molecular sieves (ion exchangers), catalysts in the petroleum industry, for wastewater treatment, in the detergent industry, control of obnoxious fumes from animal waste, removal of toxic gases from power plants, removal of ammonium ions from sewage and agriculture, purification of natural gases and sewage gas, addition to animal feed to improve weight and radio-active waste disposal by ion exchange.

Energy resource

The term energy resource refers to any natural or human-made substance or phenomenon that can be utilized to produce energy. Energy resourcesare crucial for meeting the various energy needs of society, powering industries, homes, and transportation. Energy resources are broadly classified into two categories: Renewable Energy resources and Non-Renewable Energy resources. Renewable energy is derived from natural, inexhaustible sources, while non-renewable energy is sourced from finite reserves on Earth. Examples of renewable energy resources include hydro, wind, solar, biomass, and geothermal energy. On the other hand, non-renewable energy resources encompass coal, petroleum, and other finite sources. Non-renewable energy source Coal-based power plants:

(i) Vindhyachal coal-based power plants with an installed capacity of 4760 MW are located in Sidhi. This plant is under the National Thermal Power Corporation (NTPC). The plant is sourced by coal from Nigahi mines and water sources from the discharge canal of the Singraulli superthermal power station. This plant supplies power to Madhya Pradesh, Chhattisgarh, Maharashtra, Gujarat, Goa, Daman and Diu and Dadar Nagar Haveli.

(ii) Gadarwarasuper thermal power project is a coal-based thermal power project with an installed capacity of

1600 MW. This project is located in Gadarwara Tehsil in Narsinghpur district of Madhya Pradesh. The Project is sourced by coal from the Talaipalli coal block and water source from the Narmada River. This project is under the National Thermal Power Corporation (NTPC).

(iii) Khargone Thermal Power Station is a coal-based thermal power project located in Selda and Dalchi villages in the Khargone district of Madhya Pradesh. It has an installed capacity of 1320 MW. This project is sourced by coal from Pakri Barwadhi, Jharkhand.

Thermal power plant

(i) Amarkantak Thermal power plant, owned by MPPGCL is located in Anuppur district with a power generating capacity of 450 MW. The plant obtained coal from southern coal fields and water from the Sutna Nala dam.

(ii) Satpura thermal power plant is located in Sarni village, Betul district. The plant has an installed capacity of 1142.50 MW. The plant obtained coal from the western coalfield and water needs from Tawa Dam Lake.

(iii) Sanjay Gandhi Thermal Power plant is located in Birsinghpur Umaria district. The plant has an installed capacity of 1340 MW. The plant obtained coal from southeastern coal fields and water needs from Kohila Dam.

Installed capacity

To achieve sustainability, the world leaders had pledged to expand infrastructure and upgrade technology to supply modern and sustainable energy services for all developing countries and to ensure universal access to affordable, reliable, and modern energy services (SDG-7). The growing energy demand has driven the need to shift to cleaner fuels and larger energy systems. India is increasing the installed generating capacity of power and decreasing the reliance on primary fossil fuels.

The total installed capacity of the State stands 8th in the country. At the end of the fiscal year 2022, the installed power generation capacity was around 25,385 megawatts. The installed power capacity has almost doubled from 10632 MW in 2012-13 to 25385 MW in 2021-22. The Per capita power availability in the last decade has increased from 609.8 kilowatt-hours to 1184.9 kilowatt-hours in 2021-22. The power requirement in the State has increased from 5178 (Net Crore units) in 2012-13 to 8650 (Net Crore units) in 2021-22.

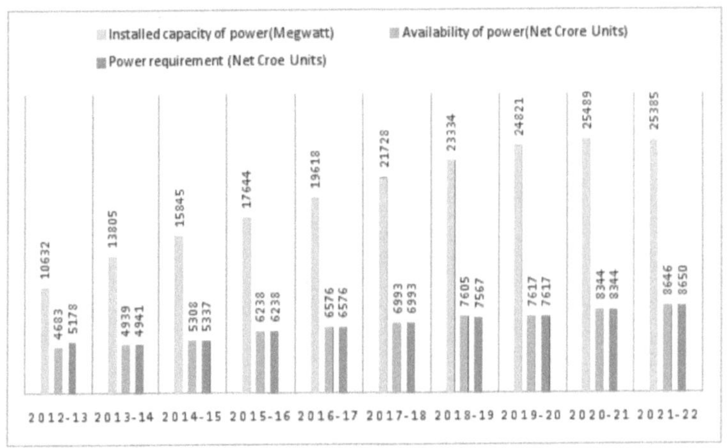

Figure 35: Installed capacity

Source: Handbook of Statistics on Indian States, Reserve Bank of India 2021-22

Renewable energy potential

India possesses substantial potential for harnessing renewable energy from diverse sources, including wind, solar, biomass, small hydro, and cogeneration bagasse.Globally, India stands 4th in renewable energy installed capacity, 4th position in wind power capacity, and 4th position in solar power capacity. Out of the total potential renewable power generation (14,90,727 MW) in the country (as of 31.03.2023), Madhya Pradesh shared 5.32 percent.

Table-13: Source-wise estimated potential of Renewable Power in Madhya Pradesh during 2021-22 (in MW)

Wind power @120m	Small Hydro-power	Biomass power	Cogenera-tion-bagasse	Waste to energy*	Solar energy	Total	Distribution (%)
15404	820	1364		78	61660	79326	5.3%

*Industrial waste

Source: Energy statistics India-2023

Table-14: Source-wise ranking of the estimated potential of renewal power (in MW)

	Wind power	Small hydro	Biomass power	Solar energy
Total energy potential in India (in MW)	6,95,509	21,134	17,538	7,48,990
Rank of Madhya Pradesh	8	4	2	4
Madhya Pradesh capacity (in MW)	15404	820	1364	61660

Source: MDES 2022-23

Hydropower energy

Hydropower is an important regenerative energy source. It is a free, renewable, and pollution- free source of energy provided by falling water driven by turbines. There are two types of hydroelectric power plants; (i) run-of-river power plants for the use of affluent water and (ii) storage power plants (power stations with reservoir) where the influx can be regulated with the help of a reservoir. Important hydroelectric projects of the State are as follows;

(i)   Gandhi Sagar Hydropower constructed on the Chambal River in the Mandsour district has a total capacity of 115MW.

(ii)   Pench/Totladoh hydropower constructed on the Pench River in Nagpur district has a total capacity of 160 MW.

(iii)   Rani Awanti Bai Sagarhydropower constructed on the Narmada River in Bargi, Jabalpur district has a total capacity of 90 MW.

(iv)   Bansagar Tons hydropower constructed on Rew Beehar river in Sirmour district has a total capacity of 315 MW.

(v)   Birsinghpur hydroelectric project constructed on Umariya/Johila River in Birsighpur district has a total capacity of 20 MW.

(vi)   Rajghat hydropower constructed on Ashoknagar /Betwa river in Guna district has a total capacity of 45 MW.

(vii)   Bansagar III hydroelectric project constructed on Shahdol/ Sone River in Deolond district has a total capacity of 60 MW

(viii) Bansagar II hydropower constructed on Rewa/Canal in Silpard district has a total capacity of 30 MW

(ix)   Bansagar IV hydropower constructed on Satna/Jhinna Dyke in Jhinne district has a total capacity of 20 MW

(x)   Madhikheda hydropower constructed on Shivpuri/ Kalisindh river in Madhikheda district has a total capacity of 60 MW

(xi)   The Indira Sagar hydroelectric project is a multipurpose project constructed on the Narmada River in Khandwa district. It has an installed capacity of 1000 MW

(xii)   The Maheshwar hydroelectric project constructed on the Narmada River in Khargon and Khandwa district has a power potential of 400 MW

(xiii) The Matatila hydroelectric project an interstate project of Madhya Pradesh and Uttar Pradesh constructed on the Betwa River in the Lalitpur (Jhansi) district of Uttar Pradesh has an installed capacity of 30 MW

(xiv) The Omkareshwar project is a multipurpose project constructed on the Narmada River in the Khandwa district with an installed capacity of 520 MW

(xv) The Sardar Sarovar hydroelectric project was constructed on the Narmada River in the Panchmahal district of Gujarat

(xvi) The Tawa hydroelectric project was constructed on the Tawa River in Hoshangabad with an installed capacity of 6.5 MW.

In the fiscal year 2017-18, the State attained a surplus in electricity. By the financial year 2021-22, the total power supply reached 82,976 million units, with 1,679 million units produced from the Indira Sagar Project and 970 million units from the Sardar Sarovar Project. Madhya Pradesh power generation companies contributed 21,933 million units to the total. In this period, the agriculture sector consumed the highest portion of the power at 42.6 percent, followed by home/residential usage at 27.6 percent. Continuous increases in power generation and transmission capacitiesare likely to maintain adequate availability of power in both industry and agriculture sectors.With increased production capacity and long-term power purchase agreements, Madhya Pradesh has achieved self-sufficiency in the field of electricity.

Wind energy

Wind is an important source of non-conventional energy. It is cheap, pollution-free, and eco- friendly energy. India hasthe fourth highest wind installed capacity in the world with a total installed capacity of 41.93 GW (as of 31st December 2022). Wind energy accounts for about 6% of the total renewable energy capacity installed. Madhya Pradesh has developed the Wind Power Project Policy of Madhya Pradesh -2012, to generate power for alternate sources of energy. The State has 38 wind energy projects of 820 MW, out of which 570 MW capacity projects have been established in the Dewas, Mandsaur, Ratlam, and Agar Malwa districts of Ujjiajn division. Prestigious wind energy sector companies such as

Gamesha, Inox-wind world, Suzlon, Hero, Renew power and Region Powerhave set up their projects in the State. The State falls under the most potential eight windy States in the country (Table 15).

Table-15: Wind power potential in India at 120 meters, above ground

Sl. No	State	wind power potential at 120 meters, above ground
1.	Andhra Pradesh	74.90
2.	Gujarat	142.56
3.	Karnataka	124.15
4.	**Madhya Pradesh**	**15.40**
5.	Maharashtra	98.21
6.	Rajasthan	127.75
7.	Tamil Nadu	68.75
8.	Telangana	24.83
	Total (8 windy states)	676.55
	Other States	18.95
	All India Total	695.50

Source: Annual report 2022-23 Ministry of New and Renewable Energy. GoI

Solar energy

Solar energy is one of the most important sources of non-conventional energy. It is non- exhaustible, reliable, and pollution-free energy. The average amount of solar energy received in the earth's atmosphere is about 1353 KW per squaremeter, which is about 1000 times the total consumption of global energy. Solar photovoltaic (SPV) technology enables the conversion of solar radiation into electricity without involving any moving part like a turbine. The State has an estimated solar energy potential of 61.66 (GWP). The cumulative solar installed capacity as of 31st December 2022 is 2774.78 (MW). The State is currently using about 2.3 percent of the available solar capacity. The list of solar parks in the State is plotted in Table 16.

Table 16: Solar parks in Madhya Pradesh

S. No	Solar park	Approved capacity (MW)
1.	Rewa solar park	750
2.	Mandsaur solar park	250
3.	Neemuch solar park	500
4.	Agar solar park	550
5.	Shajapur solar park	450
6.	Omkareswar floating solar park	600
7.	Chhattarpur solar park	950
8.	Morena solar park	1400
9.	Barethi solar park	630

Source: Annual report 2022-23 Ministry of New and Renewable Energy, Govt. of India

Rewa Ultra Mega Solar Limited (RUMSL) established in 2015 is a joint venture company of Madhya Pradesh UrjaVikas Nigam Limited (MPUVN) and Solar Energy Corporation of India(SECI). Rewa Solar project with a capacity of 750MW developed by RUMSL is the largest solar plant in Madhya Pradesh and 5th largest in India. Rewa Solar project supplies electricity to Madhya Pradesh Power Management Company (MPPMCC), the State-owned discom, and Delhi Metro Corporation Limited (DMRC). Mandsaur Solar Park with an installed capacity of 250 MW was also developed by RUMSL. Rewa Ultra Mega Solar Limited is developing 1500 MW solar parks in the Agar, Shajapur, and Neemuch districts in the Northwest region of the State. Other upcoming projects of RUMSL are the 600MW Omkarshwar floating solar park, 1500 MW Chattarpur solar park, and 1400 MW Morang Solar Park.

The Welspun solar project with a capacity of 151 MW was built in Bhagwanpura village in the Neemuch district.

                GEOGRAPHY OF MADHYA PRADESH

Power supply

The power supply in the State has increased over the years. The status of the power supply is plotted in the Table 17.

Table 17: Supply of electricity (in million units) from the year 2022-23(up to December)

Financial Year	Power supply/supply status
2018-19	76367
2019-20	76181
2020-21	83646
2021-22	86700
2022-23 (up to December)	67881

Source: Annual Administrative Report year 2022-23 Department of Energy

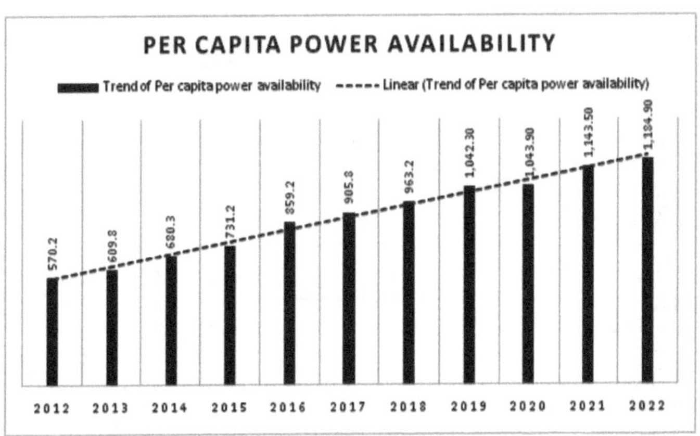

Figure 36: Per capita power availability

Source: MDES 2022-23

Water resource

The State has approximately 3956 km of river length and 553 km share boundaries with other states. Canal contributes 17.92 percent of the total irrigated area which accounts for 2766.8 thousand hectares of area. Some of the major canals are plotted in Table 18.

Table 18: Major canals in Madhya Pradesh

Sl.No	Project name	Basin	Design irrigation (in Ha.)
1.	Bansagar	Ganga basin	193359
2.	Bariyarpur	Dhasan and Ken basin	43800
3.	Barna	Narmada basin	62000
4.	Chambal canal	Yamuna basin	191380
5.	Harsi	Yamuna basin	30223
6.	Kolar	Narmada basin	60900
7.	Mahan (Gulab sagar)		9100
8.	Mahi	Mahi basin	26430
9.	Rajghat	Sindh basin	164000
10.	Rangawan	Dhasan and Ken basin	6478
11.	Samara Ashok sagar (Halali)	Betwa basin	25091
12.	Sanjay Sarovar (upper Wainganga)	Wainganga basin	69700
13.	Sindhi project	Sindh basin	40800
14.	Sukta (Bhagwant sagar)	Narmada basin	6200
15.	Tawa	Narmada basin	165472
16.	Thanwar	Wainganga	11105
17.	Urmil	Dhasan Ken basin	7692

Source: Water Resource Department, Govt. of Madhya Pradesh

Reference

1.   Annual Administrative Report year 2022-23 Department of Energy

2.   Annual report 2022-23 Ministry of New and Renewable Energy, Govt. of India

3. Coal directory of India. 2020-21. Ministry of Coal. Govt. of India. https://coal.gov.in/sites/default/files/2022-01/25-01-2022.pdf

4. Energy Statistics India-2023. Ministry of Statistics and Programme Implementation, National Statistical Office. https://.mospi.gov.in/https://www.mospi.gov.in/sites/default/files/publication_re ports/Energy_Statistics_2023/EnergyStatisticsIndia2023.pdf

5. Handbook of Statistics on Indian States, Reserve Bank of India 2021-22

6. Indian Minerals Yearbook 2018 (Part-III: Mineral reviews). 57th Edition Coal and Lignite (Advance release). Ministry of Mines, Indian Bureau of Mine. www.ibm.gov.in

7. Madhya Pradesh Economic Survey 2021-22 and 2022-23 Directorate of Economics and Statistics. Govt. of Madhya Pradesh

8. 24X7 power for all Madhya Pradesh. A joint initiative of the Government of India and the Government of Madhya Pradesh. https://powermin.gov.in/sites/default/files/uploads/joint_initiative_of_govt_of_india_ and_madhya%20pradesh.pdf

9. Madhya Pradesh renewable energy policy -2022. New and Renewable Energy Department, Govt. of Madhya Pradesh. https://india- renavigator.com/public/tender_uploads/utility_policy-62f10c923356b.pdf

10. Geology and mineral resources of Madhya Pradesh. Geological Survey of India, Miscellaneous publication. No.30, part XI, 3rd Revised edition. 2014. ISSN-0579-4706

11. Water Resource Department, Govt. of Madhya Pradesh http://mpwrd.gov.in/majorprojects/completed-2/

CHAPTER 6

INDUSTRY

The State's economy relies heavily on the agriculture sector for which industrialization is important to boost overall growth and development. Micro, small, and medium industries are indispensable for the holistic development of the rural economy. According to the MPES 2022-23 report, in the year 2021-22, a total of 1.87 lakh micro, small, and medium industries were established and 15 lakh potential jobs were generated.

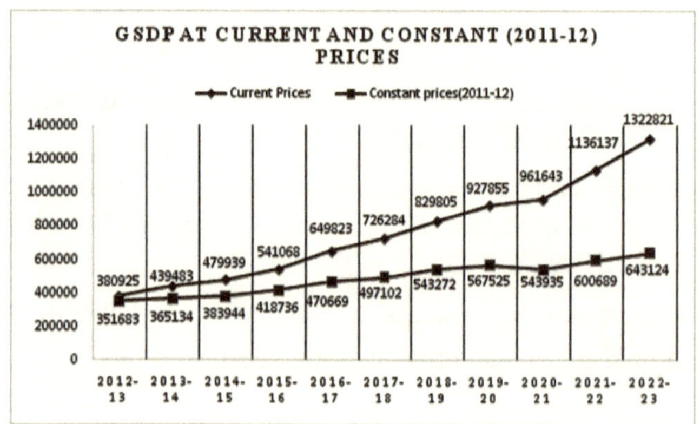

Figure 37: GSDP at current and Constant (2011-12) Prices

Madhya Pradesh is one of the fastest-growing States in the country with annual GDP growth at 8 percent Compound Annual Growth Rate (CAGR) over the last decade. According to the MPES 2022-23 report, the Gross State Domestic Products (GSDP) as per the advance estimates for the year 2022-23, has increased by 16.43 percent at current prices and 7.06 percent at constant prices as compared to the year 2021-22(Q). the State GSDP at constant prices of the base year 2011-12 is estimated to grow by 7.06 percent in the year 2022-23 (A: Advanced estimate) in comparison to 2011-22(Q: Quick estimates). While in the year 2021-22 (Q) an increase of 10.43 percent has been registered compared to the year 2020-21 (Provisional).

Source: MPES 2022-23

Its strategic geographical location provides a connectivity advantage to major markets and megacities such as New Delhi, Mumbai, Ahmedabad, Hyderabad, and Kolkata. The State has established six Inland Container Depots (ICDs) or Dry Port Facilities namely Malanpur (Gwalior), Ratlam, Mandideep (Bhopal), Pithampur (Indore), and Pawarkheda (Itarsi) and investment corridors namely., Bhopal-Indore, Bhopal-Bina, Jabalpur-Katni-Satni-Singrauli, Morena-Gwalior-Shivpuri-Guna.

The State falls under the influence area of the Delhi – Mumbai Industrial Corridor (DMIC) and has developed industrial and investment regions like (1) Pithampur-Dhar-Mhow, (2) Ratlam-Nagda (Investment regions), (3) Shajapur- Dewas, and (4) Neemach- Nayagaon (Industrial region) along the corridor.

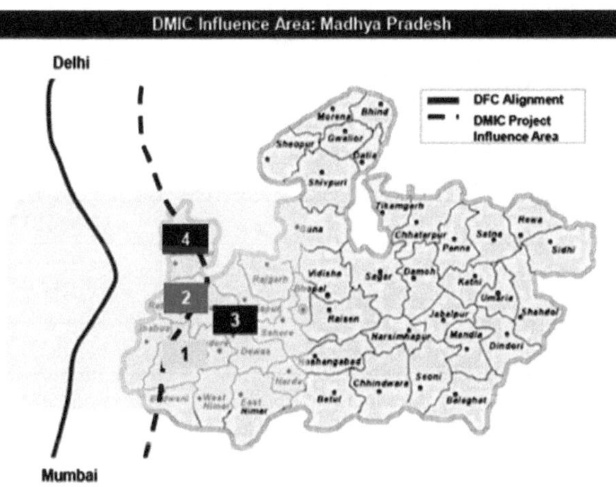

Figure 38: DMIC Influence Area: Madhya Pradesh

Source: Invest, Madhya Pradesh https://www.mpindustry.gov.in

To promote trade, the State has established eight industrial sectors i.e., (i) Agriculture and processed food (ii) technical textiles (iii) textiles (iv) pharmaceutical (v) Garment manufacturing (vi) Renewable energy-related equipment manufacturing.

Export is one of the important driving agents in economic growth. The State export has increased considerably since 2011-15 amounting to USD$ 7,834 million in 2021-22. In 2020-21, the State contributed 2.1 percent of all exports, placing 12th overall on the Export Readiness Index with a score of 49.47 percent. Medicines, oil meals, cotton, aluminum, and their products, along with other pharmaceutical formulations and organic products, were among the top 10 exported goods in 2016-17, accounting for 65.4 percent of the State's total exports.

Table 19: Top 10 exports of Madhya Pradesh (financial year 2021-22)

HS Code	Commodity description	Value of exports (Amount in Rs. Crores)
30	Pharmaceutical products	10,782
52	Cotton and cotton yarn	8,693
63	Readymade garments	4,495
76	Aluminum and articles	4,330
84	Machinery and capital goods	3,877
29	Organic chemicals	3,763
23	Residual and waste from food industries	3,024
10	Cereals	2,314
85	Electrical machinery and equipment's and parts	2,040
39	Plastic and articles thereof	2,020

Source: MDES 2022-23

Madhya Pradesh is a landlocked State and when it comes to Export such geographical conditions act as a disadvantage. The comparative analysis of landlock states in export is plotted figure.

                    GEOGRAPHY OF MADHYA PRADESH

In the 2017-18 period, Madhya Pradesh was in 4th position which moved on to 2nd position in 2021-22.

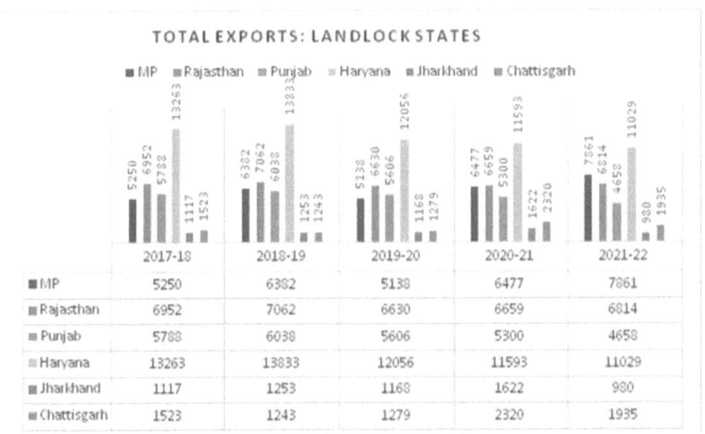

	2017-18	2018-19	2019-20	2020-21	2021-22
MP	5250	6382	5138	6477	7861
Rajasthan	6952	7062	6630	6659	6814
Punjab	5788	6038	5606	5300	4658
Haryana	13263	13833	12056	11593	11029
Jharkhand	1117	1253	1168	1622	980
Chattisgarh	1523	1243	1279	2320	1935

Figure 39: Total exports: landlock States (figures in million dollars)

Source: MDES 2022-23&Export Readiness Index, NITI Aayog, 2021

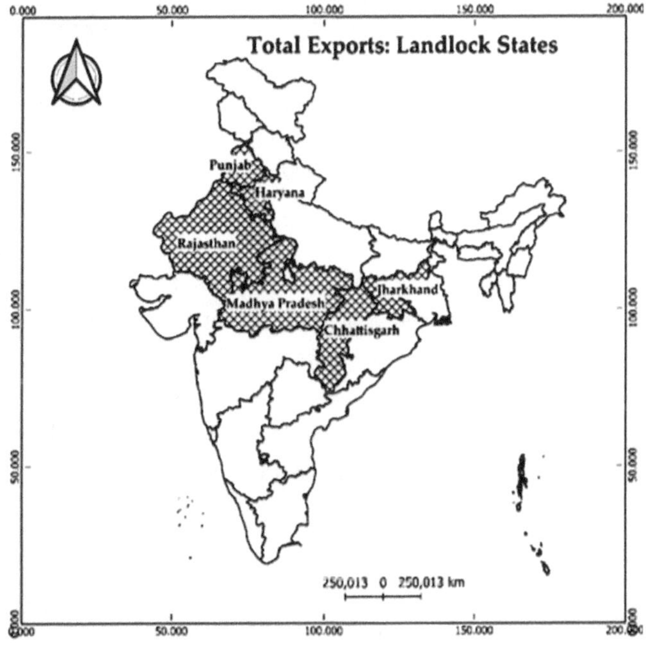

Figure 40: Total exports: Landlock states (Map) Mineral based industries

Raw minerals, both metallic and non-metallic are basic materials for the mineral base industries. The important large and medium-scale mineral-based industries in the Organized sector in Madhya Pradesh are shown in Table20.

Table 20: Principal Mineral-based Industries

Minerals	Industry/Plant
Aluminium/Alumina	– Hindalco Industries Ltd, Mahan Aluminium, Bargwan, Singruali district
Asbestos products	– Everest Building Products Ltd, Kymore – Kalani Industries Pvt. Ltd, Pitampur, Dhar – Ramco Industries Ltd, Maksi, Shajapur
Calcined Lime	– Rekha Harlalka, Jukehi, Maihar – Padampani Tripathi, Maamlime Industries Rajarwara, Katni
Cement	– ACC Ltd, Kymore, Katni district
	- Bhilai Jaypee Cement Ltd, Babupur, Satna - Birla Corpn. Ltd, (Satna Cement Works & Birla Vikas Cement), Satna - Century Textiles & Ind. Ltd, Maihar Cement, Maihar (unit I&II), Satna district - Heidelberg Cement (I) Ltd, Narsingarh, Damoh district - Jaiprakash Power Ventures, Singrauli (G) - Jaypee Rewa Cement Plant, Rewa district - Jaypee Bela Cement Plant, Rewa district - KJS Cement, Rajnagar, Satna district - Prism Cement Ltd, (Unit I & II), Satna - Satguru Cement Pvt. Ltd, Ghursal, Gandhawani - UltraTech Cement Ltd, Sidhee - UltraTech Cement, Dhar Cement Plant, Tonki, Temarnisounul, GolpuraManawar - UltraTech Cement, Vikram Cement Plant, Khor, Neemuch district - UltraTech Cement Ltd, Majhigawan, Rampur Naikin

Ceramic	- Roca Bathroom Products Ltd, Dewas - Govind Tiles Pvt. Ltd, Garra, Balaghat district
Calcined lime	- Som lime work, Jukehi, Katni - Jai Mata lime Industries Pathra, Katni - Dharampal Industries Pathra, Katni - Sampuran Singh Saluja Patra, Katni
Fertilizer	- AgroPhos. (India) Ltd, Dewas - ArihantFerts. &Chems. India Ltd, Kanawati, Neemuch - Basant Agro Tech (India) Ltd, Jawad, Neemuch - Coromandel International Ltd, (formerly, Liberty Urvarak Ltd,), Nirmani Khargone - Indra Industries Ltd, (Formerly, Swastik Ferts&Chems Ltd,), Indore, Dhar - KMN Chemicals & Fertilizers Ltd, Diwanganj, Raisen - Khaitan Chemical & Fertilizers Ltd, Nimrani, Khargone District - NFL, Vijaipur (Unit I & II), Guna district - Krishna Phoschem Ltd, Meghnagar, Jhabua - Madhya Bharat Agro Products Ltd, Rajoa, Sagar - Madhya Bharat Phosphate Pvt. Ltd, (Unit I), Diwanganj, Sanchi, Raisen - Madhya Bharat Phosphate Pvt. Ltd, (Unit II), Meghnagar, Jhabua - Mexican Agro Chemical Ltd, (Formerly, Asha Phosphates Ltd,), Jaggakhedi, Mandsaur - Mukteswar Fertilizers Ltd, Narayankhedi, Ujjain. - Rama Phosphates Ltd, Indore - Suman Phosphates and Chemicals Ltd, Indore - Varun Fertilizers Pvt. Ltd, Dewas

Ferroalloys	- Crescent Alloys Pvt. Ltd, Seoni - Jalan Ispat Castings Ltd, Meghnagar, Jhabua district - MOIL Ferro Manganese Plant, Bharveli, Balaghat district
Petroleum Refinery	- Bharat Oman Refineries Ltd, Bina, Sagar district
Refractory	- ACC Refractories, Katni - Calderys India Refractories Limited - Katni Refractory Works, KatniMurwara - Mahakoshal Refractories Pvt. Ltd, Katni - Mahakoshal Refractories Pvt. Ltd, Gudri, Bohariband - Premier Refractories India Pvt. Ltd, Katni.

Source: Indian minerals year book 2019: Madhya Pradesh

The manufacturing sector's 42.69 percent share is the highest contributor in the secondary sector during 2022-23 which is followed by the construction sector with 39.94 percent and the electricity, gas, water supply, and other utility services sector with 17.37 percent.

Table-21: Gross Value Added by Economic Activity of Secondary Sector at Current (2011-12) Prices

Economic Activity	2011-12	2015-16	2021-22(Q)	2022-23(A)
Manufacturing	38,286	51,912	89,986	1,00,019
Electricity, gas,	9,031	21,527	36,304	40,703
water supply and other utility services				
Construction	34,954	43,725	79,259	93,594
Secondary Sector	82,272	1,17,164	2,05,549	2,34,316

Source: Madhya Pradesh Economic Survey 2022-23

Tourism industry

Tourism is an important sector for economic development. It is one of the fastest-growing industries and a major source of income for many people including rural folks. Being a people's-oriented industry, it provides job and livelihood opportunities for millions of people across the globe.

Madhya Pradesh is called the "Heart of India" as it is located in the centre of the country. It is considered as the best tourist destination in the country for its rich cultural heritage, biodiversity and historic monuments. The state is the spiritual home of Hinduism, Islam, Buddhist, Sikhism and Jainism. The heritages of ancient's monuments, temples, stupas, forts, palace along with rich biodiversity has made the state the hotspot of tourism in the country. The tourism industry of the state provides a variety of options for visitors viz., cultural and heritage tourism, eco-tourism, spiritual tourism, and wildlife tourism. Madhya Pradesh is also known as the "Tiger State of India" for having the highest number of tigers in the country.

To promote tourism in the State, the Government of Madhya Pradesh has initiated the Madhya Pradesh Home Stay Establishment (Registration and Regulation) Scheme 2019, Formation of a district tourism promotion council, and rural tourism. The State has also initiated the "Madhya Pradesh Responsible Tourism Mission" with the objective to stimulate social development, economic development, and environmental protection of the local community associated with tourism.

The number of visitors to both religious and non-religious tourism destinations increased by an unprecedented volume in 2022 compared to 2021. Tourism destination-wise footfall is plotted in Table 22.

Table 22: Footfall in general tourist locations

Location	Arrival 2021	Arrival (2022)	Growth 2022 over 2021
Sanchi	1.45	3.88	168%
Udaygiri	0.34	0.78	130%
Pachmarhi	1.30	2.74	111%
Khajuraho	2.42	5.06	109%
Shivpuri	6.74	13.66	103%
Indore	26.29	50.51	92%
Bhimbetka	0.84	1.53	82%
Pench	1.23	2.07	69%
Gwalior	2.55	4.02	58%
Bhopal	15.00	23.31	55%
Kanha	1.77	2.53	43%
Bhedaghat	4.94	6.57	33%
Bandhavgarh	1.45	1.92	32%
Panna	4.20	5.28	26%
Dhammar	0.23	0.28	23%
Madhai	3.40	4.11	21%
Mandu	7.94	8.64	9%
Adamgarh	0.18	0.19	8%
Jabalpur	10.19	10.48	3%
Burhanpur	0.40	0.41	2%
Orchcha	1.35	1.33	-2%
Chanderi	0.50	0.44	-12%
Total	94.70	149.73	58%

Source: Madhya Pradesh Economic Survey 2022-23

Stupas of Sanchi: The Stupas of Sanchi is one of the oldest stone structures in the country. The Mahastupawas constructed on the order of Emperor Ashoka to preserve and spread Buddhist philosophy. The numerous stupas, temples, monasteries, and an

Ashoka's pillar are important feature to witness. UNESCO has declared Mahastupa of Sanchi as World Heritage site in 1989.

Pachmarhi: Pachmarhiis popularly known as "SatpurakiRani" (Queen of Satpura) is located in the Satpura range. It is one of the most important hill station destinations. Silver falls, aka RajatPrapat, listed among the country highest waterfall, Pandavs caves, Jata Shankar cave, Christ church etc are some important tourist attraction spots in Pachmarhi. Panchmarhi is listed in UNESCO Biosphere Reserve for its flora and fauna.

Khajuraho: Khajuraho is an important spiritual tourism spot in the country. Built in the medieval century by Chandela Dynasty, it is well known for magnificent temples and its intricate sculptures. The UNESCO site of "Khajuraho Group of Monuments" is famous for its Nagara-style architecture and graceful sculptures of Nayikas and deities. These temples fall into three distinct groups viz., Eastern, Western and Southern and belongs to two religions viz., Hinduism and Jainism. Kandariya Mahadev temple listed in UNESCO World Heritage site is one of the most imposing structures in Khajuraho

Bhimbetka: Bhimbetka is an important archaeological treasure of the country. It is an important site for recreation and education. Every year thousands of tourists both international and national visit Bhimbetka. Bhimbetka is the oldest known rock art and the largest prehistoric complex in the country. The cave painting date back approximately 30,000 years and has around 243 rock shelters. The cave paintings found in the Bhimbetka rock shelter have a striking resemblance to the Kakadu National Park in Australia, the cave painting of Bushmen in the Kalahari Desert, and upper Paleolithic Lascaux cave paintings in France. Bhimbetka has been designated a World Heritage Site by UNESCO.

Shivpuri: Shivipuri is renowned for the beautiful, ornately decorated marble Chhatris built by the Scindia rulers. The Chhatris a are stunning blend of Hindu and Islamic architecture styles with Mughal pavilions. Other important places in Shivpuri are George Castle and Madhav National Park.

Indore: Indore is one of the most important commercial centers of the State. The city is ranked as "the cleanest city in India" for the sixth consecutive year. Important places in Indore are Rajwada, Kanch Mandir, Bada Ganpati, Lalbagh Palace, Annapurna Mandir, Khahrana Ganesh Temple, and Gulawat Valley.

Pench: Pench is famous for its Tiger Reserve and well known for 'The Jungle Book' by Rudyard Kipling. Jungle walk and safari are major attractions in Pench Tiger Reserve. Gwalior: Gwalior is known for its historical monuments and heritages. The Gwalior fort dominates the city and is the most significant monument. The imposing structure of the Gwalior Fort inspired Emperor Babur to describe it as "the pearl amongst the fortresses of Hind". Other major tourist destination is, Jai Vilas Palace (the current residence of the Scindia family and Jivaji Rao Scindia Museum), Ghaus Mohammed's Tomb, Sun Temple, Teli ka Mandir, Mati Mahal, Tansen Tomb, Gujari Mahal, and GopachalParvat.

Bhopal: Bhopal is also known as the city of Begums as it was ruled by the generation of Begums for over 100 years (1819 to 1926). Bhopal is known for its natural beauty and historical monuments and heritages. Major destination of tourists are, Taj-ul-Masajid (Crown among Mosques) one of the largest Mosques in Asia, Van Vihar National Park, The lakes(Upper and lower lake), Gohar Mahal, Indira Gandhi Rashtriya Manav Sangrahalaya, Tribal Musuem, and Bhimbetka.

Kanha: Kanha National Park is the largest National Park located in the Maikal Hills of the Satpuras range spreading over the Mandla and Balaghat district of the State. Jungle safari is the main tourist attraction in the national park.

Bhedaghat: Bhedaghat is often referred as the Grand Canyon of India. The Narmada River cutting through the marble rocks produce outstanding beauty of marble rocks and their various morphological glittering and waterfalls. Several dinosaur fossils have been found in the Narmada Valley, particularly in Bhedaghat-Lametghat area of Jabalpur. In 1828 the first Dinosaur fossil was collected from Lameta

Bed by William Sleeman (UNESCO). Bandhavgarh: Bandhavgarh is significant for legendary and wildlife. The ancient Bandhavgarh Fort is believed to have been gifted by Lord Rama to his younger brother Lakshmana to keep a watch on Lanka. "Bandhav" means "Brother" and "Garh" means "Fort". Several man-made caves with inscriptions and rock painting dating back to 2000 years are found in this region. Once a hunting ground of Maharajas is now a National Park known for its highest density of Royal Bengal tigers.

Panna: Panna is well known for its diamond mines in India. The temples (Ramjanki Mandir, Baldev Ji Temple, Jugal Kishore ji temple, Prannathji Temple), waterfalls (Pandav Fall, Brihaspati Kund, Ajaygarh Fort, and Panna National Park boast the tourism industry in Panna.

Mandu: Mandavgarh or Mandav or Mandu "City of Joy" located in the Malwa region is a major tourist attraction in the State. The fort is 82 km in perimeter and is considered to be the biggest in India. The city is famous for the legendary tale of Rani Roopmati and Baz Bahadur which still hunts the palace. Important places that attract tourists are, Roopmati's Pavilion, Jahaz Mahal, Hindola Mahal, Ashrafi Mahal, Baz Bahadur palace, Darwazas, Hoshang Shah's Tomb, Jami Masjid, and Nilkanth Mahal.

Jabalpur: Jabalpur is a city with a blend of culture, river ghats, wide highways and charming surrounding. It is one of the famous tourists' destinations in the State. important tourist destinations are, Marble rocks of Bhedaghat, Chausath Yogini temple, Balancing rock formation, Madan Mahal, Kachnar city shiva temple, Dumna Nature park, Dhuandhar fall, Bhadbhada waterfalls, Nidan falls, Ghughra fall etc.

Burhanpur: Burhanpur is known for its revered heritage. The city of Burhanpur, founded in 1400 AD on the bank of the Tapti River was once the capital of the Mughal kingdom. Ruled by Shah Jahan for a very long period the city is the most beautiful symbols of Mughal Architecture and Mughal grandeur. The magnificent mosques, tombs and palace attract tourists to Burhanpur.

Orchcha: Orchcha was founded in the 16th century by Bundela Rajput chief, Rudra Pratap.

Orchcha exhibits the wonderful culture and legends of the rulers of the Bundela dynasty. Important tourist destinations are Raja Mahal, Laxmi Narayan Temple, Chhatris, Chaturbhuj temple, JahangiriMahal, Ram Raja Temple, Orchha Bird Sanctuary, Betwa river rafting, etc. Chanderi: Chanderi is an 11th-century town located in the northern part of the State. It is famous for its quaint forts, hills, and elegant hand-woven Chanderi sarees. Chanderi is known to have had 1200 Baolis in the past. Important tourist destinations are, Chanderi Museum, BattisiBaoli, ChanderiFort, Babal Mahal, Buddhi Chanderi, etc. Chanderi is an important center for Jains.

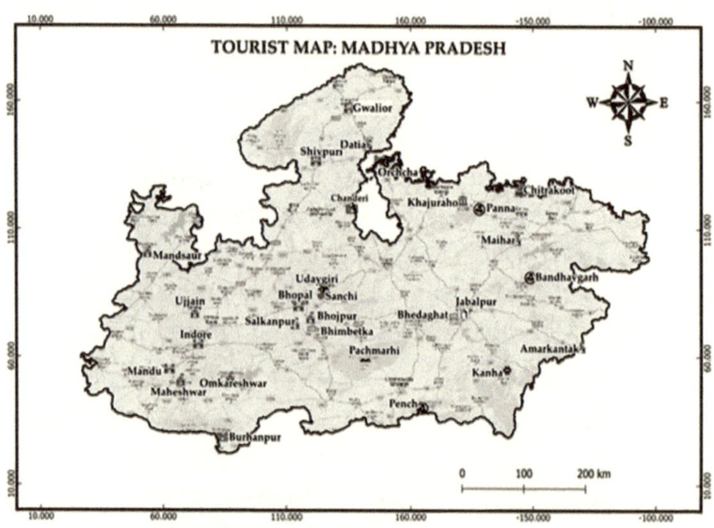

Figure 41: Tourist Map: Madhya Pradesh

Table 23: Tourist footfall in religious locations

Location	Arrival 2021	Arrival 2022	Growth 2022 over 2021
Ujjain	9.6	181.6	1796%
Maihar	57.4	110.1	92%
Omkareshwar	9.0	15.4	72%
Amrkantak	14.2	24.3	71%

    GEOGRAPHY OF MADHYA PRADESH

Salkanpur	13.9	17.3	25%
Datia	0.3	0.4	24%
Bhojpur	6.2	7.2	15%
Maheshwar	9.7	6.3	–35%
Chitrakoot	59.2	35.7	–40%
Total	179.6	398.4	122%

Source: Madhya Pradesh Economic Survey 2022-23

Ujjain: Ujjain is an important spiritual tourist spot in the country. It is known as the temple city for its numerous temples from different eras. Simhastha (Kumbha mela) is held on the banks of the Shipra River once every 12 years. The Shri Ram Ghat (Ram Ghat) is the most ancient bathing ghat in Ujjain. Important tourist destinations are Mahakaleshwar Jyotirlinga Temple, Mahakal Lok Corridor, KalBhairav Temple, Bada Ganapati Temple, Harsiddhi Temple, and Ved Shala.

Maihar: Maihar is an important spiritual tourist destination in the State. Maa Sharda Devi Temple situated at the peak of Trikoota hill in Maihar attracts thousands of devotees every year. The temple is considered as one of the 51 Shakti Peeths of Goddess Parvati. Omkareshwar: The island of Omkareshwar which is naturally shaped like an "OM", the sacred Hindu symbol is an important spiritual tourism destination in the State. Omkareshwar Jyotirlinga popularly known as 'Omkar Mandhata' is one of the 12 Jyotirlingas visited every year by a large number of pilgrims. Other important places to visit are 24 Avatars, Kajal Rani Cave, SiddhanathTemple, Gauri SiddnathTemple, etc.

Amarkantak: Amarkantak also known as "Teerthraj" (the king of pilgrimages) is a famous Hindu pilgrimage destination. Apart from spiritual significance, Amarkantak is renowned for its geographical and natural richness. The Narmada River originated here. It is the meeting point of the Vindhya and the Satpura Ranges. Important waterfalls are Kapil Dhara, DugdhDhara, and Narmada Udgam. The Kalachuri era group of old temples such as Machhendranath, Pataleshwar and Kailash Narayan, Shri Yantra

Mandir, Mrityunjay, Ashram, and BhriguKamandal are some important places to see in Amarkantak.

Datia: Datia is one of the most popular and sacred pilgrimage places in India. The seven storeyedDatia palace is a confluence of Mughal and Rajput architecture. Datia is noted for its many temples, some even dating back to pre-historic times, thus it is also known as 'Laghuvrindavan' or 'Small Vrindavan'.

Maheshwar: Magnificent Maheshwar is situated on the bank of Narmada River attracts both the pilgrim and tourist. Important places in Maheshwar are Ahilyabai fort and palace, Akhileshwar temple, EkMukhi Datta temple, Narmada Ghat, Rajwada, etc.

Chitrokoot: Chitrokoot, known as the 'place of many wonders,' is located in the northern Vindhya range has enchanting places to visit. Chitrokoot is an important religious place for its connection with Ramayanya. Kamadgiri, YagyaVedi, and Anasuya Ashram are some important places to visit.

Table 24: Important events in the State

Sl.No	Event	Month
1	Madhya Pradesh Tourism Day	24th May
2	World Tourism Day	27th September
3	Test all India Kalidasa festival	November
4	Nimar Utsav, Maheshwar	November
5	TansenSamaroh, Gwalior	December
6	Lokranjan, Khajuraho	December
7	Lokrang, Bhopal	26th to 31st January
8	Alauddin Khan Samaroh, Maihar	16th to 17th February
9	Khajuraho dance festival	20th to 26th February
10	Kumar GandharvaSamaroh, Dewas	8th April
11	Bundalkhand Utsav	December
12	Sanchi utsav	November

GEOGRAPHY OF MADHYA PRADESH

13	SharadoutsavBhedaghat	October
14	Mandu Utsav	October
15	Pachmarhiutsav, Pachmarhi	October

Source: Tourism department, Govt. of Madhya Pradesh https://tourism.mp.gov.in/

Connectivity

Road transport is an important infrastructure for economic development. The capacity of road transport in terms of handling traffic (passengers and goods) needs to keep pace with the economy. India has the second-largest road network (comprises of National Highways, Expressways, State Highways, Major district roads, other district roads, and village roads) in the world about 63.32 lakh KM.

Development in transportation and connectivity in Madhya Pradesh is one of the reasons for the State's economic growth. In the last five financial years, the length of the road has increased from 63,267 km in 2016 to 72,961 km in 2021.

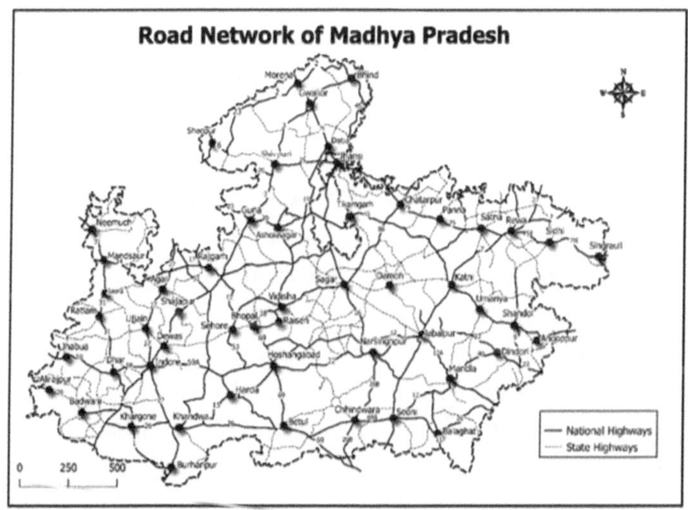

Figure 42: Road Network of Madhya Pradesh

Table 25: Road length network by road classification (figure in kilometers)

Financial year	National Highway	State Highway	District road	Other districts/ rural road	Total
2016	7806	10934	21132	23395	63267
2017	7806	11389	22129	23755	65079
2018	8858	11389	22129	28623	70999
2019	8858	11389	22191	28623	71061
2020	8858	11389	22191	28623	71061
2021	8858	11389	23401	29313	72961

Source: Madhya Pradesh Economic Survey 2022-23

The length of the National Highway in the State accounts for 6.6 percent of the total National Highways in the country. There are 46 national Highways with a total length of 9,104.64 kilometers in the State vis., National Highways 719, 27, 30, 34, 934, 135, 135B, 39, 339, 339B, 539, 43, 543, 943, 44, 45, 46, 146, 146B, 346, 47, 347, 347C, 347B, 547, 52, 552, 752B, 752C, 56, 548C, 752G, 161G, 347A, 753L, 147E, 135BB, 135BD, 135BG, 135C, 347BG, 552G, 752D, 753BE, NE4, 543K (Annual report 2022-23).

National Highway-719 starts from its junction with National Highway-19 near Etawah in Uttar Pradesh connecting Bhind and terminating at its junction with National Highway-44 near Gwalior in Madhya Pradesh. Out of 122.6 km length, 108 km lies in Madhya Pradesh. National Highway – 27 starts from Porbandar in Gujarat connecting Bamanbore, Morvi, Samakhiali, Radhanpur, Palanpur in Gujarat, Pindwara, Udaipur, Mangarwar, Chittaurgarh, Kota, Baran in Rajasthan, Shivpuri and Ganj in Madhya Pradesh, Jhansi, Kanpur, Lucknow, Faizabad, Gorakhpur in Uttar Pradesh, Gopalganj, Pipra Kothi, Muzaffarpur, Darbhanga, Forbesganj, Araria, Purnia in Bihar, Dalkola, Islampur, Shiliguri, Jalpaiguri, Mainaguri, Dhupgari, Falakata, Sonapur, Salsabari in West Bengal, Bongaigaon, Bijini, Patacharkuchi, Nalbari, Dispur, Nagaon, Lumding, Haflong and terminating at its junction with National Highway -37 near Silchar in Assam. Out of 4112.62 km total length, 121.90 km lies in Madhya Pradesh.

National Highway–30 starts from its junction with National Highway-9 near Sitarganj, Uttarakhand connecting Pilibhit, Bareilly, Shahjahanpur, Sitapur, Lucknow, Raebareli, and Allahabad in Uttar Pradesh, Mangawan, Rewa, Katni, Jabalpur, Mandla in Madhya Pradesh, Chilpi, Simga, Raipur, Dhamtari, Keskal, Jagdalpur and Konta in Chhattisgarh, Nellipaka, Bhadrachalam, Paloncha, Kottagudam, Tiravuru, Mailavaram, and terminate at its junction with National Highway – 65 near Kondapalle in Andhra Pradesh. Out of the 1987.18 km total length, 493.70 km lies in Madhya Pradesh.

National Highway–34 starts from Gangotri Dham connecting Bhatwari, Uttarkashi, Dharasu, NearTerhi, Ampata, Rishikesh and Haridwar in Uttarakhand, Najibabad, Bijnore, Meerut, Hapur, Bulandshahr, Aligarh, Etah, Kannauj, Kanpur, Hamirpur, Mahoba in Uttar Pradesh, Chattarpur, Hirapur, Damoh, Jabalpur, and terminate at the junction with National Highway – 44 near Lakhnadon in Madhya Pradesh. Out of total Highway length of 1482.83 km, 369 km lies in Madhya Pradesh.

National Highway–934 starts from its junction with Nationa Highway – 34 near Hirapur connecting Banda, Sagar, Jeruwakhera, Khurai, and termiate at Bina in Madhya Pradesh. The total length of the highway is 170 km.

National Highway–135 starts from its junction near Mirzapur connecting Lalganj, Drummondganj in Uttar Pradesh, and terminates at Mangawan in Madhya Pradesh. Out of a total 130.32 km length, 65.40 km lies in Madhya Pradesh.

National Highway-135B starts from its junction with National Highway- 35 near Mau in Uttar Pradesh connecting Dabhoura, and Sirmaur, and terminates at its junction with National Highway – 39 near Rewa in Madhya Pradesh. Out of the total 90 km length, 80 km lies in Madhya Pradesh.

National Highway–39 starts from Jhansi in Uttar Pradesh connecting Chhatarpur, Khajuraho, Panna, Satna, Rewa, and

Sidhi Madhya Pradesh, Dudhinagar in Uttar Pradesh, Garhwa, Daltenganj, Latehar, Chandwa, and terminate at its junction with National Highway–20 near Ranchi in Jharkhand. Out of the total 745.5 km, 392.80 km lies in Madhya Pradesh.

National Highway – 339 starts from its junction with National Highway – 39 near Nowgong in Madhya Pradesh and terminates at its junction with National Highway – 34 near Srinagar in Uttar Pradesh. Out of the total 36 km, 15 km lies in Madhya Pradesh.

National Highway–339B starts from its junction with National Highway – 39 at Bamitha and terminates at Khajuraho in Madhya Pradesh. The total length is 9 km.

National Highway–539 starts at the junction with National Highway- 39 near Jhansi in Uttar Pradesh connecting Pirthipur, and Tikamgarh, and terminates at its junction with National Highway – 934 near Shahgarh in Madhya Pradesh. Out of 157 km, 150 km lies in Madhya Pradesh.

National Highway–43 starts from its junction with National Highway-34 near Gulganj connecting Amanganj, Pawai, katni, Umaria, and Shahdol in Madhya Pradesh, Nagar, Ambikapur, Pathalgoan, and Jashpurnagar in Chhattisgarh, Gumla, Ranshi, Chandil, Manikul, Saraaikela, and terminates at its junction with National Highway – 20 near Chaibasa in Jharkhand. Out of 1062.47 km, 435.47 lies in Madhya Pradesh.

National Highway–543 starts from its junction with national highway- 43 at Shahdol connecting Dindori, Mandla, Nainpur, Lamta, and Balghat in Madhya Pradesh connecting Rajegaon, Dhamangaon, Rawandi, Gondia, Amgaon, Deori, Korchi. Kurkheda, Wadsa (Desaiganj), and terminate at its junction with National Highway – 353D near Bramhapuri in Maharashtra. Out of 563 km, 359 km lies in Madhya Pradesh.

National Highway–943 starts from its junction with National Highway – 43 near Pawai connecting Saleha (Jaso) Jassu, and terminates at its junction with National Highway- 39 near Nagod in Madhya Pradesh. The highway is 70 km.

National Highway–44 starts from its junction with National Highway-1 near Srinagar connectingBanihal, Jammu, Kathua in Jammu & Kashmir, Pathankot, Mukerian, Jalandhar, Ludhiana, Rajpura in Punjab, Ambala,Karnal, Panipat connecting Kundli in Haryana, Delhi [exceptportion of ring road from Mukarba Chowk (km 16.500 of old NH No. 1) toAshram Chowk (km 8.300 of old NH No. 2)], Faridabad, Palwalconnecting Hodal in Haryana, Mathura connecting Agra inUttar Pradesh, Dhaulpur in Rajasthan, Morena, Gwalior connecting Datia in Madhya Pradesh, Jhansiconnecting Lalitpur in Uttar Pradesh, Sagar, Narsmhapur,Lakhnadon connecting Seoni in Madhya Pradesh, Nagpur, Jamb connecting Pandharkawada in Maharashtra, Adilabad,Nirmal, Ramayampet, Hyderabad in Telangana {(excludingfrom Bowenpally [Km 486/200](old Km 474/00) to Assembly[497/200](Old km 485/0) on NagpurHyderabad Section} and fromAfzalganj [km 0/00] to Aramgarh [km 8/800] on Hydrabad-BangaloreSection}, Kurnool, Gooty, Anantapur connecting Penukonda in Andhra Pradesh Devanahalli connecting Bangaluru inKarnataka, Hosur, Krishnagiri, Dhramapuri, Salem connectingKanniyakumari (Cape Comonn) inTamil Nadu. Out of 3717.56 km, 571.90 km lies in Madhya Pradesh.

National Highway – 45 starts from its junction with NH-46 near Obdullaganjconnecting Bareli, Tendukheda, Jabalpur, Kundam, Shahpura, Dindori,Sagartola, Kabir Chabutra inMadhya Pradesh connectingKeonchi (Kionchi) and terminating at its junction with NH-130 nearBilaspur inChhattisgarh. Out of 593.5 km, 495.20 lies in Madhya Pradesh.

National Highway – 46 starts from its junction with NH-44 near Gwalior in Madhya Pradesh,Shivpuri, Guna, Biora, Bhopal, Obeddullaganj,Hoshangabad, and terminates at its junction with NH-47 at Betul in Madhya Pradesh. The total length of the Highway is 634 km. National Highway – 146 starts from its junction with NH-46 near Bhopal connectingVidisha and terminates at its junction with NH-44 near Sagar in Madhya Pradesh.The total length of the Highway is 167.60 km.

National Highway – 146B starts from its junction with NH-46 near Budhni connectingKosmi, and Rehti, and terminating at Nasrullahganj in MadhyaPradesh. The total length of the Highway is 50 km.

National Highway–346 starts from its junction with National Highway-46 near Jharkhedaconnecting Berasia, Vidisha, Kurwai, and Mungawali and terminating at Chanderi in Madhya Pradesh. The total length of the highway is 222 km.

National Highway–47 starts from its junction with National Highway-27 near Bamanboreconnecting Limbdi, Ahmedabad, Godhra, and Dahod in Gujarat, Indore, Betul in Madhya Pradesh, Saoner, and terminates at its junctionwith National Highway-44 near Nagpur in Maharashtra. Out of 1005.8 km, 558.60 km lies in Madhya Pradesh.

National Highway–347 starts from its junction with National Highway-47 near Multai connectingChikhli, Dunawa, Chhindwara, Chaurai and terminating at its junction withNational Highway-44 near Seoni in Madhya Pradesh. The total length of the highway is 152.30 km.

National Highway–347C starts from its junction with National Highway-47 near Dhar connecting Gujri, Kalghat, Kasarwad, Khargaon, Bistan, Baner in MadhyaPradesh Palpadlya, Raver in the state of Maharashtra and terminates atBurhanpur in Madhya Pradesh. Out of 237 km, 201 km lies in Madhya Pradesh.

National Highway-347B starts from its junction with National Highway-47 near KhericonnectingAsapur (excluding this stretch from Ashapur to Khandwa) Khandwa, Chhegaon Makhan (excluding this stretch from Chhegaon Makhan to Deshgaon)Deshgaon, Khargon, Julwania, Thikri, Anjad and terminated at Barwani in Madhya Pradesh. The total length of the Highway is 287 km.

National Highway-547 starts from its junction with National Highway-47 near Saoner inMaharashtra connecting Saunsar,

      GEOGRAPHY OF MADHYA PRADESH

Chhindwara, Amarwara,Harrari, and terminates at its junction with National Highway-44 near Narsimhapur in Madhya Pradesh. Out of 280 km, 267 km lies in Madhya Pradesh.

National Highway-52 starts from its junction with National Highway-7 near Sangrur in Punjab connecting Narwana, Hisar in Haryana, Fatehpur,Jaipur, Tonk, Kota, Aklera in Rajasthan, Rajgarh, Biora,Dewas, Indore, Sendhwa in Madhya Pradesh, Dhule,Aurangabad, Beed, Osmanabad, Solapur in Maharashtra,Bijapur, Hubli and terminates at its junction with National Highway-66 near Ankola inKarnataka. Out of 2125.75 km, 454.20 km lies in Madhya Pradesh.

National Highway-552G starts from its junction with National Highway-52 near Jhalarapatan connecting Beenda, Dawal in Rajasthan further connectingSoyat, Susner, Agar, Ghosla, Ghatia, and terminating at Ujjain in Madhya Pradesh. Out of 222 km, 192 km lies in Madhya Pradesh.

National Highway-552 starts from its junction with National Highway-52 near Tonk connectingUniara, Sawai Madhopur, in Rajasthan, Sheopur, Goras,Shampur, Sabalgarh, Morena, Porsa, Ater, Bhind (excluding this stretchfrom Bhind to Mihona) Mihona, Bhander in Madhya Pradeshand terminates at its junction with National Highway-27 near Chirgaon inUttar Pradesh. Out of 483.5 km, 402 km lies in Madhya Pradesh.

National Highway-752B starts from the Rajasthan/Madhya Pradesh Border connecting Susner, Khilchipur, Biaora on National Highway-52, Maksundangarh, and terminates at Sironj in Madhya Pradesh. The total length of the Highway is 151 km.

National Highway-752C starts from its junction with National Highway-752B near Zirapurconnecting (Pacher) Pachor, Shujalpur, and terminates at Ashta in Madhya Pradesh. The total length of the Highway is 139 km.

National Highway–56 starts from its junction with National Highway-27 near Chittaurgarh connecting Nombahera, Partapgarh, Banswara in Rajasthan,Jhalod, Umbi, Dahod in Gujarat, Bhabra,

Alirajpur in Madhya Pradesh, Bodeil, Chhota Udaipur, Rajpipla, Netrang,Vyara, Bansda, Dharampur and terminates at Vapi on NH-48 in Gujarat. Out of 716, 52 km lies in Madhya Pradesh.

National Highway-548C starts from its junction with National Highway-48 near Satara inMaharashtra and Connecting to Koregaon, Mhaswad, Malshiras, Akluj– Tembhurni – Kurudwadi, Barshi, Yermala, Kalamb, Kaij, Dharur,Majalgaon – Partur – Watur – Mantha – Lonar – Mehkar – Janephal – Khamgaon – Shegaon – Akot – Anjangaon – Wadgaon in Maharashtra and terminates at its junction with National Highway-47 near Baitul Madhya Pradesh. Out of 667.84 km, 78 km lies in Madhya Pradesh.

National Highway–752G starts from its junction with National Highway-52 near Sendwaconnecting Khetia in Madhya Pradesh, Shahada, Prakasha,Nandurbar, Visarwadi, Sakri, Satana, Deola, Chandvad, Manmad, Yeola,Kopargaon and terminates at its junction with National Highway-160 near Shirdi inMaharashtra. Out of the 403.80 km Highway, 53 km lies in Madhya Pradesh.

National Highway–161G starts from its junction with National Highway-161 near Patur connectingBalapur, Shegaon, Sangrampur, and Jalgaon Jamod in Maharashtra, and terminates at its junction with NH-930 near Khaknar inMadhya Pradesh. Out of 154.2 km of highway, 20 km lies in Madhya Pradesh.

National Highway–347A starts from its junction with National Highway-47 near Multai in Madhya Pradesh and connects to Warud, Ashti, Arvi, Pulgaon,Wardha, Sevagram,Sonegaon, Hinganghat, Jamb and terminates at itsjunction with NH-930 near Warora in Maharashtra. Out of 254 km of highway, 23 km length lies in Madhya Pradesh.

National Highway-753L starts from its junction with National Highway-753F near Pahurconnecting Jamner, Bodvad, Muktainagar in Maharashtraconnecting Burhanpur, and terminates at its junction with National Highway-347B nearKhandwa in Madhya Pradesh. Out of 251 km of highway, 93 km lies in Madhya Pradesh.

National Highway-147E starts from its junction with National Highway-47 near Jhabua (Bypass)connecting Nawagaon and terminates near Raipuriya in Madhya Pradesh. The total length of the highway is 34 km.

National Highway-135BB starts from its junction with National Highway-35 (Bargarh More) nearJamira connecting Bargarh, Gahur in Uttar Prasdeshconnecting Dubi, Magdaur and terminates at its junction with National Highway-135Bnear Dabhoura in Madhya Pradesh. Out of the 20 km length highway, 7.50 km lies in Madhya Pradesh.

National Highway-135BD starts from its junction with National Highway-135B near Sirmaur, Kolha,Rajgarh, Kyoti, Bagahaiya, Lalgaon, Pangadi and terminates at itsjunction with National Highway-30 near Kalwari in Madhya Pradesh. The total length of the highway is 36 km.

National Highway–135BG starts from its junction with National Highway-35 near Chitrakoot in Uttar Pradesh connecting Majhgawa, and Satna, and terminates at itsjunction with National Highway-30 near Maihar in Madhya Pradesh. The total length of the highway is 121.35 km.

National Highway–135C starts from its junction with National Highway-35 near Allahabadconnecting to Koraon, Drumanodganj, Haliya in UttarPradesh, Awadhadam, Pipra, Manigarha, Karondiya, Bagdara, Chtrangi,Singrauli and terminates at its junction with National Highway-39 near Waidhan in Madhya Pradesh. Out of the 176 km length of highway, 72 km lies in Madhya Pradesh.

National Highway–347BG starts from its junction with National Highway-347B near Deshgaonconnecting Sanawad, Barwah and terminates at its junction with National Highway-

52(Bhawarkua Chowk) at Indore in Madhya Pradesh. The total length of the highway is 106 km.

National Highway–552G starts from its junction with National Highway-52 near Jhalarapatan connecting Beenda, and Dawal in Rajasthan further connectingSoyat, Susner, Agar, Ghosla, Ghatia, and terminates at Ujjain inMadhya Pradesh. Out of the 222 km length highway, 192 km lies in Madhya Pradesh.

National Highway–752B starts from the Rajasthan/Madhya Pradesh Border connectingSusner, Khilchipur, and Biaora on NH-52, Maksundangarh, and terminates atSironj in Madhya Pradesh. The total length of the highway is 151 km.

National Highway–753BE starts from its junction with National Highway-753B Talodaconnecting Shahada, Shirpur, Chopda, Yawal,and Raver in Maharashtra, and terminates at its junction with National Highway-7531 near Burhanpur in Madhya Pradesh. Out of 250 km length highway, 10 km lies in Madhya Pradesh.

National Highway–NE4 is a Delhi-Mumbai Expressway that passes through Delhi (UT), Haryana, Rajasthan, Madhya Pradesh, Gujarat and Maharashtra. It enters Madhya Pradesh at DhablaMadhosingh village in Mandsaur district crosses Anas River at Dhebar village in Jahbua district and enters Gujarat. Out of the total highway length, 244 km lies in Madhya Pradesh.

National Highway-543K starts from its junction with National Highway -543 near Balaghat in Madhya Pradesh connecting Bapera, Tumsar, and Mohadi, and terminates at its junction with National Highway -53 near Bhandara in Maharashtra.

Railways

Madhya Pradesh is well connected with rail transportation. The commencement of rail transport in the State dates back to June 1867 when the Allahabad – Jabalpur branch line was inaugurated. Presently, the length of railway tracks in the State is 5150 Km which is the 5thlargest network in the country. The State has 723 major and minor railway stations and 13 major Junction railway stations namely; Indore Jn, Nagda Jn, Dewas Jn, Ratlam Jn, Khandwa Jn, Ujjain Jn under Ratlam Division (WR Zone), Jabalpur Jn, Satna Jn, Katni Jn under Jabalpur Division (WCR), Bhopal Jn, Guna Jn, Bina Jn, and Itarsi Jn under Bhopal Division (WCR). The major portion of the rail connectivity in the State is provided by the West Central Railway and some portion of the rail connectivity is served by Wester Railways, Central Railway (Khandwa), and North Central Railway (Gwalior).

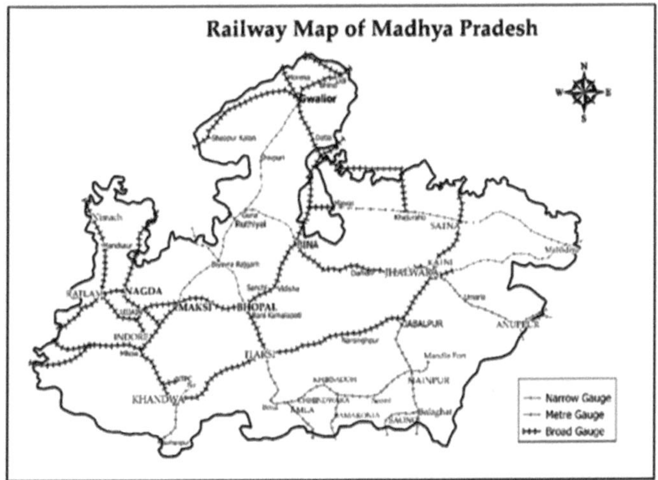

Figure 43: Railway map of Madhya Pradesh

Table 26: Railway route (As of End-March) (in KMs)

2012	2013	2014	2015	2016	2017	2018	2019	2020	2021
4954	4955	4976	4979	5000	5113	4829	4899	5148	5140

Source: Reserve Bank of India 2022

Seven major rail routes namely; Central Railway, North Central Railway, Eastern Central Railway, South East Central Railway, West Central Railway, Western Railways, and North Western Railwaypass through the State, which is the highestamong any State in the Indian Railways network system.

Airport

The State has five major airports viz., (i) Raja BhojInternational Airport, Bhopal, (ii) Devi Ahilyabai Holkar International Airport, Indore, (iii) Rajmata Vijaya RajeScindia Domestic Airport, Gwalior (iv) Jabalpur Domestic Airport, and (v) Khajuraho Domestic Airport.

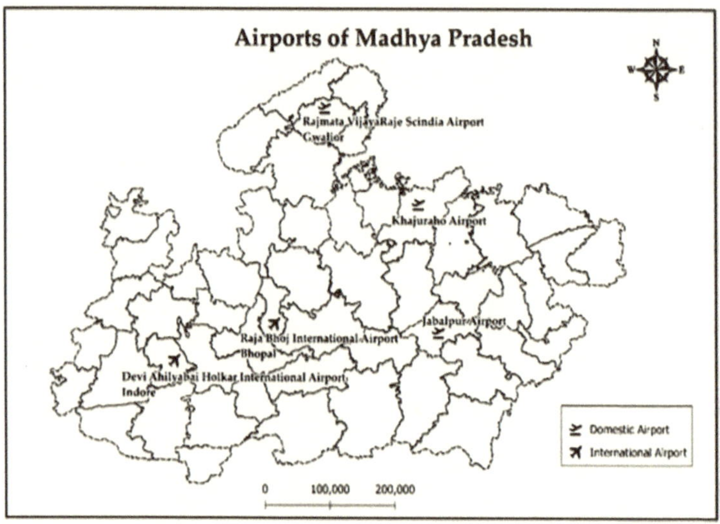

Figure 44: Airports of Madhya Pradesh

Reference

1. Annual report 2022-23 Ministry of New and Renewable Energy, Govt. of India

2. Annual report 2022-2023, Ministry of Road Transport and Highways, Govt. of India

3. Bhedaghat-Lametaghat in Narmada valley. World Heritage Convention, UNESCO. https://whc.unesco.org/en/tentativelists/6531/

4. Bhopal Division, West Central Railway. https://wcr.indianrailways.gov.in/view_section.jsp?fontColor=black&backgroundColor=LIGHTSTEELBLUE&lang=0&id=0,1,291,1419

5. Energy Statistics India 2023, Govt. of India, Ministry of Statistics and Programme Implementation, National Statistical Office. https//www.mospi.gov.in/

6. Explore destinations in Madhya Pradesh, Top tourist destinations in 32 cities. Madhya Pradesh Tourism. https://www.mptourism.com/explore.php#

7. Jabalpur Division, West Central Railway. https://wcr.indianrailways.gov.in/view_section.jsp?fontColor=black&backgroundColor=LIGHTSTEELBLUE&lang=0&id=0,1,291,360

8. Madhya Pradesh Economic Survey 2021-22, Directorate of Economics and Statistics. Govt. of Madhya Pradesh

9. Madhya Pradesh Economic Survey 2022-23, Directorate of Economics and Statistics. Govt. of Madhya Pradesh

10. Madhya Pradesh Road Development Corporation. https://mprdc.gov.in>media>map

11. Madhya Pradesh Economic Survey 2022-23 Directorate of Economics and Statistics, Govt. of Madhya Pradesh

12. Railway map of India. Survey of India. https://www.surveyofindia.gov.in/pages/railway-map-of-india

13. Ratlam Division, Western Railway. https://wr.indianrailways.gov.in/view_section.jsp?lang=0&id=0,5,575

14. Reserve Bank of India 2022. https://www.rbi.org.in/Scripts/PublicationsView.aspx?id=21523

15. Water Resource department, Govt. of Madhya Pradesh. http://mpwrd.gov.in/

CHAPTER 7

AGRICULTURE

Agriculture is the science and art of cultivating the soil, growing crops, and rearing livestock.The agriculture sector has experienced a growth of 5.46 percent during 2022-23 as compared to 2021-22(MPES 2022-23).The share of Gross State Value Added (GSVA) of Agriculture and Allied Sector in total Gross State Value Added of the State at current prices was 29.99 % in 2011-12, 34.50% in 2012-13, 35.64 % in 2013-14, 36.18% in 2014-15, 35.02% in 2015-16, 40.02% in 2016-17, 40.11 % in 2017-18, 38.20 % in 2018-19, 41.30 % in 2019-20, 44.40% in 2020-21, and 42.77 % in 2021-22.

Table 27: State Gross Value Added of Agriculture and Allied Sector at Constant (2011-12) prices

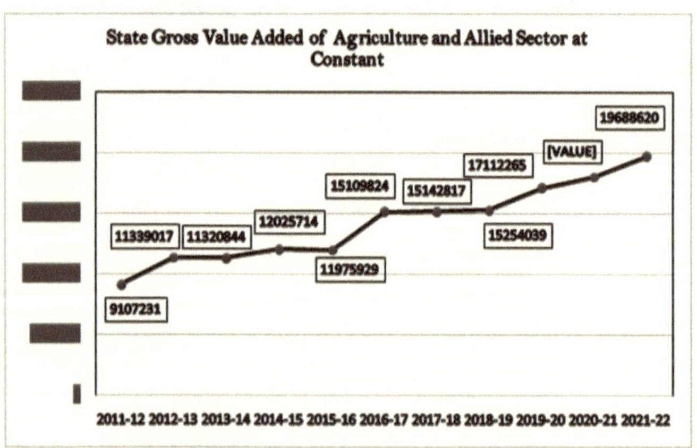

Source: Agriculture Statistics at a Glance 2022

Agriculture and Allied Sector includes Agriculture (crop and livestock), Forestry, logging and fishing. The growth rate of Gross State Value Added of Agriculture and Allied Sector at Constant (2011-12) price in 2012-13 was 24.5 % (Growth over previous year), 4.07 % in 2013-14, 6.23 % in 2014-15, - 0.41 % in 2015-16, 26.17 % in 2016-17, 0.22% in 2017-18, 0.73% in 2018-19, 12.18 % in 2019-20, 5.06 % in 2020-21 and 9.52 % in 2021-22.

Land Under Agriculture

Out of the total geographical area of the State, about 151.91 lakh hectares are arable. Out of the total arable land, about 145 lakh hectares areas are under Kharif crops, and about 119 lakh hectares are under rabi crops. The crop density of the state is about 165.70 percent. The total irrigated area in the state is about 110.97 lakh hectares from government and private sources. The land use under agriculture is plotted in Table 28.

Table 28: Land use under Agriculture

Particulars	Area in thousand hectares (2014-15)	
	Madhya Pradesh	**All India**
Gross Sown Area	23810	198360
Net Sown Area	15351	140130
Gross irrigated Area	10301	96467
Cropping intensity	155.1	141.6
Area of food grains		
Rice	2024.0	43499.2
Wheat	5911.0	30417.8
Total food grains	15658.0	123217.4

Source: Ministry of Agriculture and Famers Welfare, Govt. of India

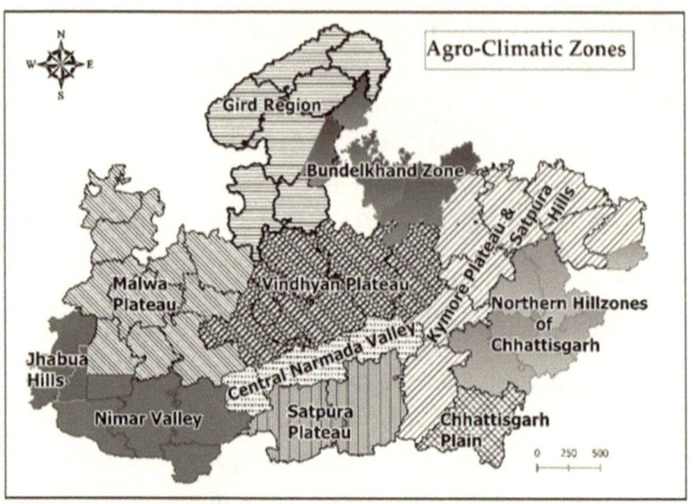

Figure 45: Agro-Climatic Zones of Madhya Pradesh

Agro-climatic diversity and topographical variations enable the State to grow a wide range of cereals, pulses, oil seeds, and cash crops, besides being home to myriad varieties of plant species, both in forest areas and outside. Various tropical fruits and vegetables and species like coriander, chili, and garlic are also widely grown. Based on the diverse climate of the State, it is divided into 11 climatic zones and 5 crop areas.

Table 29: Agro-climaticZone of Madhya Pradesh

Sl.No	Agro-Climatic regions	Soil type	Rainfall (Range in m.m.)	Districts covered	Details of Partly covered districts
1.	Chhattisgarh plains	Red &yellow (medium)	1200 -1600	Balaghat	
2.	Northern hill regions of Chhattisgarh (NHRC)	Red & yellow medium black & skeletal (medium/light)	1200–1600	Shahdol, Mandla, Dindori, Anuppur, Sindhi (partly-Singroli tehsil (Bedhan)), Umaria	
3.	Kymore plateau & Satpura hills	Mixed red & black soils(medium)	1000-1400	Rewa, Satna, Panna, Jabalpur, Seoni, Katni, Sidhi (except Singroli tehsil)	

4.	Central Narmada valley	Deep black(deep)	1200-1600	Narsinghpur, Hoshanganad, Sehore (partly), Raisen(partly)	Sehore:- Budni tehsil. Raisen:- Bareli tehsil.
5.	Vindhya plateau	Medium black & deep black (medium/ heavy)	1200-1400	Bhopal, Sagar, Damoh, Vidisha, Raisen(except Bareli teh), Sehore (except Budni tehsil), Guna(partly)	Guna:- Chanchoda, Raghpgarh & Aron Tehsils.
6.	Gird region	Alluvial (light)	800-1000	Gwalior, Bhind, Morena, Sheopur-Kala, Shivpuri(except Pichore, Karera, Narwar, Khania-dana tehsil), Guna (except Aron, Raghogarh, Chachoda tehsil) Ashoknagar	
7.	Bundelkhand	Mixed red and black (medium)	800–1400	Chhattarpur, Datia, Tikamgarh & Shivpuri(partly).	Shivpuri:- Karena, Pichhore, Narwar & Khaniadhana tehsil.
8.	Satpura plateau	Shallow black(medium)	1000-1200	Betul & Chhindwara	
9.	Malwa plateau	Medium black (medium)	800-1200	Mandsaur, Neemcuh, Ratlam, Ujjain, Dewas, Indore, Shajapur, Rajgarh & Dhar(Partly) Jhabua(partly)	Dhar:- Dhar, Badnawar & Sardarpur tehsils), Jhabua:- Petlawad tehsil.

| 10. | Nimar plains | Medium black (medium) | 800-1000 | Khandwa, Burhanpur, Khargone, Barwani, Dhar (partly) District. | Dhar:- Manawar, Dharampuri & Gandhawani tehsil. |
| 11. | Jhabua hills | Medium blackskeletal (Light/ medium) | 800-1000 | Jhabua district.(except Petlawad tehsil) & Dhar (partly) | Dhar:- Only kukshi tehsil |

Source: Jawaharlal Nehru Krishi Vishwavidyalaya, Jabalpur

Food grains

Foodgrains, classified as cereals and pulses are cultivated in the State across two crop seasons: Kharif and Rabi.

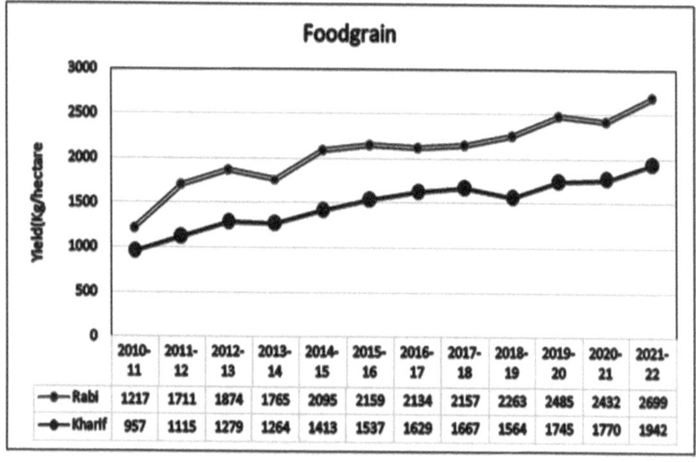

Figure 46: Foodgrain

Source: Agriculture Statistics at a Glance 2022

The State is one of the country's top producers of food grains, pulses, and oilseeds. The total area under foodgrain cultivation has increased from 15.01 million hectares in 2020-21 to 16.17 million hectares in 2021-22. Foodgrains yield (kgs/ hectare) is shown in the table 30. Table 30: Foodgrain yield (kgs/hectare)

Years	2010-11	2011 -12	2012 -13	2013 -14	2014 -15	2015 -16	2016 -17	2017 -18	2018 -19	2019 -20	2020 -21	2021 -22
Rice (Kharif)	1106	1340	1474	1474	1684	1752	1840	2024	1875	2363	2061	2283
Wheat	1757	2360	2478	2405	2850	2993	2976	2993	2993	2993	2989	3449

Source: Agriculture Statistics at a Glance 2022

Wheat and paddy/rice are the main crops under cereal in the State. The area under cereals cultivation has increased by 1.11 percent in 2022-23. The production of cereals has increased by 2.58 percent.

Paddy: The area under paddy cultivation increased by 12.00 percent in 2021-22 compared to 2020-21. Accordingly, paddy production increased from 12502 thousand metric tons in 2020-21 to 13193 thousand metric tons in 2021-22, indicating an increase of 5.53 percent. The average paddy production in the last ten years is 80.87 lakh metric tonnes. Major paddy growing districts are viz., Balaghat, Rewa, Satna, Katni, Mandala, Jabalpur etc. The districts with the largest area under paddy cultivation and production (2020-21) are plotted in Table 31.

Table 31: District-wise paddy cultivation area

Sl.No	District	Area (Ha)	Production (Metric Tonnes)
1	Balaghat	310239	1025286
2	Rewa	299099	1211780
3	Satna	239852	1004437
4	Katni	193961	874954
5	Mandala	187791	544594
6	Jabalpur	180140	696689

Source: Famer Welfare and Agriculture Development Department, M.P

Wheat: Wheat is a major rabi crop in the state. India is the second-largest wheat-producing country in the world. Among the states of India, Madhya Pradesh is the second largest producer of wheat. The area under wheat cultivation increased from 6.08 million hectares in 2021-22 to 6.50 million hectares in 2020-21. Accordingly, production increased from 18.18 million tonnes to 22.42 million tonnes in the same period. The state is well known for the "Sharbati" variety of wheat which is grown in the districts of Sheore, Vidisha, and Ashoknagar and in some parts of Bhopal and Hoshangabad districts. Sharbati wheat is also known as "Golden grain" as its color is golden. It looks heavy on the palm and tastes sweet, hence named "Sharbati". Major varieties of wheat grown in the state are viz., HI8381, HI8498, MPO1106, HD4502, PDW233, Raj1555, etc. The availability of new durum variants such as Malav Ratna, Malavshree, Malav Shakti, Sudha, and among aestivums HI1418, HI1479, HI1500, JWS17, and NP4010 are the new hopes for boosting production and productivity in the state. The diversity of wheat varieties in the state is the highest in the country.

Maize: Maize is the third most important food crop after rice and wheat in India. It is an important staple food and raw material for food processing, feed industry, and other industrial applications. It is grown in two seasons, rainy/kharif and winter/radi. Kharif maize represents more than 83 percent of the maize area in India. Madhya Pradesh is the second-largestmaize- producing state in the country. The area under maize cultivation remains the same during 2020-21 to 2021-22. The State's average production is 36.93 lakh metric tonnes and the production of maize has increased from 4430.00 thousand metric tonnes in 2020-21 to 4607 thousand metric tonnes in 2021-22 showing a 4.0 percent increase.

Major maize-growing districts are, Chhindwara, Seoni, Dhar, Rajgarh, Jhabua, Betul, Barwani, Khargone etc. Chhindwara is known as the corn city of the State. Corn is widely cultivated in the district due to suitable soil and climatic conditions. Corn festival held in Chhindwara district.

Table 32: Major maize cultivating district

Sl.No	District	Area (Ha)	Production (Metric Tonnes)
1.	Chindwara	368200	1418675
2.	Seoni	197175	663888
3.	Betul	167000	409150

Source: Famer Welfare and Agriculture Development Department, M.P

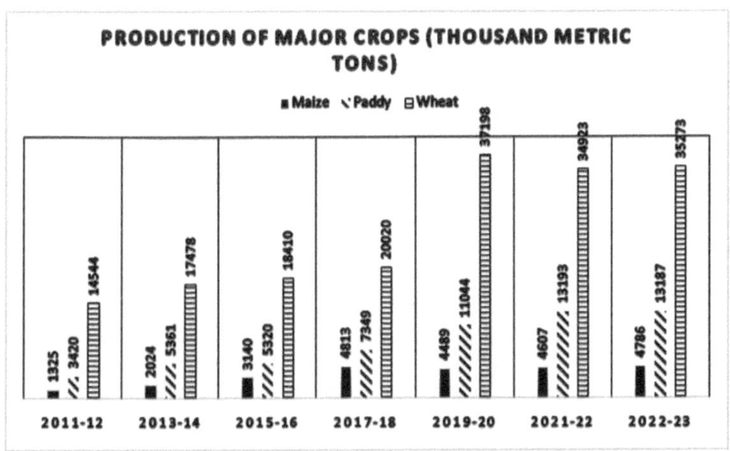

Figure 47: Production of major crops(thousand metric tons)

Source: Madhya Pradesh Economic Survey 2022-23

Pulses

Madhya Pradesh is a major producer of pulses in the country. Tur (Arhar), Gram, Masoor (Lentil), and Urad are major pulses grown in the State. The average production of gram, urad, and lentils in the last 10 years was 35.83 lakh metric tonnes, 7.35 lakh metric tonnes, and 4.78 lakh metric tonnes respectively.

Gram: Gram is a major rabi crop. India is the leading producer of chickpeas (Gram/Channa) in the world. Madhya Pradesh is the leading producer of gram in the country with a 2971.6 Ha area under cultivation and 3645.8 MT production in 2019-2020. It contributes to 45-50 percent of the total gram production of the country. The major gram-growing districts are viz., Sagar, Vidisha,

Damoh, Raisen, Rajgrah, Dewas, Satna, Sehore, Ujjain, Dhar, etc. major varieties of gram grown in the state are viz., JG-322, JG-221, JG-63, Ujjain21, 24, etc.

The districts with the largest areas and production under pulse cultivation are plotted in Table 33.

Table 33: Major Pulse cultivating districts

Gram			
Sl.No	**District**	**Area (Ha)**	**Production (MT)**
1	Sagar	118693	154301
2	Raisen	114529	218750
3	Vidisha	113505	198634
4	Damoh	106976	179185
5	Mandsaur	104995	133973
Tur(Arhar)			
1	Narsinghpur	29600	49432
2	Singrauli	22752	38109
3	Sidhi	19984	26379
4	Raisen	18608	25492
5	Chindwara	16500	24915
Mansoor			
1	Sagar	79973	86371
2	Vidisha	57991	70169
3	Rajgarh	57608	81804
4	Dindori	42371	49151
5	Damoh	29511	37480
Urad			
1	Chhatarpur	225300	99132
2	Tikamgarh	162895	22642
3	Sagar	95450	32453
4	Damoh	90975	14283
5	Panna	77714	40411

Source: Famer Welfare and Agriculture development department, M.P

                    GEOGRAPHY OF MADHYA PRADESH

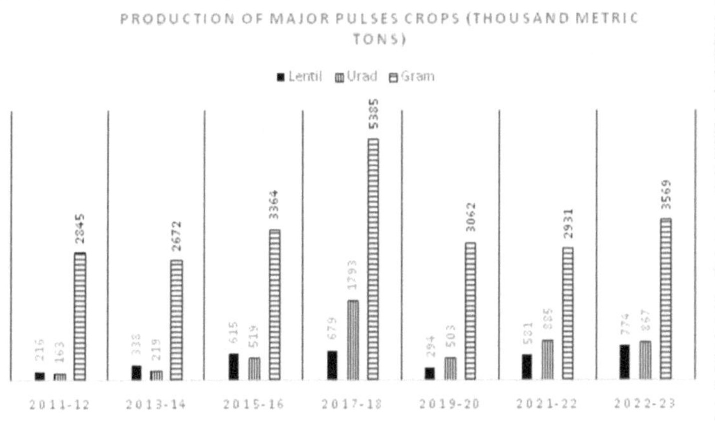

Figure 48: Production of major pulses crops (thousand metric tons) Soybean:

Soybean is a major Kharif crop of the state. The total area under soyabeen cultivation is 6.67 million hectares in 2020-21 and 5.51 million hectares in 2021-22. The production increased from 4.26 million tonnes in 2020-21 to 5.39 millin tonnes in 2021-22. The area under irrigation in 2019-20 was 0.081%. The yield – kg/hectare from 2010-11 to 2021-22 is shown in table

Table 34: The yield (Kg/hectare) 2010-11 to 2021-22: Soybean

Year	2010-11	2011-12	2012-13	2013-14	2014-15	2015-16	2016-17	2017-18	2018-19	2019-20	2020-21	2021-22
Yield (kg/hect-ares)	1200	1108	1293	831	1139	831	1231	1062	1231	789	639	978

Source: Agriculture Statistics at a Glance 2022

About 89 percent of the soybean production of the country comes from Madhya Pradesh and Maharashtra. The major soybean growing districts are viz., Ujjain, Rajgarh, Dewas, Sagar, Vidisha, Sehore, Dhar, Mandsaur, Betul, Shajapur, Guna, Ratlam, etc. major soybean varieties grown in the state are viz., 9305, JS-335, 5560, Ahilya 1(NRC2), Ahilya 3(NRC7), Ahilya 2 (NRC12), Ahilya 4(NRC37), JS71-05, JS335, JS 80-21, JS 75-46, MACS 58, JS

90-41, Indira soy9, JS 93-05, Kalitur, Porbhani sona(MAUS 47), Pratishtha (MAUS61-2),Monetta, Punjab-1, PK472, Shakti(MAUS 81). It has earned the highest award "Krishi Karman" which is given by the Govt., of India in the field of agriculture for six consecutive years.

Mustard: Madhya Pradesh, Rajasthan, Maharashtra, and Gujarat are the major oilseeds- producing States contributing more than 78 percent of the oilseeds production in the country. Mustard production in the State has increased from 1307 thousand metric tons to 1691 thousand metric tonnes between 2022-21 and 2021-22 showing an increase of 29.38 percent.

Cotton: The area under cotton cultivation in the State has decreased from 588 thousand hectares to 560 thousand hectares between 2020-21 and 2021-22. Major cotton cultivating districts are viz., Khargone, Dhar, Barwani, Khandawa, Chindwara, Jhabua etc.

Bt. Cotton is the only transgenic crop approved in the country for commercial (GEAC). The Ministry of Environment, Forests, and Climate Change is the nodal agency for the grant of permission for environmental release of Bt. Cotton hybrids under the Environmental Protection Act, 1986 in the country. At present about 1400 Bt. Cotton hybrid seeds are available for cultivation in the country. These Bt. Cotton hybrids are grown in ten States i.e., Gujarat, Madhya Pradesh, Maharashtra, Andhra Pradesh, Telangana, Karnataka, Tamil Nadu, Haryana, Punjab, and Rajasthan (Annual Report 2020-21, Department of Agriculture, Cooperation and Farmers' Welfare, Ministry of Agriculture and Farmers' Welfare, GOI)

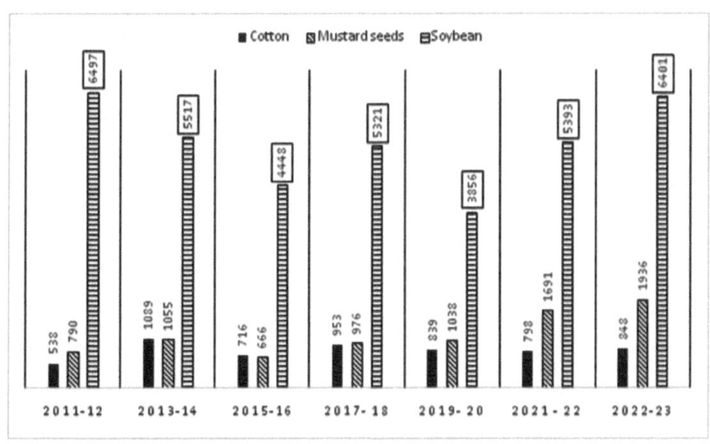

Figure 49: Production of major commercial crops (thousand metric tons)

Source: MDES 2022-23

Sugarcane: Sugarcane production increased from 544 thousand metric tons in 2020-21 to 651 thousand metric tons in 2021-22 showing an increase of 19.67 percent. Narsinghpur is known as the sugar bowl of Madhya Pradesh. About 65 percent of the total sugarcane in the State is in Narsinghpur district (approximately 75000 ha).

Major agriculture scheme in the State

1. Pradhan Mantri Kisan Samman Nidhi (PMKISAN)

2. Mukhya Mantri Kisan Kalyan Yojana

3. Pradhan Mantri Fasal Bima Yojana

4. Paramparagat Krishi Vikas Yojana (PKVY)

5. National Agriculture Development Plan

6. National Mission on Agriculture Extension "ATMA"

7. National food security mission

8. Soil health card scheme

9. Agricultural mechanization

10. Pradhan Mantri Krishi Sinchai Yojana (micro irrigation)

11. Certified seeds of distribution

Seeds

The use of quality seeds is an important input to increase agricultural production. Beej Nigram recognizes three generations of seeds, viz., Breeder, Founder, and Certified seeds, and provides adequate quality assurance safeguards in the seed multiplication chain to maintain the purity of the variety as it flows from the breeder to the farmer, following the Indian seed programme system.

Table 35: Seed variety with seasons

Sl.No	Crop	Season	Variety
1.	Pea	Rabi	Central Field Pea IPFD-12-2, Central Field Pea, IPFD-11-5, Prakash (IPFD1-10)
2.	Barley	Rabi	RD-2786, J.B.110
3.	Mustard	Rabi	Giriraj-31, Pusa mustard 30(LES-43), Pusa mustard-28(NPJ-124), NRCHB 101
4.	Linseed	Rabi	JLS-79, LC-4 (Kotabarani), Pratap Alsi-2, JLS-73, JLS-67, PKDL-41, Azad alsi – 1 (LMS9-2K), Kartika (IA-18)
5.	Wheat tall	Rabi	C-306, HI-3173, HI-1531, Sujata
6.	Wheat dwarf	Rabi	HI-1605, HI-8759, DBW-110, MP-3382, RAJ-4238, HI-8737, HI-8713(Pusa mangal), MP/HI-3336, MP 4106(Rajvijay), MP-3288, MP-1201, MP-1202, MP-3211, MPO-1215, MP-1203, HI-1544(purnima), GW-366, Gw-322
7.	Gram	Rabi	J.G, RAJVIJAY-202, RAJVIJAY-201, RAJVIJAY-203, RVKG-101(KABULI), J.G. 6, J.G. 14, JAKI 92-18, J.G. 63, JG.11
8.	Lentil	Rabi	RVL-11-6, L-47, RVM-31, IPL-316
9.	Soybean	Kharif	JS 20-98, Rajsoya -18 pragya, Rajsoya -24 RVS 2002-4, JS-20-69,JS-20-34, JS 20-29, JS 97-52, JS 95-60,JS 93-05, NRC-37
10.	Paddy	Kharif	Jeerashankar, Chinnor, JR-81, JRB-1, MTU -1156, CO-51, CR-303, CNR-2 (Sujala), IET 20235, DRR-51, MTU- 1153, Swarna Shreya ET24003, JR 767, IR-64 DRT-1, SJR-50(IET19972), ps-1, Sanbhagi Dhan IET 19576, (IR74371-70-1-1) Crr-1, PUSA SUGANDHA-5, CS(MTU-1010), Kranti R-2022, IR 64

11.	Arhar	Kharif	Rajeswari(Phule-12), Rajeevlochan(RA-6), TJT-501,ICPL-87 (Pragati), Pant291
12.	Urad	Kharif	Indra (URD-1), Visvash (NUL-7), UH-1, Pratap-1, IU-8-6, IPU-2-43, IPU 94-1, KU-300 (Shekhar-2), KU-309, KU-479
13.	Til	Kharif	BNS-11, TKG-308, TKG-306, JAWAHAR TIL(Pkds-11), Gujrat til -2/li>
14.	Niger	Kharif	Jawahar Niger Selection 28, JNS-30,JNC-9
15.	Jowar	Kharif	RAJ Vijay 1862, CSV-24, Aksb
16.	Maize	Kharif	Maize jm-218, JM-216, Patap 3
17.	Kutki	Kharif	Jawahar kutki-4, JK-36
18.	Kodo	Kharif	JNS-30, JK-109
19.	Moong	Kharif	IPM-205-7 (Virat), IPM 410-3 (Shikha), Suketi, SWATI (KM-2195), Term-3 TJM-3

Source: M.P. Rajya Beej Evam Farm Vikas Nigam

Breeder seed: the production of genetic seeds is prepared under the supervision of an authorized specialist in the Research Centers and Agricultural universities of the states under the control of the Indian Council of Agricultural Research, New Delhi. The golden yellow color of the seed details level is used on this seed bag which is signed by the crop breeder specialist.

Foundation seed: This seed is the progeny of the breeder seed which is certified after being found on the prescribed standards under the supervision of the seed certification body. The foundation seed bags are affixed with a white colored label which is signed by the organization's officer.

Certified seed: the progeny of foundation seed grown by registered seed growers under the supervision of seed certification agencies to ensure seed quality meets minimum seed certification standards. Certified seed bags carry a blue certification tag signed by the authorized officer.

Fertilizer is a major input in the production of various crops. Fertilizer comes under the Essential Commodities Act, 1955(ECA) and Fertilizers(control) order, 1985. There are six fertilizer quality control laboratories in the state viz., Bhopal, Indore, Gwalior, Jabal, Ujjain, and Sagar. Fertilizer consumption in the state is in increasing trend.

Table 36: Per hectare consumption of fertilizer (N+P+K) (Kg per hectare)

State	2004-05	2005-06	2006-07	2007-08	2008-09	2009-10	2010-11
Madhya Pradesh	53.4	47.1	61.5	63.8	69.7	81.4	97.2

Source: Agricultural Statistics at a Glance, Ministry of Agriculture and Farmer Welfare, Govt. of India

Horticulture

Horticulture is the science and art of cultivating fruits, vegetables, and ornamental plants or flowers.

Red chilli, garlic, coriander, and ginger are the important spices grown in the State. The total area under species in the State has increased from 8.24 lakh hectares in 2020-21 to 8.57 lakh hectares in 2021-22. Accordingly, the production of spices has increased from 46.75 lakh metric tons in 2020-21 to 50.90 lakh metric tons in 2021-22.

Table 37: Important spices of Madhya Pradesh (2019-2020 second estimate (Area in Hectare, production in MT)

Sl.No	Name of Spices	Area	Production	Productivity
1.	Dry Red chilly	103712.31	371435.69	3.58
2.	Green chilly	32881.69	515204.87	15.67
3.	Ginger	20337.91	325429.58	16.00
4.	Garlic	114786.73	1243135.67	10.83
5.	Turmeric	9616.06	164635.31	17.12
6.	Coriander seed	249102.44	351051.61	1.41
7.	Fenugreek	49398.45	105613.93	2.14
8.	Cumin	472.60	439.37	0.93
9.	Fennel	1225.08	97.38	0.80
10.	Other spices	41468.35	21130.07	5.24
	Total	623001.62	3295053.48	5.29

Source: Department of Horticulture and Food Processing, Madhya Pradesh

 GEOGRAPHY OF MADHYA PRADESH

Chilli: India is the world's leading producer of chilli. It is cultivated in both the kharif and rabi seasons. Madhya Pradesh is the third largest producer of dry chilies in the country with a 103712.31 Ha area under cultivation, 371435.69 MT production in 2019-2020 estimate. The area under green chilli cultivation covers 32881.69 Ha. Major variants of chilli grown in the state are viz., Pusa jwala, Sona-21, Jawahar, Sadabahar, Agni. Major chilli growing districts are viz., Khargone, Chhatarpur, Dhar, Khandwa, Shivpuri, Tikamgarh, Rewa, Gwalior, Katni, Barwani, etc. chilli festival is held in Khargone district.

Garlic: India is one of the leading producers of Garlic (Allium Sativum) in the world. Garlic is planted in both the kharif and rabi seasons in India. Madhya Pradesh is one the leading producers of garlic with 180580.96 Ha area under cultivation, 1833175.54 MT production, and 10.15 productivity in 2019-2020. The major varieties of garlic grown in the state are viz., Yamuna Safed-3(G282), Yamuna safed-4 (G-323), Yamuna safed-5(G-189), Agrifound parvati-2(G-408), G-282, Agrifound white (G-41), Phule Baswant, etc. major garlic growing districts are viz., Ujjain, Indore, Mandsaur, Neemuch, Ratlam, Shajapur, Rajgarh, Chhatarpur, Sagar, Agar Malwa etc.

Coriander: India is the largest producer and consumer of coriander in the world. Madhya Pradesh is the third largest producer of coriander in the country with 249102.44 Ha area under cultivation, 351051.61 MT production, and 1.41 productivity in 2019-2020 estimate. It is mostly grown as a rabi crop. Major varieties of coriander grown in the state are viz., Swati, Sadhana, Rcr-41, Rajendra swati, Moroccan, Gwalior No 5365, CO1, CO2, and CO3. Major coriander growing districts are viz., Guna, Rajgarh, Mandsaur, Agar Malwa, Neemuch, Ashoknagar, Sheopur, Rewa, Ujjain, Sagar, etc.

Sl.No	Vegetable Name	Area (Ha)	Production	Productivity
1	Potato	151413.36	3457319.97	22.83
2	Sweet potato	5647.47	86040.89	15.24
3	Onion	164667.18	4082901.06	24.79
4	Tomato	90971.04	2655294.2	29.19
5	Lady finger	49361.97	714156.31	14.47
6	Brinjal	54372.3	1135041.61	20.88
7	Cauliflower	51313	1153798.74	22.49
8	Cabbage	33245.66	774625.95	23.30
9	Colocasia	16617.33	276895.2	16.66
10	Green Peas	101521.72	1046837.31	10.31
11	Bottle gourd	21069.53	393026.68	18.65
12	Bitter gourd	15622.93	233110.72	14.92
13	Raddish	11381.25	174821.14	14.92
14	Leafy vegetable/Spinach	32054.33	370512.26	11.56
15	Sponge gourd	14602.76	200930.82	13.6
16	Carrot	8242.59	154563.4	18.75
17	Cucumber	12333.86	212108.85	17.20
18	Capsicum	1599.03	28487.58	17.82
19	Pointed gourd	669.81	10519.74	15.1
20	Other vegetable	85507.83	1265547.95	14.80
	Total	922214.97	18426540.38	19.98

Source: Department of Horticulture and Food Processing, Govt.,
of Madhya Pradesh

Potato: India is the second largest producer of potatoes in the world after China. Madhya Pradesh is the fifth largest producer of potatoes in the country with 151413.36 Ha area under cultivation,

3457319.97 MT production, and 22.83 productivity in 2019-2020. Major variants of potato grown in the state are viz., Kufri-chipsona, Kufri-chipsona-2, Kufri-chipsona-3, Kufri chandramukhi, kufrijyoti, kufrijawahar, kufri sultej etc.The major potato-growing districts are etc Indore, Ujjain, Shajapur, Chhindwara, Sagar, Dewas, Marena, Gwalior, Katni, Singrauli, etc.

Peas: Pea (Pisum Sativum) is a major rabi crop in Madhya Pradesh. The state is one of the leading producers of peas in the country with a cultivated area of 101521.72 Ha and 1046837.31 production and 10.31 productivity in 2019-2020. Major pea-growing districts are viz., Jabalpur, Ratlam, Chhindwara, Ujjain, Narsinghpur, Dewas, Tikamgarh, Gwalior, Datia, Seoni etc. Shubra, KMPR-400, KMPR-552, Pusamukta Prakesh, Arkel, Kasha Nandin, Pusa Pragati, Bonneville, PSM-3, GS-10, etc are major variants of pea grow in the state.

Onion: India is the second largest producer of onion in the world after China. Madhya Pradesh is the second largest producer of onion after Karnataka.The total area under onion cultivation increased from 186.92 million hectares in 2020-21 to 196.70 million hectares in 2021-22(3rd Adv.Est). the production increased from 4548.56 million tonnes to 4740.60 million tonnes in the same period.

The major varieties of onion grown in the state are viz., AFDR, AFLR, Bhima light red, Bhima dark red, Bhima super, Bhima shakti, Early Grano, Pusa white round, Arkakirtiman, N-53, etc. the major onion-growing districts are viz., Dewas, Indore, Rewa, Khandwa, Ujjain, Shivpuri, Shajapur, Sagar, Ratlam, Agar Malwa, etc.

Tomato: India is the second largest producer of tomatoes in the world. Madhya Pradesh is the largest producer of tomatoes in the country with a 90971.04 Ha area under cultivation, 2655294.2 MT production, and 29.19 productivity in 2019-2020. Major tomato growing districts are viz., Shivpuri, Chhindwara, Jhabua, Sagar, Raisen, Dhar, Jabalpur, Katni, Dewas, Shajapur etc.

Table 39: Fruits (2019-2020 second estimate (Area in Hectare, production in MT)

Sl.No	Name of Fruit	Area (Ha)	Production	Productivity
1.	Mango	49568.8	704067.05	14.20
2.	Guava	39763.69	767928.51	19.31
3.	Aonla	22547.99	334883.33	14.85
4.	Kinnow/Mandarin Orange	127878.75	2168455.42	16.96
5.	Lime	22003.17	333855.84	15.17
6.	Sweet lime	6549.92	113047.65	17.26
7.	Banana	26863.04	1873328.99	69.74
8.	Pomegranate	8963.78	106811.88	11.92
9.	Papaya	10986.43	435910.19	39.68
10.	Muskmelon	6203.89	108574.6	17.50
11.	Watermelon	10079.23	272260.53	27.01
12.	Water chestnut	824.98	2079.34	2.52
13.	Bengal quince	11080.91	122529.27	11.06
14.	Jackfruit	5167.34	107107.76	20.69
15.	Grapes	84.00	1344.00	16.00
16.	Custard apple	7298.44	93879.69	12.86
17.	Others fruits	19574.76	211119.1	10.79
	Total	375448.12	7757183.19	20.66

Source: Department of Horticulture and Food Processing, Madhya Pradesh

Orange: India is the third largest producer of oranges in the world. It contributes about 10 percent of the world's total production. Madhya Pradesh is the leading producer of oranges in the country with a cultivated area of 127878.5 Ha, 2168455.42 MT production, and 16.96 productivity in 2019-2020. Major variants of orange grown in the state are viz., Nagpur mandarin, Kinnow, Coorg mandarin, Mosambi, etc. The major orange growing districts are viz., Agar Malwa, Chhindwara, Shajapur, Rajgarh, Mandsaur, Betul, Ujjain, Neemuch, Hoshangabad, Sehore, etc.

Mango: India is the world leader in the production of mango with 40 percent of total production. India is also known as the "mango capital of the world". Madhya Pradesh is among the top ten mango-producing states in India with 49568.8 Ha area under cultivation, 704067.05 MT production, and 14.20 productivity in the 2019-2020 second estimate. A major variant of mango grown in the state are viz., Alphonso, Bombay green, Langra, Chausa, Sunderja, Dashehari, Fazli, Amrapalli, Mallika, etc. The Major mango growing districts are viz., Betul, Anuppur, Katni, Balaghat, Alirajpur, Rewa, Singrauli, Sidhi, Chhindwara, Vidisha etc.

Guava: India is the largest producer of guava in the world. Madhya Pradesh is the second largest producer of guava in the country with 3976.69 Ha area under cultivation, 767928.51 MT production, and 19.31 productivity in 2019-2020. Major varieties of guava grown in the state are viz., Sardar(L-49), Allahabad Safeda, Gwalior-27, Seedless, Lalit, Shweta etc. The major guava growing districts are viz., Khargone, Sehore, Rewa, Vidisha, Katni, Indore, Singrauli, Bhopla, Sheopur, Morena etc.

Banana: India is the largest producer of bananas in the world. Madhya Pradesh produces 1873328.99 MT with 69.74 productivity in 26863.04 Ha area under cultivation in the 2019-2020 estimate. The main transit points of bananas are Khandwa, Burhanpur, Dhar, and Barwani. Dwarf cavendish (Basrai), is the 3rd most commercially grown variety of bananas in India due to their superior fruit quality, dwarfness, and sweet aroma. Major banana growing districts are viz., Burhanpur, Dhar, Barwani, Khandwa, Khargone, Katni, Harda, Jabalpur, Balaghat, Sidhi, etc.

Pomegranate: India is the world's largest producer of pomegranate. Madhya Pradesh is the fifth largest producer of pomegranate in the country with a total production of 106811.88 MT and an 8963.78 Ha area under cultivation in the 2019-2020 estimate. The cultivation of pomegranate as a commercial crop was started in 2013. The major pomegranate growing districts are viz., Khargone, Dhar, Agar Malwa, Shajapur, Dewas, Ratlam,

Ujjain, Khandwa, Barwani, Chhindwara etc. Bhagwa, Jyoti, Ruby, Mridulla etc are major variants grown in the state.

Table 40: Flower (2019-2020 second estimate (Area in Hectare, production in MT)

Sl.No	Name of flowers	Area	Production	Productivity
1.	Marigold	18227.38	238260.34	13.07
2.	Rose	3555.68	34933.73	9.82
3.	Chrysanthemum	1145.82	14316.85	12.49
4.	Tuberose	222.38	2753.53	12.38
5.	Gladiolus	827.12	7001.03	8.46
6.	Other flowers	6820.93	66566.52	9.67
	Total	30799.31	363832	11.81

Source: Department of Horticulture and Food Processing, Madhya Pradesh

Table 41: Medicinal plants (2019-2020 second estimate (Area in Hectare, production in MT)

Sl.No	Name of medicinal plants	Area	Production	Productivity
1	Ashwagandha	3929.38	5504.84	1.40
2	White Musli	1653.13	5695.59	3.45
3	Isabgol	14806.2	16153.13	1.09
4	Coleus	435.18	2334.61	5.36
5	Other medicinal plants	16793.51	65989.54	3.93
	Total	37617.4	95677.71	2.54

Source: Department of Horticulture and Food Processing, Madhya Pradesh

In order to promote horticulture in the State, the following schemes have been implemented

(i)   Fruit plantation scheme

(ii) Spices area expansion scheme

(iii) Incentive scheme for protected cultivation of commercial horticulture crops

(iv) Prime Minster Agricultural Irrigation scheme

(v) PM micro food upgradation scheme (MEME)

Livestock

Animal husbandry is an integral part of agriculture and contributes significantly to the rural economy. Livestock-rearing activities significantly create employment in rural areas, particularly for landless, small, and marginal farmers, as well as women. The livestock also acts as a source of protein in the form of milk, eggs, and meat for millions of people.

Madhya Pradesh is the third largest producer of milk (8.60 percent in 2021-22) in the country. The production of milk has increased from 179.99 lakh tonnes in 2020-21 to 190.00 lakh tonnes in 2021-22 indicating an annual growth of 5.58 percent. The per capita availability of milk in the State is 616 grams per day (based on projected population according to population census 2011). About 48 percent of milk production comes from buffaloes and 36 percent from indigenous/non-descript cows.

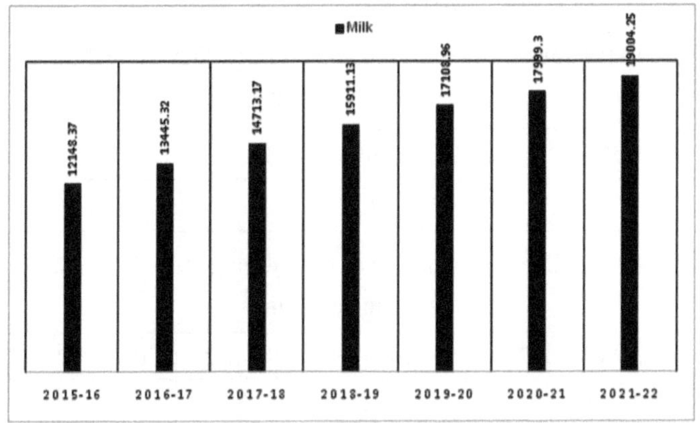

Figure 50: Estimates of milk production during 2015-16 to 2021-22 (Figures in '000 tonnes) Source: Basic Animal Husbandry Statistics – 2022

Milk

India is the third largest producer of eggs in the world. The annual growth rate of eggs in the State is 9.72 in 2021-22. The percentage share of the State is about 2.24 percent in 2021-22. The Per Capita availability during 2021-22 is 34 eggs per person per year.

Table 42: Estimates of Egg production during 2015-16 to 2021-22

(figures in lakh nos.)

2015-16	2016-17	2017-18	2018-19	2019-2020	2020-21	2021-22
14414.28	16939.63	19421.61	21431.92	23793.88	26515.73	29092.25

Source: basic animal husbandry statistic 2022

Table 43: Per Capita Availability of Egg during 2015-16 to 2021-22

(figures in number/annum)

2015-16	2016-17	2017-18	2018-19	2019-2020	2020-21	2021-22
19	21	24	26	29	32	34

Source: Basic Animal Husbandry statistic 2022

Meat production in 2021-22 is about 127.04 percent indicating an increase of 9.2 percent as compared to 2020-21. The Per Capita availability of meat in 2021-22 is around 1.50 kg per person per year. The maximum contribution in total meat production comes from poultry (54.14 percent), goat(24.99 percent), and buffalo(33.49 percent) during 2021-22.

Table 44: Estimates of meat production from 2015-16 to 2021-22

(figures in '000 tonnes)

2015-16	2016-17	2017-18	2018-19	2019-2020	2020-21	2021-22
69.83	78.64	89.24	97.37	106.50	116.34	127.04

Table 45: Per Capita availability of meat during 2015-16 to 2021-22

(figures in kg/annum)

2015-16	2016-17	2017-18	2018-19	2019-2020	2020-21	2021-22
0.90	1.00	1.12	1.20	1.30	1.40	1.50

Source: Basic animal husbandry statistic 2022

Reference

1. Agriculture Statistics at a glance 2022. Department to of Agriculture and Farmers Welfare, Govt. of India. https://agriwelfare.gov.in/en/Agricultural_Statistics_at_a_Glance

2.   Annual report 202-21, department of Agriculture, Cooperation and Farmers' welfare, Ministry of Agriculture and Farmers' Welfare, Govt. Of India

3.   Basic animal husbandry statistic 2022. Ministry of Fisheries, Animal Husbandry and Dairying, Department of Animal Husbandry and Dairy, Govt. of India

4.   Directorate of Research Services, Jawaharlal Nehru Krishi Vishwavidyalaya, Krishi Nagar Aadhartal, Jabalpur, M.P

5.   Department of Horticulture and Food Processing, Govt. of Madhya Pradesh
     http://www.mphorticulture.gov.in/en

6.   District Narsinghpur, Govt of Madhya Pradesh, https://narsinghpur.nic.in/en/district- produce/sugarcane/

7.   Madhya Pradesh Economic Survey 2022-23, Govt. of Madhya Pradesh

CHAPTER 8

PEOPLE AND CULTURE

The amalgamation of the diverse groups' varied traditions has made Madhya Pradesh's culture vibrant. The State is the fifth most populated State in the country. As per Census 2011, the State has 72,626,809 persons of which 39,610986 (51.79%) is male and 35,015,826 (48.21%) are female. The population of the State forms about 6.00 percent of the country's population in the 2011 census. Out of the total population of the State, 27.63 percent (20,069405) of people live in the urban regions. Of the total urban population, 52.1 percent (10462918) are males and 47.8 percent (9606487) are females. 72.3 percent (52557404) of the total population of the State live in a rural area. Out of the total population of rural areas, 51.6 percent (27149388) are males and 48.3 percent (25408016) are females.

The population of Madhya Pradesh increased from 60,348,023 in the census 2001 to 72,626,809 in 2011 showing a decadal growth rate of 20.35 which is more than the country's growth rate of 17.64 percent. The Growth Rate (GR) for the last 10 decades of the State has been plotted in Table 46.

Table 46: Madhya Pradesh population 1901 – 2011

Year	Population	Growth	
		Net Change	Rate %
1901	12,679,214	–	–
1911	14,249,382	1,570,168	12.38
1921	13,906,774	-342,608	-2.40
1931	15,326,879	1,420,105	10.21

   GEOGRAPHY OF MADHYA PRADESH

1941	17,175,722	1,848,843	12.06
1951	18,614,931	1,439,209	8.38
1961	23,217,910	4,602,979	24.73
1971	30,016,625	6,798,715	29.28
1981	38,168,507	8,151,882	27.16
1991	48,566,242	10,397,735	27.24
2001	60,348,023	11,781,781	24.26
2011	72,626,809	12,278,786	20.35

Source: Census of India

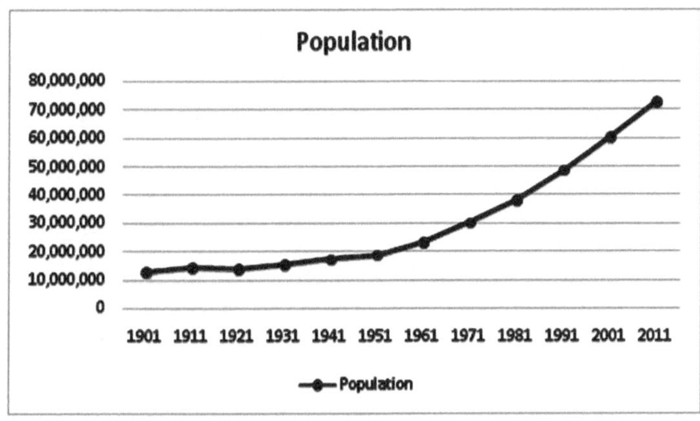

Figure 51: Population Growth 1901 to 2011

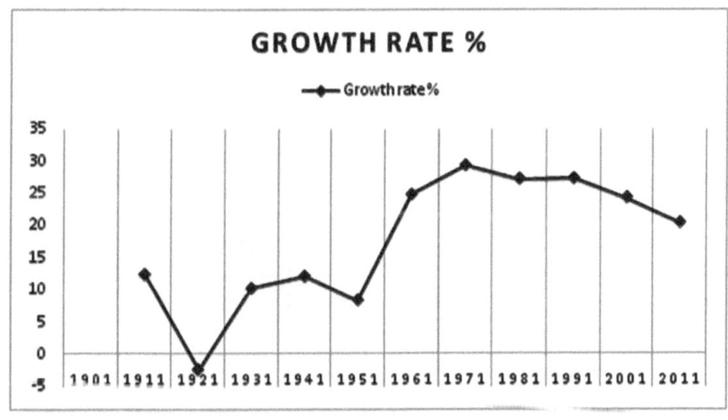

Figure 52: Growth Rate (population)

The population growth rate from 1901 to 1951 shows a slow pace of growth. 1921 growth rate of -2.40 is the only negative growth rate until today. After 1921, the growth rate bounced back to 10.21 in 1931 and 12. 06 in 1941 and show a decreasing trend in 1951.

A steady growth rate was observed during the decade 1951 to 1971. From an 8.38 percent growth rate in 1951, the growth rate shows a steady growth rate to 29.28 percent in 1971. The 1971 growth rate is the highest growth rate recorded so far in the State. The declining trend in population Growth Rate started from 1971 onwards.

As per the census 2011, the highest Growth Rate among the districts was recorded in Indore with 32.7 percent followed by Jhabua (30.6%), Bhopal (28.5%), Singrauli (28.0 %), Barwani (27.6%),etc and the lowest Growth Rate among the districts was recorded in Anuppur with (12.3%) followed by Betul (12.9%), Chhindwara (13.0%), Mandsaur (13.2%) and Balaghat (13.6%). The Decadal Growth Rate among the division between 1991-2001 and 2001 to 2011 shows an interesting picture. In 1991-2001, the highest Growth Rate observed in the Bhopal division with 29.5 %. However, from 2001-2011, the highest Growth Rate was observed in the Indore division with 26.3%. In 1991-2001, the lowest Growth Rate was observed in the Jabalpur division at 17.6% while in 2001-2011, the lowest Growth Rate was observed in the Narmadapuram division at 14.6%.

Table 47: Decadal Growth Rate: India and Madhya Pradesh 1901-2011

Year	India	Madhya Pradesh	Year	India	Madhya Pradesh
1901	238,396,327	12,679,214	1961	439,234,771	23,217,910
1911	252,093,390	14,249,382	1971	548,159,652	30,016,625
1921	251,321,213	13,906,774	1981	683,329,097	38,168,507
1931	278,977,238	15,326,879	1991	846,302,688	48,566,242
1941	318,660,580	17,175,722	2001	1,027,015,247	60,348,023
1951	361,088,090	18,614,931	2011	1,210,193,422	72,597,565

                                    GEOGRAPHY OF MADHYA PRADESH

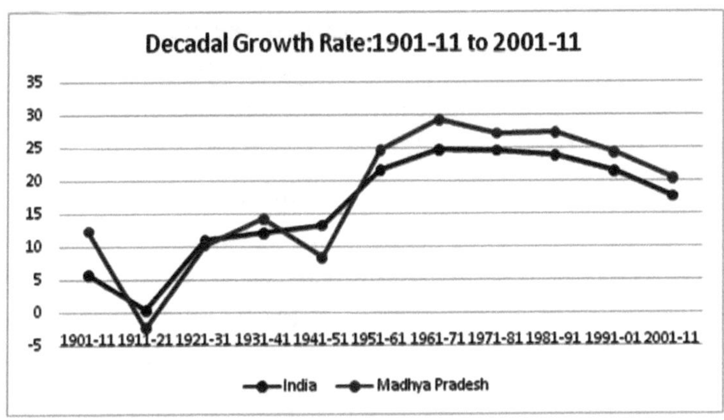

Figure 53: Decadal Growth Rate: 1901-11 to 2001-11

Source: Census 2011

Population density is expressed in terms of the total number of persons per sq km. The population density of Madhya Pradesh and India is plotted in Table 48.

Table 48: Population density: India and Madhya Pradesh, 1901-2011

Country/State	1901	1911	1921	1931	1941	1951	1961	1971	1981	1991	2001	2011
India	73	77	76	85	97	110	134	167	208	267	324	382
Madhya Pradesh	41	46	45	50	56	60	75	97	124	158	196	236

Source: Census

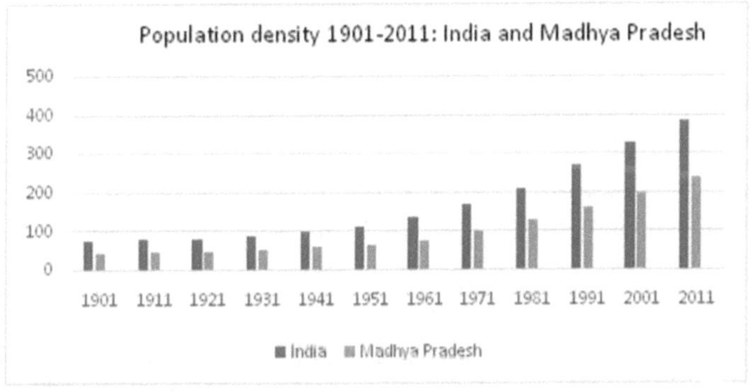

Figure 54: Population density: 1901 – 2011: India and Madhya Pradesh

Source: Census

The comparative analysis shows that the population density of the country has increased by 57 points from 2001 (325) to 2011(382). The population density of the State increased by 40 points from 2001 (196) to 2011 (236).

The population density varies greatly from district to district across the State. As per the census 2011, the highest population density was observed in the Bhopal district at 854 per sq km followed by Indore (839), Jabalpur (472), Gwalior (445), and Morena (394). The lowest density was observed in the Raisen district at 157 per sq km followed by Betul (157), Panna (142), Sheopur (104), and Dindori (94).

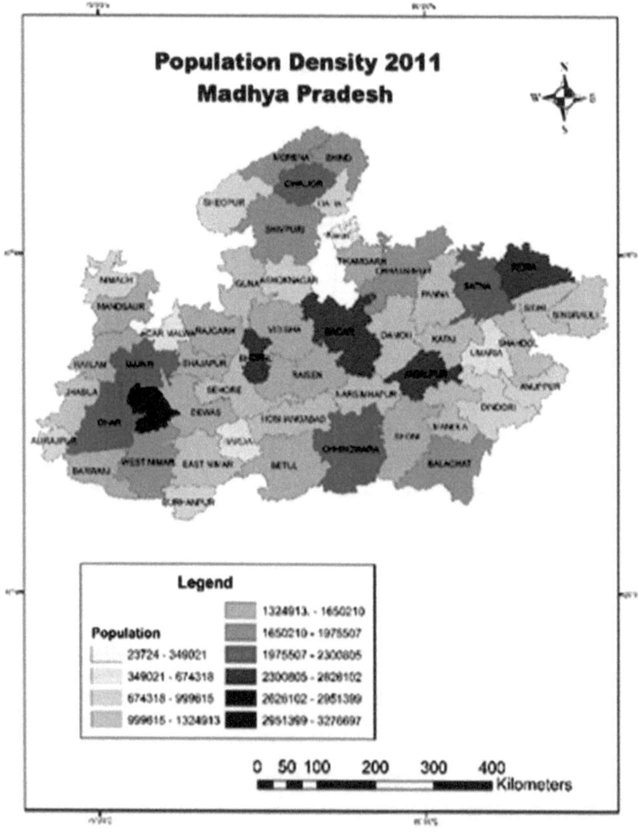

Figure 55: Population density 2011: Madhya Pradesh

                      GEOGRAPHY OF MADHYA PRADESH

Sex ratio

The sex ratio is defined as the number of females per thousand males. It is an important demographic indicator to measure the extent of prevailing equality between males and females in a society at a given point in time. Changes in sex composition largely reflect the underlying socioeconomic and cultural patterns of society in different ways.

The comparative sex ratio of India and Madhya Pradesh is plotted in Table49 and Figure56

Table 56: Sex Ratio 1901 to 2011: India and Madhya Pradesh

Country/State	1901	1911	1921	1931	1941	1951	1961	1971	1981	1991	2001	2011
India	972	964	955	950	945	946	941	930	934	927	933	940
Madhya Pradesh	972	967	949	947	946	945	932	920	921	912	919	930

Source: Census 2011

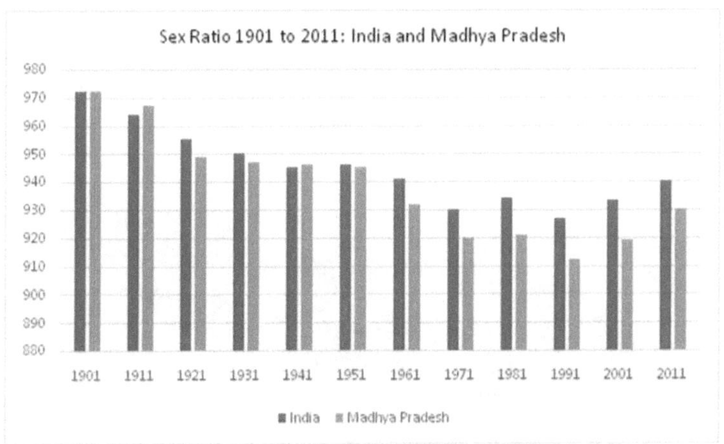

Figure 56: Sex Ratio 1901 to 2011: India and Madhya Pradesh

Source: Census 2011

The sex ratio of the State gradually declines from 1901 to 1971. In 1981 it shows a slightly increased and fall in the 1991 census. In the subsequent census, the sex ratio tends to increase. As per the 2011 census, 23 districts viz., Satna, Jabalpur, Indore,

Sehore, Narsimhapur, Singrauli, Damoh, Hoshangabad, Bhopal, Guna, Panna, Sheopur, Tikamgarh, Ashoknagar, Raisen, Vidisha, Sagar, Chhatarpur, Shivpuri, Datia, Gwalior, Morena, and Bhind recorded sex ratio less than the State. Rewa district recorded a sex ratio of 930 is at par with the State sex ratio.

Table 50: Top five and bottom five districts by Sex Ratio: 2011

Top five districts		Bottom five districts	
District	Sex Ratio	District	Sex ratio
Balaghat	1021	Bhind	838
Alirajpur	1009	Morena	839
Mandla	1005	Gwalior	862
Dindori	1004	Datia	875
Jhabua	989	Shivpuri	887

Source; Census of India 2011

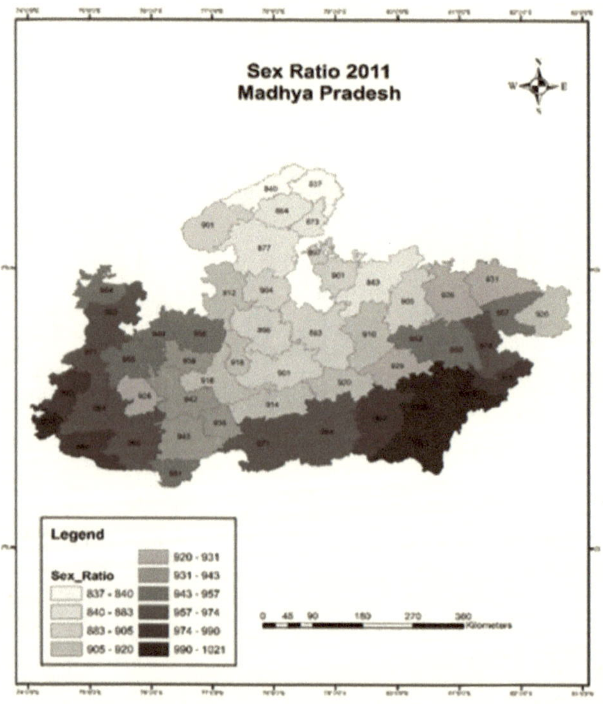

Figure 57: Map-Sex Ratio 2011

 GEOGRAPHY OF MADHYA PRADESH

The child sex ratio declined by 2,33,919 in the decade 2001-2011. The total number of children in the age group of 0-6 years is 1,05,48,295 which is about 14.5% of the total population of the State. Jhabua district recorded the highest proportion of child population followed by Alirajpur, Barwarni, Singrauli, Sheopur, etc, and the lowest child population is observed in Jabalpur, Balaghat, Bhopal, Indore, Gwalior, etc.

Table 51: Top ten division-wise proportions of child population (0-6 years): 2001 and 2011

State/Division	2001	2011
Madhya Pradesh	17.87	14.53
Chambal	18.59	15.07
Gwalior	18.11	14.81
Sagar	18.91	15.29
Rewa	19.35	15.30
Shahdol	17.33	14.64
Ujjain	17.10	13.73
Indore	18.80	15.85
Bhopal	17.96	14.33
Narmadapuram	16.85	13.31
Jabalpur	15.88	12.74

Source: Census of India 2011

Table 52: Top five and bottom five districts by Child population (0-6 years): 2011

Top five districts		Bottom five districts	
District	Proportion of child population	Districts	Proportion of child population
Jhabua	20.3	Jabalpur	11.7
Alirajpur	19.8	Balaghat	12.2
Barwani	18.8	Bhopal	12.4
Singrauli	17.3	Indore	12.5
Sheopur	16.8	Gwalior	12.5

Source: Census of India 2011

The proportion of children 0-6 age group to the population in the State has declined sharply from 17.87 % in 2001 to 14.53 % in 2011. A decline of 3.34 percentage points (refer to table52)

Literacy rate

Literacy and education are important indicators in society and play a central role in human development that impacts the overall socio-economic development milieu. Higher levels of literacy and education lead to the better attainment of health and nutritional status, economic growth, population control, and empowerment of the weaker sections and the community as a whole (Census of India)

As per the census of India, a person aged seven and above who can both read and write with understanding in any language is treated as literate. A person who can only read but cannot write is not literate. In the census before 1991, children below 5 years of age were treated as illiterates. However, the ability to read and write with understanding is not ordinarily achieved until one has time to develop these skills. Therefore, it was decided at the 1991 census that all children in the age group of 0-6, would be treated as illiterate by definition and the population aged seven years and above only would be classified as either literate or illiterate. The same criterion has been retained in the censuses of 2001 and 2011.

As per the Census 2011, 43827193 persons have been counted as literate in the State, out of which 2584813 are male and 1799058 are females. The literacy rate in 2011 was 70.6 percent as compared to 63.7 percent in 2001 which indicates a rise of 6.9 points. However, the State has dropped from 25th position in the 2001 census to 28th position in the census 2011. The decadal growth rate in literacy rate is plotted in Table 53.

     GEOGRAPHY OF MADHYA PRADESH

Table 53: Decadal variation in Literacy rate: Madhya Pradesh 1981-2011

Year	Literacy Rate		
	Person	**Male**	**Female**
1981	28.3	39.7	16.0
1991	44.7	58.6	29.4
2001	63.7	76.1	50.3
2011	70.6	80.5	60.0

Source: Census of India 2011

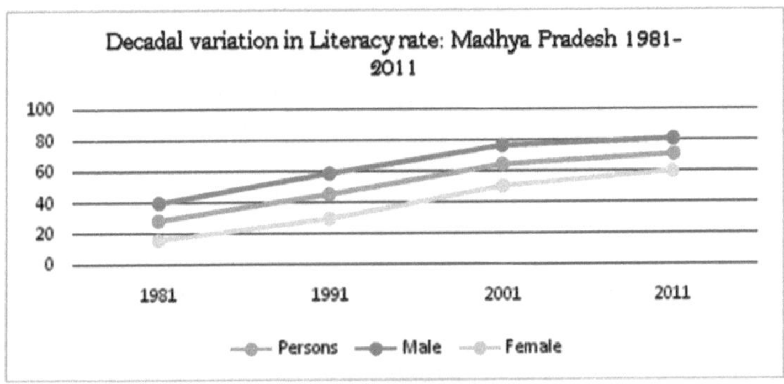

Figure 58: Decadal variation in Literacy rate: Madhya Pradesh 1981-2011

Table 54: Five top districts and five bottom districts by Literacy rate: 2011

Five tops		Five bottoms	
State/District	**Literacy Rate**	**State/District**	**Literacy Rate**
Jabalpur	82.47	Alirajpur	37.22
Indore	82.32	Jhabua	44.45
Bhopal	82.26	Barwani	50.23
Balaghat	78.29	Sheopur	58.02
Gwalior	77.93	Dhar	60.57

Source: Census of India 2011

The literacy rate for 1981 was calculated in crude literacy rate whereas, from 1991 onwards effective literacy rate has been taken into consideration.

According to the census 2011, Indore district recorded the highest male literacy rate at 82.2 percent and Bhopal district recorded the highest female literacy rate at 76.6 percent. Among the districts, Alirajpur district has the lowest male literacy rate at 43.6 percent as well as a female literacy rate at 31.0 percent. Although the total number of illiterates in the State has increased from 1,79,73,246 in 2001 to 1,82,22,077 in 2011 during the decade, in 26 districts absolute number of illiterates has declined. Narsimhapur district recorded the highest literacy rate in the State in the 2001 census, at 77.7 percent, which increased by 22.1 percent from the decade 1991-2001. In 2011, the rate decreased marginally to 76.8 percent.

Lang uage There is a wide numb er of langu ages spoke n in Madh ya Prade

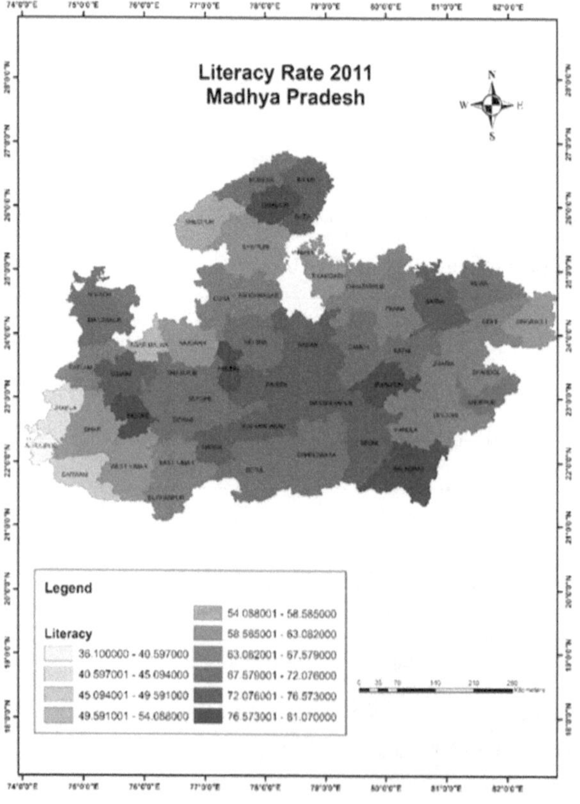

Figure 59: Literacy rate 2011

Table 55: Madhya Pradesh: Indo-European language speakers, their proportion to total population and percentage, distribution of each Indo-European language speakers 2011

Total population 2011 (Madhya Pradesh)	7,26,26,809
Indo – European Language 2011	
Total speakers	7,08,29,951
Percentage to total population	97.53
Percentage distribution of Indo-European language speakers	
Bengali (S)	0.15
Bhil/Bhilodi	5.07
Gujarati (S)	0.26
Hindi(S)	90.82
Khandeshi	0.05
Lahnda	0.01
Maithili (S)	0.01
Marathi (S)	1.74
Nepali (S)	0.01
Odia (S)	0.03
Punjabi (S)	0.20
Sindhi (S)	0.35
Urdu (S)	1.29

Table 56: Madhya Pradesh: Dravidian language speakers, their proportion to total population and percentage distribution of each Dravidian language speakers 2011

Total population 2011 (Madhya Pradesh)	7,26,26,809
Dravidian Language 2011	
Total speakers	12,55,734

Percentage to total population	1.73
Percentage distribution Dravidian language speakers	
Gondi	92.72
Kannada	0.33
Kui	0.01
Kurukh/Oraon	0.33
Malayalam (S)	3.01
Malto	0.02
Tamil (S)	1.64
Telugu(S)	1.94
Tulu	0.01

Source: Language Atlas of India 2011, Census of India

Table 57: Madhya Pradesh, Austro-Asiatic language speakers, their proportion to total population and percentage distribution of each Austro-Asiatic language speakers 2011

Total population 2011 (Madhya Pradesh)	7,26,26,809
Austro–Asiatic Language 2011	
Total speakers	4,76,362
Percentage to total population	0.66
Percentage distribution Dravidian language speakers	
Ho	0.54
Kharia	0.03
Korku	98.75
Korwa	0.45
Munda	0.05
Mundari	0.09
Santali(S)	0.08

Source: Language Atlas of India 2011, Census of India

Table 58: Madhya Pradesh, Tibeto-Burman language speakers, their proportion to total population and percentage distribution of each Tibeto-Burman language speakers 2011

Total population 2011 (Madhya Pradesh)	7,26,26,809
Tibeto-Burman Language 2011	
Total speakers	2,760
Percentage to total population	0.00
Percentage distribution Tibeto-Burman language speakers	
Adi	15.43
Angami	0.98
Ao	0.58
Bhotia	2.07
Bodo(S)	3.15
Dimasa	0.40
Garo	0.69
Kabui	0.11
Karbi/Mikri	0.14
Lotha (Lodha)	0.51
Lushai/Mizo	6.56
Manipur(S)	36.56
Mao	0.25
Nissi/Dafla	2.36
Tangkhul	0.98
Radha	0.25
Thado	0.18
Tibetan	2.57
Tripuri	0.94
Other (Below 1 %)	25.29

Source: Language Atlas of India 2011, Census of India

Scheduled Language

As per the Census 2011, there are 6,72,80,520 Scheduled language speakers in Madhya Pradesh which account for 92.64 percent of the state population.

Table 59: Percentage distribution of Scheduled languages in Madhya Pradesh 2011

Total population 2011 (Madhya Pradesh)	7,26,26,809
Scheduled Language 2011	
Total speakers	6,72,80,520
Percentage to total population	92.64
Percentage distribution of speakers of Scheduled Language	
Assamese	0.01
Bengali	0.16
Gujarati	0.28
Hindi	95.61
Kannada	0.01
Maithili	0.01
Malayalam	0.06
Marathi	1.83
Nepali	0.01
Odia	0.03
Punjabi	0.21
Sindhi	0.36
Tamil	0.03
Telugu	0.04
Urdu	1.36

Source: Language Atlas of India 2011, Census of India

Assamese is the official language of Assam. The language comes under the Indo-Aryan language family. Assamese Bengali script is used with specified distinction in writing Assamese. Out of the total Assamese speakers in the country, 0.01 percent (1,870) is recorded in Madhya Pradesh.

Bengali is the official language of West Bengal. The language comes under the Indo-Aryan language family. The Assamese-Bengali script which owns its origin in Brahmi and is a descendant of the 'Kutila' variety of Gupta script of eastern India is used in writing Bengali. Out of the total Bengali speakers in the country, 0.11 percent (1,09,185) is recorded in Madhya Pradesh. Bodo comes under the Tibeto-Burman language family. Devanagari script is used to write Bodo. Out of the total Bodo speakers in the country, 0.01 percent (87) are recorded in Madhya Pradesh.

Dogri comes under the Indo-Aryan language family. Dogri is recognized as one of the literary languages of the country by the Sahitya Academy. In general, the Devanagari script is used for writing Dogri. However, in Jammu and Kashmir, the Perso-Arabic script is used for writing the Dogri language. Out of the total Dogri speakers in the country, 0.03 percent are recorded in Madhya Pradesh.

Gujarati comes under the Indo-Aryan language family. It is the official language of Gujarat state. The Gujarati language is written using the saraphi (banker's), vaniasai (merchant's), and mahajani (trader's) script. The syllabary is Sanskrit and the shape of the letters bears a close resemblance to Devanagari. Out of the total Gujarati speakers, 0.34 percent (1,87,211) are recorded in Madhya Pradesh.

Hindi comes under the central group of the Indo-Aryan language family. Linguistically Hindi area encompasses broad dialect group areas viz., Western Hindi (Braj Bhasha, Bundeli, Kanauji, Bangaru, etc.), Eastern Hindi (Awadhi, Chhattisgarhi, Bagheli, etc), the speech of Rajasthan (Rajasthani, Marwari Mewati, etc.), Bihari (Bhojpuri, Maithili, Magahi, etc) and Pahari (Garhwali, Kumauni, Mandeali, Kulvi, etc.). Hindi is written in Devanagari script. Out of the total Hindi speakers, 12.17 percent (6,43,24,963) are recorded in Madhya Pradesh. Hindi is the official language of Madhya Pradesh which is spoken by 95.61 percent of the total State population.

The Kannada language comes under the Dravidian language family. It was declared "classical language" by the Government of India in 2008. Kannada script has evolved from southern varieties of Ashokan Brahmi script. It has a close resemblance with the Telugu script as both emerged from an old Kannarese script. Out of the total Kannada speakers, 0.01 percent (4,175) are recorded in Madhya Pradesh.

The Kashmiri language comes under the Dardic sub-group of the Indo-Aryan language family. Devanagari, Perso-Arabic, and Sharda are used in writing the Kashmiri language. Out of the total Kashmiri speakers, 0.02 percent (1,050) are recorded in Madhya Pradesh.

Konkani language comes under the Indo-Aryan language family. It is the official language of Goa. Devanagari script is used for writing Konkani. Out of the total Konkani speakers, 0.04 percent (814) are recorded in Madhya Pradesh.

Maithili comes under the eastern Bihari branch of the Indo-Aryan language family and is closely related to the Bhojpuri and Magahi languages. Maithili was included in the Scheduled VIII of the constitution of India in the 92nd Amendment Act enacted in 2004. Prior to it, the Maithili speakers were grouped under the Hindi language. Tirhuta was formerly the primary script for writing Maithili. Now it is written in the Devanagari script. Out of the total Maithili speakers, 0.03 percent (4129) are recorded in Madhya Pradesh.

Malayalam comes under the Dravidian language family. It is the official language of Kerala. The alphabet known as 'Arya Ezhuttu' (introduced in the 17th century) is used in writing Malayalam. Out of the total Malayalam speakers, 0.11 percent (37,761) are recorded in Madhya Pradesh.

Manipuri comes under the Kuki Chin group of the Tibeto-Burman language family. Manipuri is written in Bengali script and Meitei Mayek. Out of the total Manipuri speakers, 0.06 percent (1009) are recorded in Madhya Pradesh.

Marathi comes under the Indo-Aryan language family. It is the official language of Maharashtra. The Marathi language is written in Devanagari script with specific distinctions. Out of the total Marathi speakers, 1.48 percent (12,31,285) are recorded in Madhya Pradesh, especially in Burhanpur, Balaghat, Betul, and Chhindwara districts.

Nepali is the official language of Sikkim and West Bengal. Nepali comes under the eastern Pahari sub-branch of the Indo-Aryan language family. It is written in Devanagari script. Out of the total Nepali speakers, 0.30 percent (8724) are recorded in Madhya Pradesh.

Odia is the official language of Odisha. Odia belongs to the Indo-Aryan language family. It is written using a particular script that derives from the Kalinga alphabet (a descendant of the Brahmi script of ancient India). Out of the total Odia speakers, 0.05 percent (18,765) are recorded in Madhya Pradesh.

Punjabi is the official language of Punjab. Punjabi belongs to the central group of the Indo- Aryan language family. Gurmukhi script is used to write the Punjabi language. Out of the total Punjabi speakers, 0.42 percent (1,39,658) are recorded in Madhya Pradesh.

Sanskrit is one of the oldest documented languages from the Indo-European language family and is the key to understanding the history and culture of India. It is written in Devanagari script. Out of the total Sanskrit speakers, 7.54 percent (1,871) are recorded in Madhya Pradesh, especially in Hoshangabad, Bhopal, and Shajapur districts.

Santali comes under the Munda branch of the Austro-Asiatic language family. It is written in five scripts viz., Devanagari, Bengali, Odia, Alchiki, and Roman. Out of the total Santali speakers, 0.01 percent (404) are recorded in Madhya Pradesh.

Sindhi is included in the Scheduled languages of the Indian constitution by the 21st Amendment Act, of 1967. According to Grierson, Sindhi comes under the Indo-Aryan language family. It has a tradition of writing in Perso-Arabic script. In India, Sindhi is written in Devanagari script. Out of the total Sindhi speakers, 8.84 percent (2,45,161) are recorded in Madhya Pradesh, especially in Bhopal, Indore, and Katni districts.

Tamil comes under the Dravidian language family. It is the official language of Tamil Nadu. The script used in writing Tamil is known as VaTTeLuttu (the script having a round shape), it owns its origin in Brahmi script. Out of the total Tamil speakers, 0.03 percent (20,544) are recorded in Madhya Pradesh.

Telugu is the official language of Andhra Pradesh. the Pahlava script of the 7th century A.D., which evolved from the old Brahmi script, is known to have taken shape by 1000 A.D, and is used in writing the Telugu language. Out of the total Telugu speakers, 0.03 percent (24,411) are recorded in Madhya Pradesh.

Urdu is written in Perso-Arabic script. It is spoken mainly in the states of Bihar, Uttar Pradesh, Andhra Pradesh and Karnataka. According to Grierson, Urdu comes under the Central Sub-Group of the Indo-Aryan language family. Out of the total Urdu speakers, 1.81 percent (9,16,608) are recorded in Madhya Pradesh.

Non- Scheduled languages

Non-scheduled languages are spoken languages that are not included in the Eight Schedule of the Constitution of India. As per the census 2011, There are 99 Non-Scheduled languages in the country. Out of which 56 Non-Scheduled languages (with at least five percent share of speakers in any State/Union Territory) are prominent and the rest are included in 'Others'. The highest number of Non-Scheduled language speakers is recorded in Madhya Pradesh (53,46,289).

Arabic/Arbi is one of the Non-Scheduled languages spoken in India. Out of the total Arabic/Arbi speakers, 2.16 percent (1,188) are recorded in Madhya Pradesh. The language comes under the Western Semitic sub-group of the Semito-Hamitic language family. It is written in Arabic script.

Bhili/Bhilodi is one of the Non-Scheduled languages spoken in India. Out of the total Bhili/Bhilodi speakers, 34.45 percent (35,87,810) are recorded in Madhya Pradesh, especially in Alirajpur, Jhabua, Barwani, Khargone(west Nimar), Dhar, Burhanpur,

Ratlam, Khandwa(East Nimar), and Dewas districts. Bhili/Bhilodi comes under the Western branch of the Indo-Aryan language family. In census 2011, 17 (seventy) mother tongues viz., Baori, Barel, Bhilali, Bhili/Bhilodi, Chodhari, Dhodia, Gamti/Gavti, Garasia, Kikna/Kokni/Kukna. Mawchi, Paradhi, Pawri, Rathi, Tadavi, Varli, Vasava, and Wagdi with 10,000 plus population at all India level are grouped under the Bhili/Bhilodi language as a variant (Language Atlas 2011).

English is one of the most common languages spoken worldwide. Out of the total English speakers, 00.92 percent (2,381) are recorded in Madhya Pradesh. English comes under the West Germanic sub-group of Indo-European languages and it is written in Roman script. Gondi is one of the Non-Scheduled languages spoken in India. Madhya Pradesh has the highest number of Gondi speakers in the country with 39.01 percent (11,64,290). 1.60 percent of the State population speaks the Gondi language. High concentration of Gondi speakers is recorded in Betul, Dindori, Balaghat, Mandla, Seoni, Chhindwara, Anuppur, Harda, Singrauli, Dewas, and Khandwa (East Nimar). Gondi is classified under the Dravidian group of languages. Devanagari script, Gunjala Gondi, and Masaram Gondi scripts are used to write the Gondi language.

Ho is one of the Non-Scheduled languages spoken mainly in Jharkhand and Odisha. Out of the total Ho speakers, 0.18 percent (2,579) are recorded in Madhya Pradesh. Ho language comes under the Austro-Asiatic language family. It is written in Roman and indigenous Varang Kshiti script.

Khandeshi is one of the Non-Scheduled languages spoken in the Khandesh region. Out of the total Khandeshi speakers, 2.04 percent (37,882) are recorded in the Barwani, Burhanpur, Balaghat, Neemuch, and Sehore districts of Madhya Pradesh. The language comes under the Indo-Aryan language family. No regular scripts are used for writing Khandeshi.

Kurukh/ Oraon is one of the Non-Scheduled languages in India, it is mainly spoken in Jharkhand, Chhattisgarh, West Bengal,

Odisha, and Bihar. As per Census 2011, there are 19,88,350 Kurukh/Oraon speakers which account for 0.16 percent of the country's total population and ranks third among Non-Scheduled languages speakers. Out of the total Kurukh/Oraon speakers, 0.21 percent (4,132) is recorded in Madhya Pradesh. Kurukh/Oraon language comes under the Dravidian group of language family. It is written in Tolong Siki script.

Mundari is one of the Non-Scheduled languages in India. It is mainly spoken in Jharkhand. As per Census 2011, there are 11,28,228 Mundari speakers are recorded which account for

0.09 percent of the total population of the country. Out of the Mundari speakers, 0.04 percent (424) are recorded in Madhya Pradesh. The language comes under the Austro-Asiatic language's family. Roman and Devanagari scripts are used in Bihar, Jharkhand, and Assam and Odia script is used in Odisha.

Table 60: Percentage distribution of Scheduled and Non-Scheduled languages with rural and urban break up 2011

Total population 2011 (Madhya Pradesh	7,26,26,809
Urban population 2011	2,00,69,405
Percentage of urban to total population	27.63
Scheduled languages	
Rural	
Number	4,73,41,482
% to pop.	65.18
Urban	
Number	1,99,39,038
% to pop.	27.45
Non-Scheduled Languages	
Rural	
Number	52,15,922

     GEOGRAPHY OF MADHYA PRADESH

% to pop.	7.18
Urban	
Number	1,30,367
% to pop.	0.18

Source: Language Atlas of India 2011

There are 71 (seventy-one) important mother tongues spoken by different major scheduled tribes in the country. The largest Scheduled Tribe population in the country is registered in Madhya Pradesh (1,53,16,784). The tribal communities of the State viz., Bhil, Bhilala, Barela, Patelia with 59,93,921 population are the largest Scheduled Tribes in the country which account for 39.13 percent of the total population of the State. The majority of this population speak Bhili/Bhilodi (34,51,689) as their first mother tongue followed by Hindi (24,81,554) as their second mother tongue and Gujarati as their third mother tongue whereas 41, 287 of these Scheduled Tribes use other mother tongues. Gond, Arakh, Arrakh, Agaria, Asur, Bada Maria, etc of the State with a population of 50,93,124 which account for 33.25 percent of the total Scheduled Tribe population of the State. The majority of this population speak Hindi (39,97,229) as their first mother tongue followed by Gondi (10,44,810) as their second mother tongue and Marathi (34,285) as their third mother tongue whereas 16,800Scheduled Tribes in this group use other mother tongues.

The majorlanguages spoken and their strength from 1961 to 2011 are plotted in the table 58. Table 61: Major language spoken in Madhya Pradesh

Major Language	Speakers strength					
	1961	1971	1981	1991	2001	2011
Hindi	25217723	34698020	43807729	56619090	52658687	64324963
Bhili/Bhilodi	875916	1299411	1622008	2215399	2973201	3587810

| Marathi | 1259682 | 1036193 | 1222581 | 1283977 | 1266038 | 1231285 |
| Others | 4965087 | 4620495 | 5526526 | 6062704 | 3450097 | 3482751 |

Source: Language Atlas of India 2011

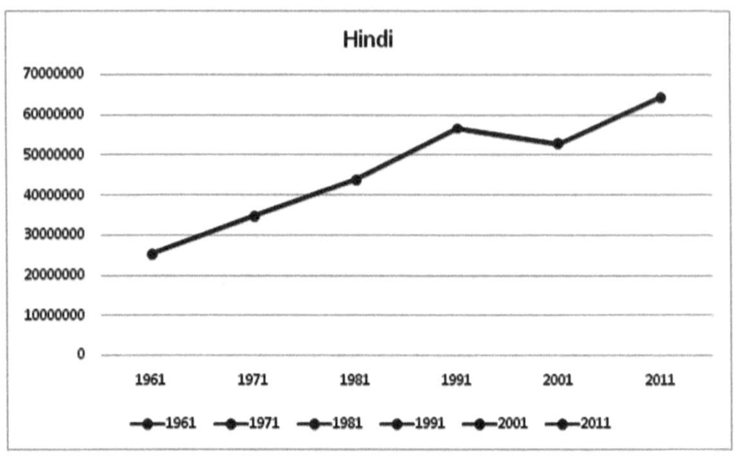

Figure 60: Growth of the Hindi language
Source: Language Atlas of India 2011

Tribes

A tribe has been defined as a group of people claiming a common ancestry and sharing a common culture. As per the National Census, tribes are classified as "Aboriginals" and are listed as 'Tribes'. Adivasi (ancient inhabitants) is a Hindi term used for Tribe.

Article 366 (25) of the Constitution of India refers to Scheduled Tribes as those communities who are scheduled in accordance with Article 342 of the Constitution. According to this article, Scheduled Tribes are only those communities that have been declared as such by the President through an initial public notification or through a subsequent amending Act of Parliament. The criteria followed for specification of a community as a Scheduled Tribes are; Indications of primitive traits, distinctive culture, Geographical isolation, Shyness of contact with the community at large, and backwardness.

The State has the largest Scheduled Tribe population in the country. As per the Census 2011, the Scheduled Tribe population in the State is 153.16 lakhs which accounts for 21.10 percent of the total population of the State. There are 46 (forty-six) distinct tribes in the State viz., (1) Agariya, (2) Andh, (3) Baiga (4) Bhaina (5) BhariaBhumia, BhuinharBhumia, Bhumiya, Bharia, Paliha, Pando (6) Bhattra (7) Bhil, Bhilala, Barela, Patelia (8) Bhil Mina (9) Bhunjia (10) Biar, Biyar (11) Binjhwar (12) Birhul, Birhor (13) Damor, Damaria (14) Dhanwar (15) Gadaba, Gadba (16) Gond; Arakh, Arrakh, Agaria, Asur, Badi Maria, Bada Maria, Bhatola, Bhimma, Bhuta, Koilabhuta, Koliabhuti, Bhar, Bisonhorn Maria, Chota Maria, DandamiMaria, Djuru, Dhurwa, Dhoba, Dhulia, Dorla, Gaiki, Gatta, Gatti, Gaita, Gond Gowari, Hill Maria, Kandra, Kalanga, Khatola, Koitar, Koya, Khirwar, Khirwara, Kucha Maria, Kuchaki Maria, Madia, Maria, Mana, Mannewar, Moghya, Mogia, Monghya, Mudia, Muria, Nagarchi, Nagwanshi, Ojha, Raj, SonjhariJhareka, Thatia, Thotya, Wade Maria, Vade Maria, Daroi (17) Halba, Halbi (18) Kamar (19) Karku (20) Kawar, Kanwar, Kaur, Cherwa, Rathia, Tanwar, Chattri (21) Keer (in Bhopal, Raisen and Sehor(sic) district) omitted by Govt. of India Gazette(sic) Notification dated 08-01-2003 (22) Khairwar, Kondar (23) Kharia (24) Kondh, Khond, Kandh (25) Kol (26) Kolam (27) Korku, Bopchi, Mouasi, Nihal, Nahul Bondhi, Bondeya (28) Korwa, Kodaku (29) Majhi (30) Majhwar (31) Mawasi (32) Mina (in Sironj Subdivision of Vidisha district) Omitted by Govt. of India Gazette(sic) Notification dated 08-01-2003 (33) Munda (34) Nagesia, Nagasia (35) Oraon, Dhanka, Dhangad (36) Panika (in (i) Chhatarpur, Panna, Rewa, Satna, Shahdol, Umaria, Sidhi and Tikamgarh districts, and (ii) Sevda and Datia tehsils of Datia districts) (37) Pao (38) Pardhan, Pathari, Saroti (39) Pardhi (in Bhopal, Raisen and Sehore(sic) districts) Omitted by Govt. of India Gazette(sic) Notification dated 08-01-2003 (40) Pardhi, Bahelia, Bahellia, Chita Pardhi, Langoli Pardhi, Phans Pardhi, Shikari, Takankar, Takia (in (i) Chhindwara, Mandla, Dindori and Seoni districts, (ii) Baihar tahsil of Balaghat district, (iii) Betul, Bhainsdehi and Shahpur tahsils of Betul district, (iv) Patan tahsil and Sihora and Majholi blocks of Jabalpur district, (v) Katni (Murwara) and

Vijaya Raghogarh tahsils and Bahoriband and Dhemerkheda blocks of Katni district, (vi) Hoshangabad, Babai, Sohagpur, Pipariya and Bankhedi tahsils and Kesla block of Hoshangabad district, (vii) Narsinghpur district, and (viii) Harsud tahsil of Khandwa district) , (41) Parja (42) Sahariya, Saharia, Seharia, Sehria, Sosia, Sor (43) Saonta, Saunta (44) Saur (45) Sawar, Sawara (46) Sonr.

Out of 46 (forty-six) tribes, 3 (three) tribes viz., Bharia, Baiga, and Sahariya) have been classified as Particularly Vulnerable Tribal Groups (PVTGs) (earlier known as Primitive Tribal Groups). The criteria followed for the determination of PVTGs are; (i) A pre- agriculture level of technology, (ii) A stagnant or declining population, (iii) Low literacy, and (iv) A subsistence level of the economy.

Table 62: Scheduled Tribe-wise population

State	ST population	Male	Female
Madhya Pradesh	1,53,16,784	77,19,404	75,97,380
Tribe			
Agariya	41,243	20,706	20,537
Andh	137	70	67
Baiga	4,14,526	2,07,588	2,06,938
Bhaina	6,357	3,192	3,165
BhariaBhumia, BhuinharBhumia, Bhumiya, Bharia, Paliha, Pando	1,93,230	97,574	95,656
Bhattra	1,155	599	556
Bhil, Bhilala, Barela, Patelia	59,93,921	30,16,445	29,77,476
Bhil Mina	2,244	1,194	1,050
Bhunjia	1,469	767	702
Biar, Biyar	10,452	5,390	5,062
Binjhwar	15,805	7,766	8,039

                    GEOGRAPHY OF MADHYA PRADESH

Birhul, Birhor	52	27	25
Damor,Damaria	1,815	936	879
Dhanwar	2,175	1,109	1,066
Gadaba, Gadba	578	295	283
Gond; Arakh, Arrakh, Agaria, Asur, Badi Maria, Bada Maria, Bhatola, Bhimma, Bhuta, Koilabhuta, Koliabhuti, Bhar, Bisonhorn Maria, Chota Maria, Dandami Maria, Djuru, Dhurwa, Dhoba, Dhulia, Dorla, Gaiki, Gatta, Gatti, Gaita, Gond Gowari, Hill Maria, Kandra, Kalanga, Khatola, Koitar, Koya, Khirwar, Khirwara, Kucha Maria, Kuchaki Maria, Madia, Maria, Mana, Mannewar, Moghya, Mogia, Monghya, Mudia, Muria, Nagarchi, Nagwanshi, Ojha, Raj, SonjhariJhareka, Thatia, Thotya, Wade Maria, Vade Maria, Daroi	50,93,124	25,49,973	25,43,151
Halba, Halbi	14,438	7,148	7,290
Kamar	666	333	333
Karku	265	156	109
Kawar, Kanwar, Kaur, Cherwa, Rathia, Tanwar, Chattri	18,603	9,380	9,223
Khairwar, Kondar	76,097	39,193	36,904
Kharia	2,429	1,258	1,171
Kondh, Khond, Kandh	109	54	55
Kol	11,67,694	5,95,694	5,72,356
Kolam	224	112	112
Korku, Bopchi, Mouasi, Nihal, Nahul Bondhi, Bondeya	7,30,847	3,72,552	3,58,295
Korwa, Kodaku	920	459	461

Majhi	50,655	26,513	24,142
Majhwar	443	226	217
Mawasi	1,09,180	55,234	53,946
Munda	5,041	2,669	2,372
Nagesia, Nagasia	359	180	179
Oraon, Dhanka, Dhangad	28,431	14,275	14,156
Panika (in (i) Chhatarpur, Panna, Rewa, Satna, Shahdol, Umaria, Sidhi and Tikamgarh districts, and (ii) Sevda and Datia tehsils of Datia districts)	97,767	49,546	48,221
Pao	44,312	21,706	22,606
Pardhan, Pathari, Saroti	1,23,742	62,189	61,553
Pardhi, Bahelia, Bahellia, Chita Pardhi, Langoli Pardhi, Phans Pardhi, Shikari, Takankar, Takia (in (i) Chhindwara, Mandla, Dindori and Seoni districts, (ii) Baihar tahsil of Balaghat district, (iii) Betul, Bhainsdehi and Shahpur tahsils of Betul district, (iv) Patan tahsil and Sihora and Majholi blocks of Jabalpur district, (v) Katni (Murwara) and Vijaya Raghogarh tahsils and Bahoriband and Dhemerkheda blocks of Katni district, (vi) Hoshangabad, Babai, Sohagpur, Pipariya and Bankhedi tahsils and Kesla block of Hoshangabad district, (vii) Narsinghpur district, and (viii) Harsud tahsil of Khandwa district)	5,896	3,029	2,867
Parja	137	70	67
Sahariya, Saharia, Seharia, Sehria, Sosia, Sor	6,14,958	3,16,541	2,98,417
Saonta, Saunta	190	113	77
Saur	1,67,340	86,357	80,983

| Sawar, Sawara | 881 | 464 | 417 |
| Sonr | 12,905 | 6,644 | 6,261 |

Source: Census 2011

Out of many tribes in the State, the Bhil tribe is one of the most populous mainly concentrated in the Jhabua, Khargone, Dhar, and Barwani districts. The Bhil tribe constitutes about 39.13 percent of the total Scheduled Tribe population of the State. The name Bhil is derived from the word 'Billu', meaning 'bow'. According to Russell and Hiralal, this name came into use in 600 AD, before this tribe was probably known by the names "Pulind and Van- Putradi". They are known for their excellent archery and sculpture skills. Bhil women wear traditional saris while men dress in long frocks and pyjamas. Bhagoriya is the main festival of the Bhil tribe.

Gond tribe constitute about 33.25 percent of the total Scheduled Tribe population of the State. The name Gond derived from Kond, meaning Green Mountain in Dravidian idiom. Gonds are largely concentrated in the districts of Betul, Hoshangabad, Chhindwara, Balaghat, Shahdol, Mandla, Sagar, Damoh, Satna, Khandwa, Burhanpur, Sehore, Raisen, and Narsinghpurexcept the northern part of Madhya Pradesh. The main festivals of the Gond tribe are Jathra, Madai, and Nayakhani.

Kol tribe constitutes about 7.62 percent of the total tribe population in the State. There are many opinions regarding the nomenclature of the Kol tribe. scholars are of the opinion that Kol or Mundari call themselves by the names 'Har', 'Hor', 'Ho', and 'Koro' in their dialect which means 'Human'. Kol is largely concentrated in the districts of Rewa, Sidhi, Satna, Shahdol, Jabalpur, Raigarh, and Mandla. The main festival of Kol are Hariyali Amavasya and Jawara.

Korku, Bopchi, Mouasi, Nihal, Nahul Bondhi, and Bondeya tribes constitute about 4.77 percent of the total tribe population of the State. The name derives from 'Kor' or 'Koron' which means 'Man'. The literal meaning of Kurku is a group of men. Korku is largely concentrated in the districts of Chhindwara, Betul,

Hoshangabad, and East Nimar. The main festivals of Korku are Gudi Padwa and Jiroti.

Sahariya, Saharia, Seharia, Sehria, Sosia, and Sor constitute about 4.01 percent of the total Scheduled Tribe population of the State. Sahariya are listed in Particularly Vulnerable Tribal Groups (PVTGs) (earlier known as Primitive Tribal Groups). They are mainly concentrated in Morena, Sheopur, Bhind, Gwalior, Datia, Shivpuri, Guna, Vidisha, and Raisen districts. The Sahariya tribe mainly worships Goddess Durga and celebrates Dussehra, Diwali, Holi, Rakshabandhan, etc. Teja Navami is a special festival celebrated by the tribe.

The Baiga tribe constitutes about 2.7 percent of the total tribe population in the State. The Baiga tribe is one of the most ancient tribes found in the Bajag block of the Dindori district. The name Baiga literally means 'Medicine man'. Baiga tribe is listed in Particularly Vulnerable Tribal Groups (PVTGs) (earlier known as Primitive Tribal Groups). Baiga celebrates Nava/Nayaparv, Hareli Parv, Cherta, Javara, Holi, Dussehra, etc.

Table 63: District-wise Scheduled Tribe population distribution

Sl.No	Districts	District population	ST population	% out of the district population
1	Sheopur	6,87,952	1,61,448	23.47
2	Morena	19,65,137	17,030	0.87
3	Bhind	17,03,562	6,131	0.36
4	Gwalior	20,30,543	72,133	3.55
5	Datia	7,86,375	15,061	1.92
6	Shivpuri	17,25,818	2,27,802	13.20
7	Tikamgarh	14,44,920	67,857	4.70
8	Chhatarpur	17,62,857	73,597	4.17
9	Panna	10,16,028	1,70,879	16.82
10	Sagar	23,78,295	2,21,936	9.33

    GEOGRAPHY OF MADHYA PRADESH

11	Damoh	12,63,703	1,66,295	13.16
12	Satna	22,28,619	3,19,975	14.36
13	Rewa	23,63,744	3,11,985	13.20
14	Umaria	6,43,579	3,00,687	46.72
15	Neemuch	8,25,958	71,441	8.65
16	Mandsaur	13,39,832	33,092	2.47
17	Ratlam	14,54,483	4,09,865	28.18
18	Ujjain	19,86,597	48,730	2.45
19	Shajapur	15,12,353	37,836	2.50
20	Dewas	15,63,107	2,72,701	17.45
21	Dhar	21,84,672	12,22,814	55.97
22	Indore	32,72,335	2,17,679	6.65
23	West Nimar	18,72,413	7,30,169	39.00
24	Barwani	13,85,659	9,62,145	69.44
25	Rajgarh	15,46,541	53,751	3.48
26	Vidisha	14,58,212	67,603	4.64
27	Bhopal	23,68,145	69,429	2.93
28	Sehore	13,11,008	1,45,512	11.10
29	Raisen	13,31,699	2,05,006	15.39
30	Betul	15,75,247	6,67,018	42.34
31	Harda	5,70,302	1,59,678	28.00
32	Hoshangabad	12,40,975	1,97,300	15.90
33	Katni	12,91,684	3,17,699	24.60
34	Jabalpur	24,60,714	3,75,231	15.25
35	Narsimhapur	10,92,141	1,45,879	13.36
36	Dindori	7,04,218	4,55,789	64.72

37	Mandla	10,53,522	6,10,528	57.95
38	Chhindwara	20,90,306	7,69,778	36.83
39	Seoni	13,78,876	5,19,856	37.70
40	Balaghat	17,01,156	3,83,026	22.52
41	Guna	12,40,938	1,90,819	15.38
42	Ashoknagar	8,44,979	82,072	9.71
43	Shahdol	10,64,989	4,76,008	44.70
44	Anuppur	7,49,521	3,58,543	47.84
45	Sidhi	11,26,515	3,13,304	27.81
46	Singrauli	11,78,132	3,83,994	32.59
47	Jhabua	10,24,091	8,91,818	87.08
48	Alirajpur	7,28,677	6,48,638	89.02
49	East Nimar	13,09,443	4,59,122	35.06
50	Burhanpur	7,56,993	2,30,095	30.40

Source: Census 2011

Alirajpur district has the largest proportion of the Scheduled Tribe population with 7,28,677 (89%) of the total population of the district followed by Jhabua with 10,24,091 (87%), Barwani with 1385,659 (69.44%) and Dindori with 7,04,218 (64.72%). The districts with less Scheduled Tribe populations are Bhind with 1703,562 (0.36%), Morena with 19,65,137 (0.87%), Datia with 7,86,375 (1.92%), and Ujjain with 19,86,597 (2.45%).

Festivals and Fairs

Madhya Pradesh hosts rich traditional cultural and heritage festivals and fairs. People of various cast, religions, and tribes celebrate fairs and festivals in vibrant. Some of the important festivals and fairs are mentioned below;

Simhastha: The Kumbh Mela is considered the holiest fair in the country. It is held in four cities of the country viz., Haridwar, Ujjain, Prayagraj, and Nashik. The male is held every four years in one of the four cities. The Kumbh Mela held in Ujjain is known as Simhastha Kumbh Mahaparv and is held on the banks of the Kshipra River. It is regarded as a Hindu pilgrimage in which devotees from all over the world gather to bathe in the sacred river. Tansen Samaroh: Tansen Samaroh is celebrated every year in the month of December in Behat village of Gwalior district. Artists and music lovers from all over the world gather to pay tribute to the Great Indian Musical Maestro Tansen. Madhya Pradesh government has renamed Behat village to Tansen Nagar.

Fair of Pir Budhan: Fair of Pir Budhan is more than 250 years. This fair is held near the tomb of Muslim saint Pir Budhan at Samvara in Shivpuri district. The fair is organized in the months of August – September.

Fair of Nagaji: this fair is organized in memory of Nagaji saint who lived during the period of Akbar. This fair is held in the month of November – December in Porsa village of Morena district. Previously, monkeys were sold here but now other animals are also sold.

Tetaji fair: Tetaji is believed to be a great man and had the power to remove sanke poison from the body. For the last 70 years, the Tetaji fair has been organized on his birthday in Bhamavad village of Guna and Nimar districts.

Jageshwari Devi fair: Since time immemorial, Jageshwari Devi fair is held annually in Chanderi of Guna district. The story goes that the king of Chanderi who was a great devotee of Goddess Jageshwari Devi contracted leprosy. The Goddess asked him to meet her at a particular place after an interval of 15 days but the impatient king visited there only on the third day. The king's leprosy was cured by he could only see the Goddess's head. Since that day, a fair was dedicated to the goddess.

Shivrati fair of Amarkantak: The Shivratri fair has been held at the origin of the Narmada River in Shahdol district for the last eighty years.

Mahamrityunjaya fair: This fair is organized on the day of Basant Panchami and the Shivarati in the Mahamrityunjaya temple of Rewa district.

Chandi Devi fair: The temple of Chandi Devi in Ghoghara village of Sidhi district is believed to be an incarnation of Goddess Parvati. This fair is held every year in March-April. Baba Shahabuddin Auliya's Urs: Baba Shahabuddin Auliya's Urs is held for four days in the month of February in Neemuch district where the tomb of Baba Shahbuddin is located. Kaluji Maharaj: kaluji Maharaj fair is held for a month at Piplya Khurd in West Nimar district. It is said that about 200 years ago, Kaluji Maharaj used to cure diseases of humans and animals. In this fair, Keema bulls of the Nimari breed are bought and sold.

Fair of Singaji: The Singaji fair is held for a week in August-September in Piplya village in West Nimar district. Singaji was an enigmatic man and was considered a deity.

Dhamoni Urs: DhamoniUrs is held in the month of April-May at the tomb of Mastan Ali Shah located in Dhamoni in Sagar district.

Barman's Fair: The Barman fair is organized for thirteen days on the occasion of Makar Sankranti at Gadarwara in the Narsinghpur district.

Fair of Math Ghoghara: On the occasion of Shivaratri, this fair is held for fifteen days at Bhairavnath in the Seoni district.

Alami Tablighi Ijtima: Ijtima is organized every year for three days in Bhopal. During Ijtima Jamaat from countries like Russia, Kazakhstan, France, Indonesia, Malaysia, Zambia, South Africa., Kenya, Iraq, Saudi Arabia, Yemen, Ethiopia, Somalia, Turkey, Thailand, and Sri Lanka participated in the religious festival.

Khajuraho Dance Festival: The Khajuraho dance festival was started in the year 1975. The event is hosted every year at Khajuraho in the Chhatarpur district where the artists perform in the backdrop of historical monuments. The one-week-long dance festival aims to promote and encourage dance, artists, culture, and heritage of India. Indian classical dances such as Kathak, Odissi, Manipuri, Bharatnatyam, Kuchipudi, and Mohiniattam. The temples at Khajuraho were built by the Chandella dynasty which reached its apogee between 950 and 1050. There are now just about 20 temples left, which are divided into three district groups and belong to Hinduism and Jainism.

Bhagoriya festival: Bhagoriya festival is one of the main festivals of the Bhil tribe celebrated in the districts of West Nimar, Jhabua, and Alirajpur. The festival marks the onset of the spring season and falls a few days before Holi. The festival is notable for being a large-scale Svayamvara or marriage market. As the name suggests, 'Bhag' means 'Run' in Hindi, in this festival young people choose their partners and elope. Eventually, they become husband and wife.

Ghadalya festival: Ghadalya is the main festival in the Malwa region. In this festival, the girls dance together on the occasion of Navratri. The girls visit each home in their locality and sing songs related to this festival. After the recital of songs, they are offered grains and money.

Lokrang festival: Lokrang festival is celebrated every year on January 26th (Republic Day) in Bhopal. The five-day cultural extravaganza emboldens rich tribal and folk traditions of India through various cultural activities such as Ramayni, Dharohar, Lokrag, Deshantar, 'Peer Parayi Jane Na', Aakar, Ullas, Swad, and Lokwarta.

Lokranjan festival: The Lokranjan festival is a national festival of fold dance organized every year in Khajuraho. Artists from all over the country gather and present popular folk and tribal dances, and attractive traditional crafts by the artisan.

Reference

1. Annual Report 2021-22, Ministry of Tribal Affairs, Govt. of India. https://tribal.nic.in/Statistics.aspx

2. Annual Report 2018-19, Ministry of Tribal Affairs, Govt. of India. https://tribal.nic.in/Statistics.aspx

3. Bhagoriya festival, Alirajpur. Govt. of Mdhya Pradesh. https://alirajpur.nic.in/en/festival/bhagoriya-festival/

4. Khajuraho Group of Monuments, World Heritage Convention, UNESCO. https://whc.unesco.org/en/list/240/

5. Language Atlas of India 2011, Census of India, Ministry of Home Affairs, Govt., of India

6. Indira Gandhi National Centre for the Arts, Ministry of Culture, Govt. Of India. https://ignca.gov.in/divisionssjanapada-sampada/tribal-art culture/adivasi-art- culture/the gond-of-madhya-pradesh/

7. Nagaji festival. District Morena. Madhya Pradesh Government. https://morena.nic.in/en/festival/nagaji-festival/

8. Utsav. Khajuraho Dance Festival, Govt. of India. https://utsav.gov.in/view- event/khajuraho-dance-festival

About the Author

Dr. Soyhunlo Sebu is anM.Sc Geography (Gold Medal), UGC-NET, and Ph,D in Geography. He has authored a book "Geography of Nagaland" and has published Research papers related to geography, environment, school education, etc in National and International journals.

He is currently an Assistant Professor atthe Regional Institute of Education (A constituent unit of the National Council of Educational Research and Training) in Bhopal, Madhya Pradesh. He isinvolved in training In-service teachers, Pre-service teachers, and research.